EMERSON LAKE & PALMER

Together and Apart

Laura Shenton

EMERSON LAKE & PALMER

Together and Apart

Laura Shenton

WP
WYMER
PUBLISHING
Bedford, England

First published in Great Britain in 2020
by Wymer Publishing
www.wymerpublishing.co.uk
Tel: 01234 326691
Wymer Publishing is a trading name of Wymer (UK) Ltd

Every effort has been made to trace the copyright holders of the
photographs in this book but some were unreachable. We would
be grateful if the photographers concerned would contact us.

Typeset / Design by Andy Bishop / Tusseheia Creative
Printed by Halstan, Amersham, Buckinghamshire.

A catalogue record for this book is available from the British Library.

Front and back cover images: Pictorial Press / Alamy Stock Images

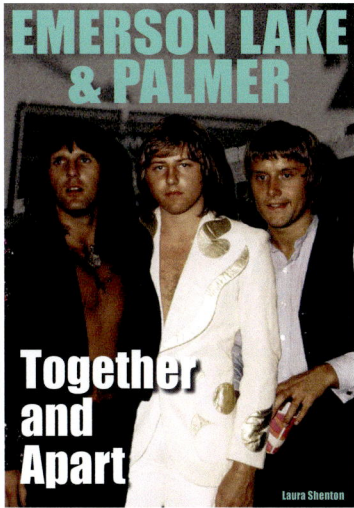

EMERSON LAKE & PALMER

Together and Apart

Laura Shenton

Emerson Lake & Palmer ★
7月22日(土)
後楽園球場
PM3:00開場 PM6:30開演
東京 ART-576 INC PRESENTANON ● ロック・ミラクルジョン'72 其7年
エマーソン・レイク&パーマー
A ¥2,300
1 階3塁側 N 列 102番

ROYAL FESTIVAL HALL
GENERAL MANAGER JOHN DENISON, C.B.E.
EMERSON, LAKE and PALMER
MONDAY, 26 OCTOBER, 1970
9 p.m.
Management: Marquee Block Ltd
GREEN SIDE
Please enter the auditorium by DOOR
6B
LEVEL 6
R.F.H.
26 Oct., 1970
9 p.m.
BOX 70p 14/-
BOX SEAT 27 C
BOX 70p 14/- 27 C

LYCEUM STRAND
E.L.P
(Emerson Lake & Palmer in concert)
WEDNESDAY 9th DECEMBER 1970
doors open 7pm
Concert between 8 and 11pm   Price 18/-
Issued subject to the rules and conditions of the ballroom
775

EMPIRE POOL, WEMBLEY
Harvey Goldsmith
John Smith Entertainments presents
EMMERSON LAKE & PALMER
IN CONCERT
FRIDAY, 19 APRIL, 1974
at 8 p.m.
Official Programmes available only inside
SOUTH UPPER TIER
£2.20
TO BE RETAINED See conditions on back
APRIL
19
ENTER AT SOUTH DOOR
ENTRANCE
58
ROW L
SEAT 82

CAPITOL - CARDIFF
EMERSON - LAKE - PALMER
WEDNESDAY MARCH **10**
at 7-45 p.m.
DRESS CIRCLE £1·25
BLOCK **B**   **C26**
No ticket exchanged nor money refunded
THIS PORTION TO BE RETAINED

Stadio Flaminio - Roma
E & PALMER
Mercoledì 2 maggio - ora 21
Posto unico
L. 1.500
Il presente biglietto deve essere conservato per il controllo
N° 1568

WIENER STADTHALLE
Eingang: Märzpark
Halle D   Amtlich aufgelegt
STIMMEN DER WELT präsentiert
MONTAG **12.**
●19.30 UHR
JUNI 1972
EMERSON LAKE & PALMER $ 120.-
REIHE **11**
SITZ 0029   TRIBUNE RECHTS
100
Eintritt in das Zuschauerraum
Durch den Erwerb dieser Karte unterwirft sich der Besucher der Hausordnung. Diese Karte ist nicht übertragbar u. ohne Abriß ungültig. Bei Verlassen des Hallengeländes verliert die Karte ihre Gültigkeit.   V. Klaushofer, Wien IV

WILD WEST PRODUCTIONS presents
Emerson.Lake & Palmer
DALLAS MEMORAL AUDITORIUM
Dallas, Texas
Wednesday Eve.
8:00 P.M.
FEBRUARY **27** 1974
BALCONY 8
FEB. 27, 1974
$6.00
SEC ROW SEAT
6 6 8
BALCONY 8

ENTER TOWER **B** | GATE **21**
2nd PROMENADE $5.50
316 L **9**
SEC. ROW SEAT
EMERSON, LAKE & PALMER
8:00 P.M.
THUR. EVE.
NOV. 25 1971

THE GUILDHALL PORTSMOUTH
Emerson Lake & Palmer
IN CONCERT
Monday 28th September
at 7.30 p.m.
GRAND CIRCLE
10/- (50p.)
TICKETS CANNOT BE EXCHANGED OR MONEY REFUNDED
TO BE RETAINED
Acme Printing Co. Ltd. Portsmouth
BLOCK **G**
ADMIT AT NORTH DOOR
ROW **N** SEAT **46**

FREE TRADE HALL (Peter Street) MANCHESTER
WARNING
Official Programmes & Posters sold INSIDE Hall only. Beware of pirate sellers operating outside
JOHN & TONY SMITH present
Emerson Lake & Palmer
+ Supporting Act
FRIDAY, 10th DECEMBER, 1971
2nd House 10-30 p.m. 2nd House
STALLS - - 100p (£1)
G 5

ROW **UU**   SEAT **32**
FLOOR
Retain Stub — Good Only
FRI. 8.00 P.M.   **DEC. 7**
Davis Printing Limited
EMERSON LAKE AND PALMER
PRICE -6.00 + RST .60 - $6.60
ADMIT ONE. Entrance by Main Door or by Church Street Door.
Maple Leaf Gardens LIMITED
CONDITION OF SALE

THE OPERA
NATIONAL ARTS CENTRE
OTTAWA CANADA
L'OPÉRA CENTRE NATIONAL DES ARTS
GAUCHE LEFT
Allée Aisle
The Treble Clef presents
EMERSON, LAKE and PALMER
WEDNESDAY EVENING 10:00
MERCREDI EN SOIRÉE 22 h 00
FRONT ORCHESTRA – L'AVANT DE L'ORCHESTRE
$5.00
Tax .50
$5.50
no refunds - non remb. – see reverse / voir verso
AUG. **25** AOUT 1971
FF 5

FREE TRADE HALL (Peter Street) MANCHESTER
JOHN and TONY SMITH present
Emerson Lake & Palmer
IN CONCERT
MONDAY, 22nd MARCH, 1971
at 7-45 p.m.
CENTRE CIRCLE 85p (17/-)
M   19

SWING AUDITORIUM
NATIONAL ORANGE SHOW GROUNDS
CONCERT ASSOCIATES PRESENTS
Emerson, Lake & Palmer
SAT. EVE. 8:00 P.M.
FEB'RY 9
$6.00 AT DOOR
NO REFUND - NO EXCHANGE
1974
No. 004542
UNRESERVED
SWING AUDITORIUM
FEB'RY **9** 1974
No. 004542

Introduction

Emerson, Lake & Palmer. What a band! Progressive, enigmatic and downright entertaining. In the 1970s, they were easily one of the most successful groups, both artistically and commercially.

Despite some of the dramas behind their fallings out, the group was founded on a strong extent of musical rapport. Carl Palmer recalled, "Keith and I had this thing, that we really enjoyed classical music. I come from a really classical background, with my father being a professor of music and so on, and so Keith and I always used to rib each other, 'Have you heard this?' and 'Have you heard that?' We'd be talking about various pieces of music and something would come up, and I'd say, 'I used to listen to that at home with my grandfather!' so there was a bit of synergy going on there straight away."

Of a hard-working band consisting of individuals dedicated to their musical cause, Greg Lake said, "This band runs on the co-operation between us. That element is the power of ELP. It's the combination and the battles between that romance of mine and that technical development of Keith's which makes this an interesting and exciting group. Not that it wouldn't be just as valid and exciting if Keith were to do a strictly instrumental thing or if I were to do a complete album of simple songs, but at this moment this is the way it is and right now we're committed to that, because being in a band isn't something you enjoy. It's not a fairground ride. It's something you're a part of creatively and it's often a very painful experience, if you're sincere. The reality of being in a band like ELP is an artistic reality, it's not an entertainment reality. For promotional purposes it would be great to say, 'Yeah, we had a fantastic time making this album' — but we didn't."

An endearing aspect of ELP is that each individual had their own distinct musical interests. In such regard, what they achieved as a group is legendary. In February 1974, Keith Emerson said, "I've been trying to get a solo album for ages and ages. For about a year I've got about five tracks done, in bits and pieces which I like, and I think that will continue. Whenever I like something, I want it for ELP, because that is my prime objective. It's not really that important to me because I am doing what I want to do. Usually, solo albums are done because the cat is not being allowed to do what he really wants to do. All of us do whatever he wants on stage, and on record, so there is no real hurry."

With regards to the scope of ELP doing solo albums, Lake mused in 1973; "They'd just be made up of things we felt we couldn't do within the band. Maybe Keith would get into some specialist piano things — twenties boogies or something. Things like that would be better on more personal albums. I don't know whether we'll do it. It'd just be as a kind of hobby if we did."

And who's to say that having the ambition and scope to do solo projects is a bad thing anyway? Emerson confirmed in 1972; "This band is designed so that everybody gets featured equally. I think it's working out that way; we're all getting recognised in our own right and we're very pleased about that. That's why we're called Emerson, Lake and Palmer. The fact is, if we want to do our own projects, then we have a chance."

Keith Emerson purchased his Moog synthesiser with funds provided by ELP's record deal. He recalled, "It cost a lot of money and it arrived and I excitedly got it out of the box stuck it on the table and thought, 'Wow! That's great! A Moog synthesiser. How do you switch it on?' There were all these leads and stuff, there was no instruction manual." The patch for Emerson's Moog was provided by Mike Vickers. It came with six unique sounds that became a vitally distinctive ingredient in ELP's music.

With an established sound and innovative ideas in abundance, ELP certainly earned the right to declare, "Welcome Back, My Friends, To The Show That Never Ends…"

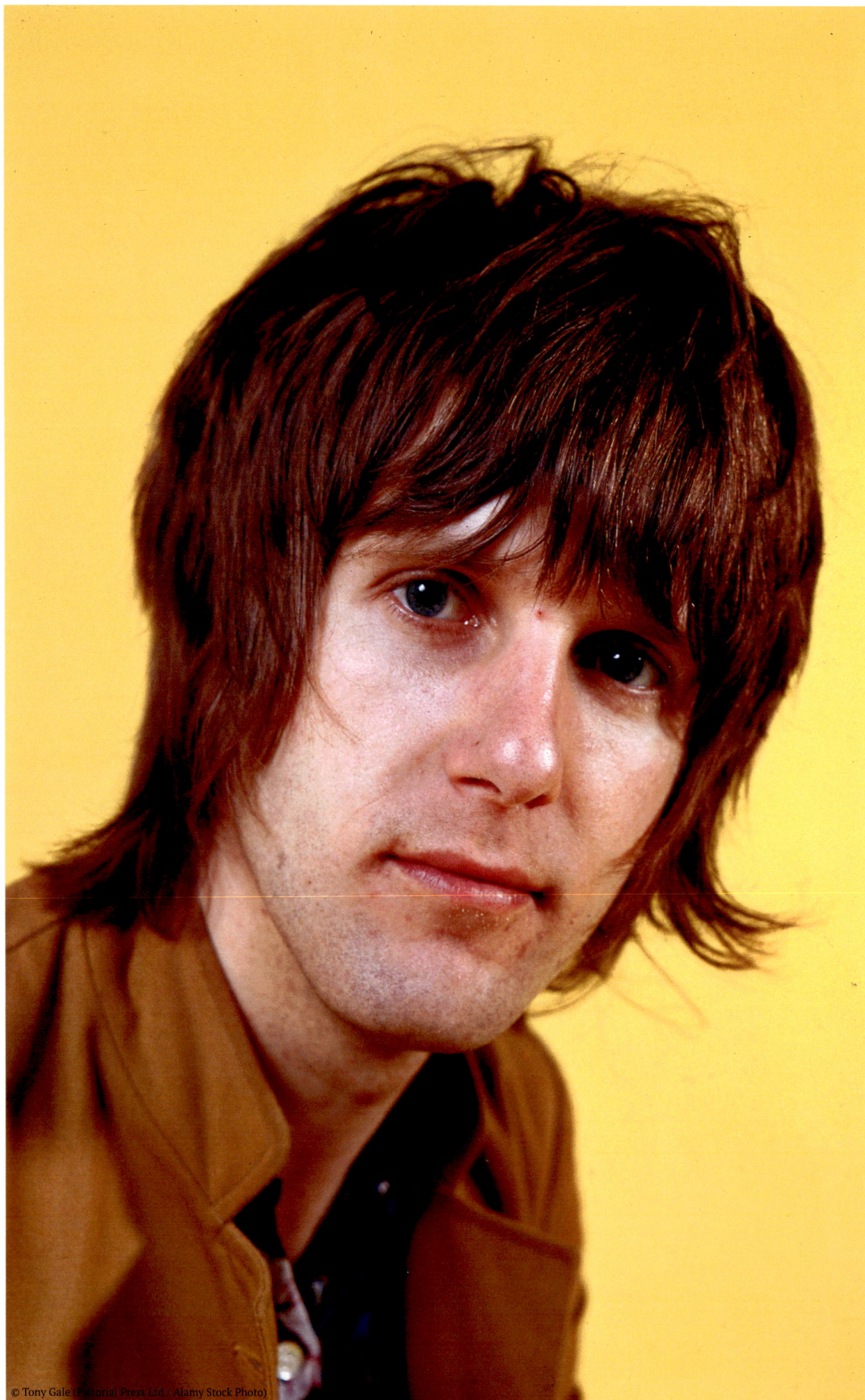

Emerson's
Early Days

Keith Noel Emerson was born on 2nd November 1944 in Todmorden, West Yorkshire to a family who had been evacuated from the south of England during the second world war. When they returned south and settled in Goring-by-Sea in West Sussex, Emerson attended West Tarring School. Although Emerson's mother wasn't musical, his father played the piano. By the age of eight, Emerson was supported by his parents to attend piano lessons from local tutors. His tuition included how to read music and although emphasis was placed on Western classical music as part of his studies, it wasn't long before Emerson started to develop his own style based on jazz and rock music.

Emerson didn't own a record player but upon listening to the radio, he found that Floyd Cramer's 1961 slip note style 'On The Rebound' resonated with him, as well as the work of Dudley Moore.

In many ways, Emerson was a self-starter when it came to his early music education. He studied the sheet music of Dave Brubeck and George Shearing and learnt about jazz piano from books.

Other sources of Emerson's inspiration were diverse. He listened to boogie-woogie, and to country-style pianists including Joe "Mr Piano" Henderson, Russ Conway and Winifred Atwell. Emerson later said of himself: "I was a very serious child. I used to walk around with Beethoven sonatas under my arm. However, I was very good at avoiding being beaten up by the bullies. That was because I could also play Jerry Lee Lewis and Little Richard songs. So, they thought I was kind of cool and left me alone."

Emerson's interest in the Hammond organ was ignited after hearing jazz organist Jack McDuff perform 'Rock Candy'. So much so that the Hammond became his instrument of choice in the late 1960s. Emerson rented his first Hammond organ around the age of fifteen. It was an L-100 model.

Initially, Emerson functioned on the basis that music would be a hobby on the side. He played the piano in pubs whilst working at Lloyds Bank during the day. This wasn't to last though; as music became more and more prevalent in how he spent his time, Emerson was fired from his job at the bank.

It was whilst he was performing in the Worthing

Brother Jack McDuff's 1963 recording that instigated Keith's passion for the Hammond organ.

11

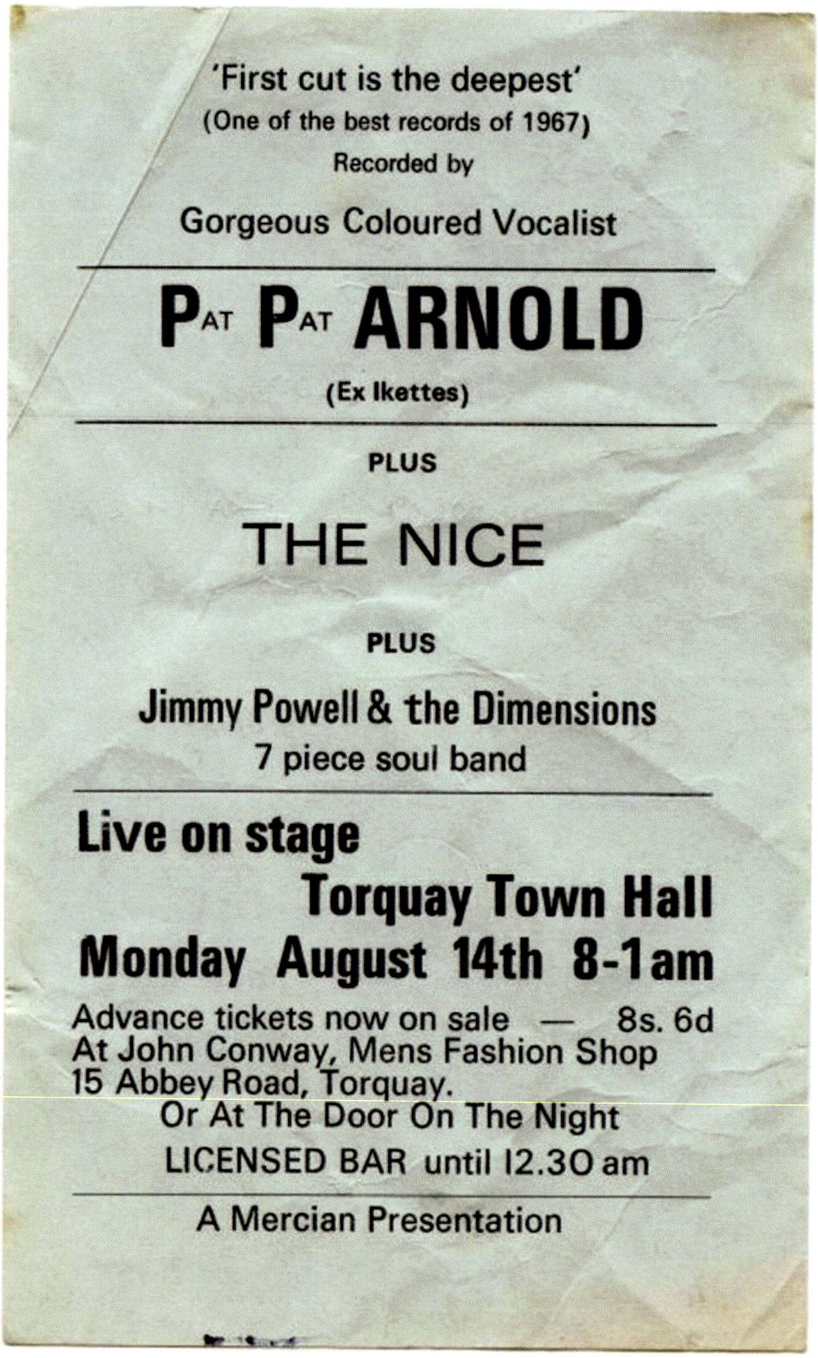

'First cut is the deepest'
(One of the best records of 1967)
Recorded by

Gorgeous Coloured Vocalist

PAT PAT ARNOLD

(Ex Ikettes)

PLUS

THE NICE

PLUS

Jimmy Powell & the Dimensions
7 piece soul band

Live on stage
Torquay Town Hall
Monday August 14th 8-1am

Advance tickets now on sale — 8s. 6d
At John Conway, Mens Fashion Shop
15 Abbey Road, Torquay.
Or At The Door On The Night
LICENSED BAR until 12.30 am

A Mercian Presentation

The Nice only backed PP Arnold for a short while. From May '67 through to their last gig with her at The Pink Flamingo in London, two weeks after this Torquay show. They didn't have a problem getting gigs under their own name although some have alluded archivists such as a unique show they did for an engineering work's private Christmas concert in Bedford in December '67.

Keith with Gary Farr and the T-Bones. Keith is on the far right and Lee Jackson is wearing the shades.

area that Emerson received an offer to join his first professional band, the T-Bones. They were the backing group of blues singer Gary Farr. The T-Bones toured the UK and France before they all went their separate ways. It was after this that Emerson joined a band called The V.I.P.'s.

In 1967 though, the connections that Emerson had made with the T-Bones would come back to the fore, and fantastically so too. With Lee Jackson who he had worked with in the T-Bones, Emerson formed The Nice. The other members were David O'List and Ian Hague, after soul singer P. P. Arnold had asked him to form a backing band.

Ultimately, Hague was replaced with Brian Davison. The Nice set out on their own and they quickly acquired an intense following on the basis of their live performances. The group had a solid foundation in Emerson's Hammond organ showmanship as well as from his theatrical use of the instrument. Their bold rearrangements of classical music themes have often been described by some as "symphonic rock".

A flyer for the November / December '67 package tour with an impressive line-up. As in keeping with package tours of the day, low down on the bill The Nice only played for about twelve minutes, performing 'Rondo' and 'The Thoughts Of Emerlist Davjack'.

The Nice, July 1968

BLUESVILLE '68 CLUBS

Our new address is:

"THE HORNSEY WOOD TAVERN"

376 SEVEN SISTERS RD., N.4, 2 MINS. WALK FROM MANOR HOUSE

NANDA AND RON LESLEY PRESENT

FRIDAY, OCTOBER 4th ★
The **Savoy Brown Blues Band**

FRIDAY, OCTOBER 11th ★
THE NICE

FRIDAY, OCTOBER 18th ★
THE CHICKEN SHACK

FRIDAY, OCTOBER 25th ★
THE **Savoy Brown Blues Band**

FRIDAY, NOVEMBER 1st ★
FLEETWOOD MAC

FRIDAY, NOVEMBER 8th ★
John Mayall's Blues Breakers

We apologise for increased admission prices
This is due to the smaller capacity of the room

**Top Rank Brighton Suite
Friday, 27th December**

Beat that Christmas anti-climax . . . . See

Britain's most exciting Group

THE NICE

and

The Orange Bicycle

Syd Dean Band

SIX HOURS OF DANCING

8 p.m. — 2 a.m.

TICKETS 12/6 in advance   (15/- on the door)
ON SALE NOW AT Hanningtons - Exspantion, Middle St.
Fine Records, Brighton Square - Gondola, Hove and at the
Top Rank Suite

16

Ever keen to add to the visual aspect of his performance, Emerson used his Hammond L-100 organ aggressively — sometimes far beyond what was needed for the music — hitting it, beating it with a whip, pushing it over, riding it across the stage like a horse, playing with it lying on top of him, and wedging knives into the keyboard but nevertheless it became iconic. As much as some of Emerson's actions were very much for show, they also produced great musical sound effects. Hitting the organ caused explosive sounds. Turning the organ over resulted in feedback. The knives held down keys and provided the scope for notes to be generously sustained. As a showman, Emerson's appetite for destruction predates many of his peers in the field of rock music.

Unsurprisingly, Emerson was starting to become well known for not only his work with The Nice, but for his work outside of the group. In 1969, he participated in the Music From Free Creek supersession project. It included big names such as Eric Clapton and Jeff Beck. For the session, Emerson performed with bassist Chuck Rainey and Hendrix's drummer Mitch Mitchell. The group covered, among

© Tony Gale (Pictorial Press Ltd / Alamy Stock Photo)

Left to right: Brian "Blinky" Davison, David O List, Lee Jackson, and Keith Emerson

(Tony Pye/Alamy Stock Photo)

18

other tunes, the Eddie Harris instrumental 'Freedom Jazz Dance', although it was not released until 1973.

It was in a record shop that Emerson had first heard a Moog. The store owner played Switched-On Bach for him. Emerson said of his response at the time; "My God that's incredible, what is that played on?" The owner then showed him the album cover. "So I said, 'What is that?' And he said, 'That's the Moog synthesiser.' My first impression was that it looked a bit like electronic skiffle."

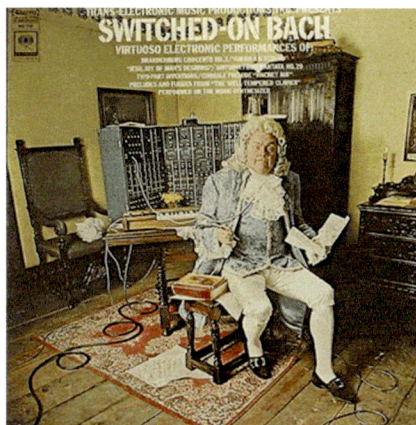

Walter Carlos's album that was a major influence on Keith, who became arguably the greatest exponent of the Moog synthesiser.

Entranced by the instrument, Emerson borrowed Mike Vickers' Moog for an upcoming Nice concert with the Royal Philharmonic Orchestra at London's Royal Festival Hall. Vickers helped patch the Moog. The concert was a success. Emerson's performance of 'Also Sprach Zarathustra' (a composition most famous for its use in the 1968 film 2001: A Space Odyssey) was met with much critical acclaim. Emerson later recalled how much the concert made him realise that the Moog was the instrument for him; "I thought, 'this was great. I've got to have one of these'."

The Nice performing at the Actuel Music Festival of Jazz, Rock and New Music in Amougies, Belgium, 26th October 1969. It was proclaimed at the time to be Europe's answer to Woodstock. The festival was organised by BYG Actuel, a French record label. The five-day, twenty-four-hour, open-air festival was to be held at the Parc de Saint Cloud in Paris but the French authorities banned the festival a few days before it was due to start. The organisers moved the festival to Amougies in Belgium — a three-hour drive east of Paris. Over 15,000 people attended despite the seasonal cold, damp and fog.

BATH FESTIVAL
OF BLUES

SATURDAY JUNE 28TH
RECREATION GROUND PULTENEY STREET ENTRANCE

with

FLEETWOOD MAC
JOHN MAYALL
TEN YEARS AFTER
LED ZEPPELIN
THE NICE
CHICKEN SHACK
JOHN HISEMAN'S COLOSSEUM
MIKE ABRAHAM'S BLODWIN PIG
KEEF HARTLEY · GROUP THERAPY
LIVERPOOL SCENE · TASTE
SAVOY BROWN BLUES BAND
CHAMPION JACK DUPRE
CLOUDS · BABYLON
PRINCIPAL EDWARD'S MAGIC THEATRE
DEEP BLUES BAND · JUST BEFORE DAWN
COMPERE JOHN PEEL

IN CASE OF BAD WEATHER THERE WILL BE A SUBSTANTIAL AMOUNT OF UNDER COVER ACCOMODATION

REFRESH-MENTS AND HOT SNACKS WILL BE AVAILABLE ALL DAY

12 NOON TO 11 P.M.

TICKETS IN ADVANCE ALL DAY 18'6 EVE. ONLY (6·30 P.M.) 14'6
ON THE DAY ALL DAY 22'6 EVE. ONLY (6·30 P.M.) 16'6

TICKETS ARE OBTAINABLE FROM
Bath Festival Box Office, Abbey Chambers, Abbey Churchyard, Bath, Som.
Please enclose S.A.E. with Postal Applications

© Tony Byers (Alamy Stock Photo)

Keith at the Bath Festival of Blues 1969 held at the city's Recreation Ground on Saturday 28th June. The following year promoter Freddy Bannister expanded the event to run over a weekend, moving it to the Bath and West Showground at Shepton Mallet and renaming it the Bath Festival of Blues and Progressive Music. That festival inspired Michael Eavis to start a festival of his own at Glastonbury later in 1970.

22

December 1969 during the last American tour.

USA, December 1969.

Putting the Hammond through its paces USA, December 1969.

27

CITY HALL · SHEFFIELD
7.30 — THURSDAY, 29th JANUARY — 7.30

JOHN MARTIN and DEREK BLOCK
with TONY STRATTON-SMITH presents
in assoc. with
JOHN & TONY SMITH

THE NICE
IN CONCERT

PRICES: 15/- 12/6 10/6 7/6
Obtainable from: Wilson Peck Ltd., 64/70 Leopold Street, Sheffield S1 1RP (Tel. 27074)

In February '69 The Nice shared a bill with Deep Purple at London's University College. Deep Purple's Jon Lord and Emerson became good friends throughout this period. Towards the end of the year both keyboard men also premiered their first works combining the band with an orchestra. Lord's *Concerto For Group & Orchestra* was premiered on 24th September at the Royal Albert Hall, and Emerson's *Five Bridges Suite* just sixteen days later at the Newcastle Arts Festival.

A second recorded performance followed a week later at the less salubrious Fairfield Halls. Something that Emerson jokingly remarked about after Lord's death in 2012: "In the early years I remember being quite jealous of Jon Lord — may he rest in peace. In September 1969 I heard he was debuting his Concerto For Group & Orchestra at the Royal Albert Hall, with none other than Malcolm Arnold conducting. Wow! I had to go along and see that. Jon and I ribbed each other, we were pretty much pals, but I walked away and thought: 'Shit, in a couple of weeks time I'm going to be recording The Nice's Five Bridges Suite... not at the Albert Hall but at the Fairfield Halls, Croydon!' A much more prosaic venue."

It's probably worth pointing out however that The Nice had been banned from playing the Royal Albert Hall following a performance there on 26th June 1968 when Emerson burned an American flag onstage during a performance of 'America' at a Come Back Africa charity event.

As the poster here shows, The Nice and Deep Purple shared the same stage again on 30th March 1970 at the Berlin Peace Pop World Festival, which was supposedly The Nice's last concert, although a poster for the Progressive Pop Festival in Cologne on April 4th lists them, along with Deep Purple as amongst the acts performing, although The Nice had split, making Berlin the last show.

Deep Purple took the stage first, performing a typically usual set for the time. For the encore they returned with Keith Emerson joining them for rousing versions of Roy Orbison's 'Go! Go! Go! (Down The Line)' and Little Richard's 'Lucille'.

The Nice's set was 'Intermezzo From Karelia Suite', 'Hang On To A Dream', 'Country Pie/Brandenburg Concerto No. 6', 'My Back Pages' and 'Blue Rondo à la Turk'.

For the encore Deep Purple's Ritchie Blackmore and Ian Gillan joined The Nice for a lengthy jam — a nice way to conclude the band's career.

The rather whacky poster for the Cologne gig that The Nice never performed at.

Lake's
Early Days

Greg Lake was born on 10th November 1947 in the Parkstone area of Poole in Dorset. His father, Harry, was an engineer, and his mother, Pearl, was a housewife. Lake grew up in Oakdale. He recalled of his childhood that he was "born in an asbestos prefab housing unit" into a "very poor" family where he experienced several cold winters at home. Equally though, Lake spoke highly of his parents for sending him money and food in the days when he was a struggling musician at the start of his career. Overall, Lake asserted that he had a happy upbringing.

It was upon buying Little Richard's 'Lucille' in 1957 that Lake first got into rock 'n' roll music. By the age of twelve, he first learned to play the guitar and it was with a mere fundamental knowledge of the instrument that he composed his first song, 'Lucky Man'. He committed it to memory and didn't write it down.

Lake's mother played the piano and in wanting to encourage her son, she got him a second-hand guitar. Lake had lessons with Don Strike, who had a shop in Westbourne. As well as how to read music and exercises based on violin pieces by Niccolò Paganini, Strike taught Lake "these awful Bert Weedon things." Although Lake engaged more with the pop tunes from the 1930s that Strike encouraged him to play, it wasn't much longer than a year after that Lake stopped having lessons with Strike because he wanted to play music that the teacher was keen to discourage — songs by The Shadows. As Lake's journey with the guitar continued, his second was a pink Fender Stratocaster.

Lake went to Oakdale Junior School and then Henry Harbin Secondary Modern School, which he left circa 1963/64. He went straight to work in a job where he was required to load and unload cargo at the Poole docks. He also worked as a draughtsman for a short period. It wasn't long after that Lake made the decision to become a full-time musician — he was seventeen by that point.

Lake's first band was a group by the name of Unit Four. He contributed guitar and vocals. They played cover songs. When they split up in 1965, Lake and the band's bassist, Dave Genes, formed another covers group called the Time Checks. They remained together until 1966.

Greg with Unit Four on top of their old ambulance outside the Oakdale pub in Poole. Formed in 1963 with guitarist David Genes, keyboard player John Dickenson and drummer Kenny Beveridge. The band transported their gear to venues in this old converted ambulance. The band line-up soon changed as depicted here. Tony Batey replaced Kenny Beveridge, Greg switched from bass to guitar when John Dickenson left and Don Strike's son Bev took over on bass. The gigs at the Oakdale had a reputation for ending in punch ups, upended furniture and flying beer glasses. To avoid their gear getting trashed in the ensuing melee they devised a plan of passing their equipment through the window at the side of the stage to Greg's dad, who loaded it into the van as soon as the bell rang for last orders. Greg's two finger salute in this photo suggests that he had already developed a rock 'n' roll attitude.

It was after this that Lake then became a member of The Shame. He is featured on their single, 'Don't Go Away Little Girl'. The song was written by Janis Ian. It was during his stay in Carlisle for a gig that Greg contracted pneumonia. He continued to perform on stage but his bandmates refused to drive back home that night. As a result, he "woke up blue" from having had no other choice but to sleep in the van overnight. He recalled, "When we got home I was nearly dead... That was probably the worst I went through."

The Shame circa 1967, Left to Right: Greg Lake, John Dickenson, Malcolm Brasher & Bill Nims.

After a brief stint in the Shy Limbs, by 1968 Lake was in a band called The Gods. Based in Hatfield, he described his experience of being in the group as "a very poor training college." Despite this, they did manage to secure a residency at the Marquee Club in London. Unhappy with the creative direction the band was taking, Lake left them in 1968, just as they were to enter the recording studio! Their keyboard player Ken Hensley later confessed that Lake "was far too talented to be kept in the background."

With The Gods in 1968. Success was just around the corner for Greg, as it was for fellow band members Lee Kerslake and Ken Hensley in Uriah Heep.

King Crimson at their breakthrough moment performing at Hyde Park on 5th July 1969 as part of The Rolling Stones concert to an audience estimated to be somewhere between 250,000–500,000. They had yet to release the ground-breaking debut album *In The Court Of The Crimson King* and were invited to play on the strength of word of mouth after their live performances in venues such as the Marquee Club. Sam Cutler introduced them on stage, stating the "new band is gonna go a long way".

The setlist was '21st Century Schizoid Man', 'In The Court Of The Crimson King', 'Get Thy Bearings', 'Epitaph', 'Mantra', 'Travel Weary Capricorn' and 'Mars'. The performance was released by Fripp in 2002.

You can clearly see in the photo hand-held film cameras and some footage of the show does exist.

Robert Fripp was also from Dorset and had also had guitar lessons with Don Strike. Fripp had seen Lake perform in Poole when he was in Unit Four. Fripp and Lake first began playing guitar together when Fripp was asked to be a roadie for a gig at Ventnor in the Isle of Wight. When no audience tuned up, the duo began jamming and playing songs that they had both learnt in their lessons with Strike.

Fripp formed King Crimson when his previous group, Giles, Giles And Fripp failed to gain any traction commercially. On top of this, their record company had already suggested getting a proper lead singer. In response, Fripp chose Lake for the role of vocalist. He asked him to play bass instead of guitar on the basis that it eliminated the need to find a bass player for the group. Lake had predominantly been a guitarist for eleven years and the personnel dilemma handed to him by King Crimson was such that it was his first-time playing bass.

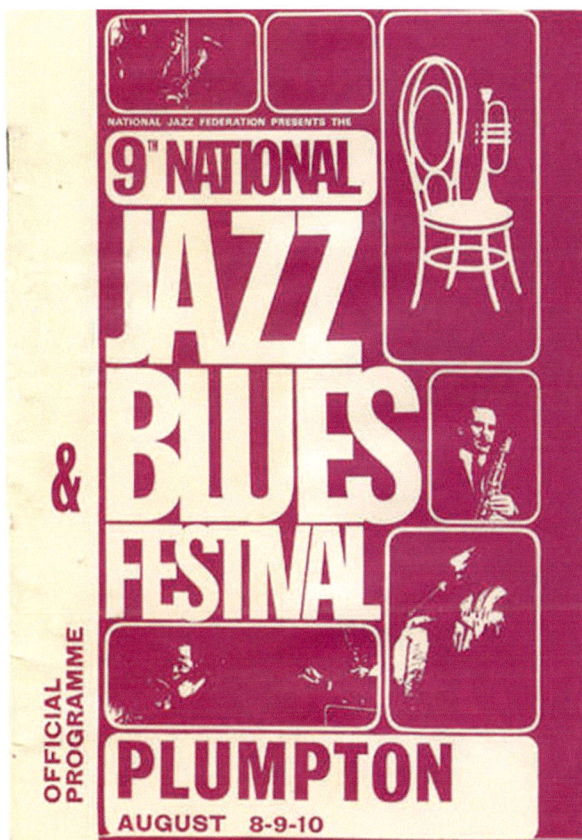

The month following Hyde Park Crimson played at the 9th National Jazz, Blues & Rock Festival. In 1969 the Festival had relocated yet again with the promoters having trouble finding a new home. Plans were made to move to West Drayton in Middlesex but the local council refused permission to use the site, so the venue was hurriedly changed to the Plumpton Racecourse in East Sussex.

King Crimson played on the second night, headlining in what was described as the Village. Basically the festival had two performance areas; the main stage, and a second one inside a marquee, dubbed as "The Village".

One member of the audience that night, Dave Bee, recalls, "I have a vivid memory of being at a festival around this time when a friend dragged me into a marquee. It was at night, there was no stage, just a band tuning up and people drifting in. It soon got crowded but we were ringside.

"I noted the name on the drum kit, King Crimson, which meant nothing to me. They then started playing the whole *Court Of The Crimson King* set. I am certain no one in that tent had ever heard anything like it. We were totally silent throughout. Okay so we didn't know or care where prog rock would end up, this was stunning."

King Crimson was paid £25 for the performance. Interestingly, The Nice headlined the main stage the following evening.

Although Peter Sinfield was the lyricist for King Crimson, Lake had some involvement in the process when it came to the writing for the band's debut album, *In The Court Of The Crimson King*. Lake also produced the album as a result of their originally contracted producer, Tony Clarke, walking out midway through the project. When the album came out in October 1969, it was met with both critical acclaim and commercial success. Lake said, "There was this huge wave of response. The audiences were really into us because we were an underground thing — the critics loved us because we offered something fresh."

© Tony Gale (Pictorial Press Ltd / Alamy Stock Photo)

Greg with King Crimson on *Top Of The Pops*, 25th March 1970 performing 'Cat Food'. It was broadcasted the following day. Initially acts performing on the show mimed to the commercially released record, but in 1966 after discussions with the Musicians' Union, miming was banned. After a few weeks during which some band's attempts to play as well as on their records were somewhat lacking, a compromise was reached whereby a specially recorded backing track was permitted, as long as all the musicians on the track were present in the studio.

King Crimson supported their debut album with tours of the UK and the US. At some shows The Nice was also on the bill. It was during the US tour that Lake struck up a friendship with Keith Emerson. They both had similar musical interests in common and it was through this that they began to consider the benefits of forming a new group together. King Crimson returned to the UK in early 1970. Lake agreed to sing on the band's second album, *In The Wake of Poseidon,* as well as to appear on Top Of The Pops with them, to perform the song 'Cat Food'.

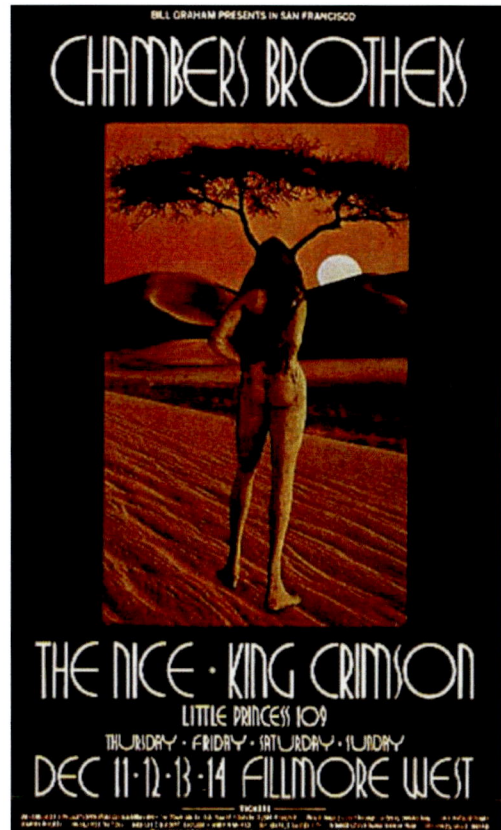

Greg crossed paths with Keith when King Crimson shared the bill with The Nice at the Fillmore West in December '69.

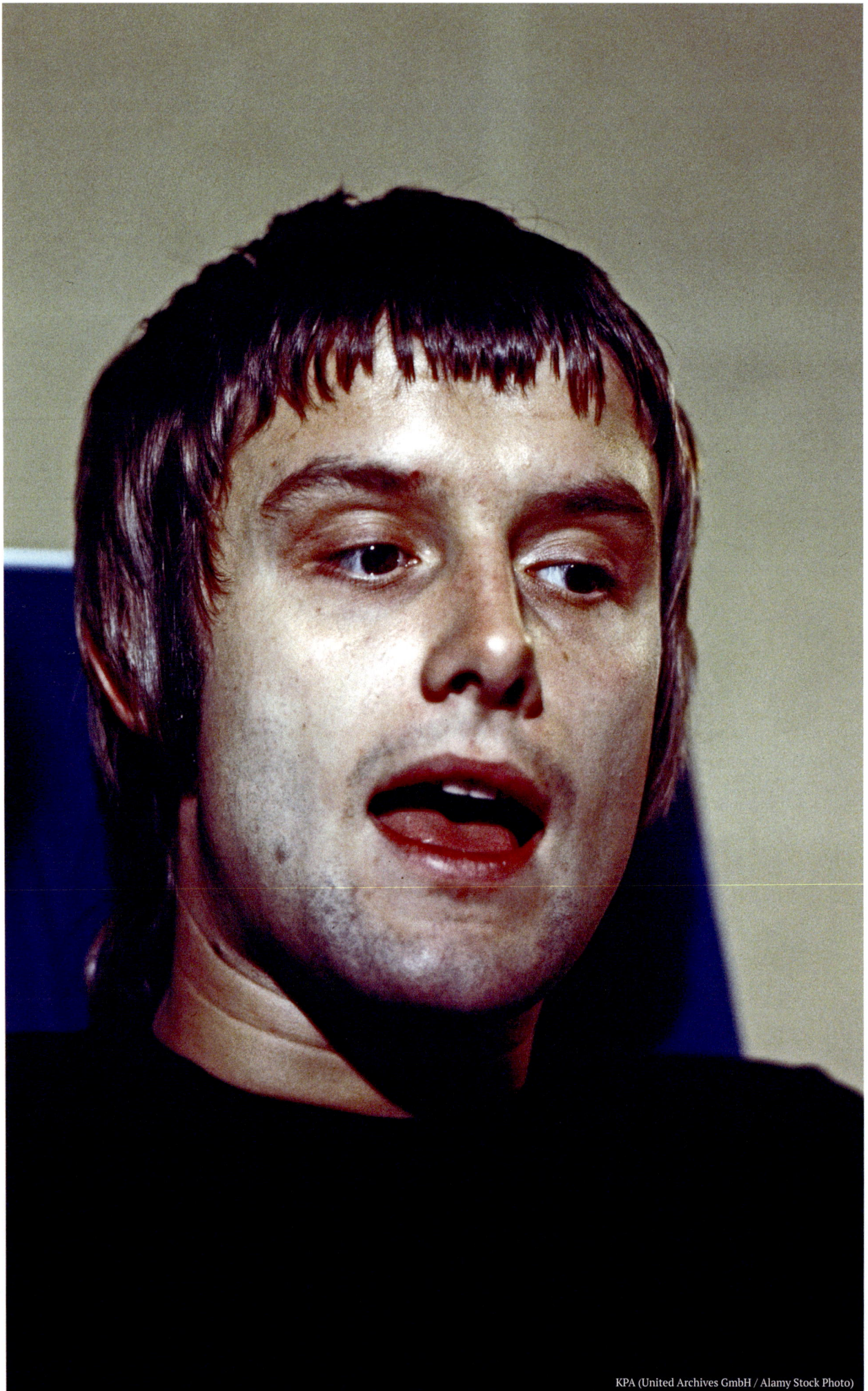

Palmer's
Early Days

Carl Frederick Kendall Palmer was born on 20th March 1950. He began taking drum lessons as a young boy. He formed his first band with others from the Midlands area; they initially named themselves the King Bees but soon changed their name to The Craig. In 1966, they made their first record. On the A-side was a song called 'I Must Be Mad' and on the B-side was 'Suspense'. It was produced by Larry Page.

It was around this time that Palmer also started to do his early session work. He played on the song, 'Love Light' for a band from Liverpool, The Chants. Palmer was invited to join Chris Farlowe And The Thunderbirds later that year.

Palmer's next move saw him joining The Crazy World Of Arthur Brown. They had already had their big hit single, 'Fire'. The original drummer, Drachen Theaker, played on that track and indeed on their eponymous album. When Theaker suddenly left part way through a tour of the US in 1969, Palmer was quickly brought in as a replacement but he soon became a permanent member of the band.

Carl in a breaker's yard with the Crazy World Of Arthur Brown

© Tony Gale (Pictorial Press Ltd / Alamy Stock Photo)

The Crazy World Of Arthur Brown performing 'Fire' at London's Marquee, 6th August 1968. There are many legendary but unverified stories about Arthur Brown setting himself alight with his fire stunt as well as apparently at one show declaring "I am the god of hellfire…" with someone supposedly saying "no you're not Arthur, we can't find the matches!" For Carl it was his first major experience of showmanship and would have held him in good stead for plenty of Keith's exploits that followed. Incidentally, The Nice were regular performers at The Marquee and actually played two nights later.

It didn't last for long though; things hadn't been working out well for anyone in The Crazy World Of Arthur Brown. Palmer recalled that Brown had "gone missing on a commune on Long Island". Along with keyboard player Vincent Crane they left Arthur Brown and with the addition of Nick Graham on vocals and bass, Atomic Rooster was born and that was pretty much that.

Atomic Rooster went through a number of personnel changes in a short period of time and their first album was released in 1970. Atomic Rooster's sound was one of high energy organ-driven rock. Palmer's contribution was both elaborate and reliable. Whilst he wasn't the driving force of the band, the studio album that he features on reached number forty-nine in the UK charts and is still regarded by many as a progressive rock classic.

Ever the innovative musician, Palmer played congas on 'Before Tomorrow' and 'Play The Game'. He played glockenspiel on 'Winter'. The album also features Atomic Rooster's rendition of the John Mayall penned song, 'Broken Wings'.

Although the album was originally released as a trio, guitarist John Cann soon joined the band and went into the studio to add his guitar to three tracks on the already released debut album. It was then reissued but with exactly the same sleeve and credits, with no mention of Cann whatsoever. The only way to tell the albums apart without playing them is that the label on the original UK release is rough in texture.

The sessions that Atomic Rooster did for BBC Radio were not released until 1998. Palmer's contribution is featured on 'Friday The 13th' and 'Seven Lonely Streets'.

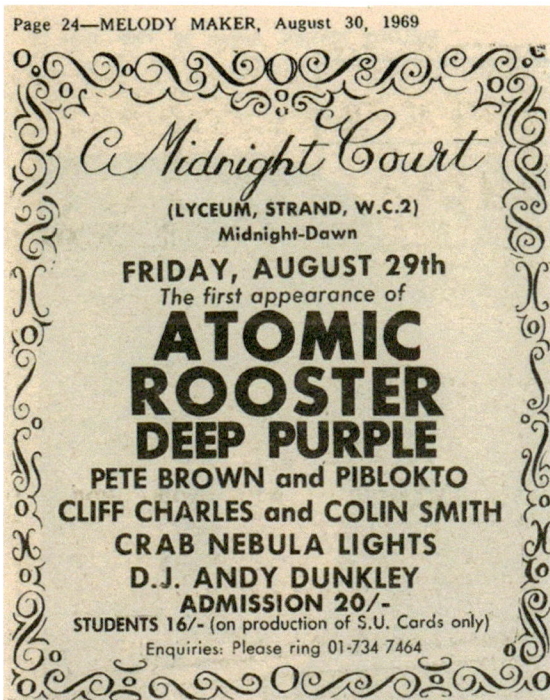

Page 24—MELODY MAKER, August 30, 1969

Midnight Court

(LYCEUM, STRAND, W.C.2)
Midnight-Dawn

FRIDAY, AUGUST 29th
The first appearance of

ATOMIC ROOSTER
DEEP PURPLE
PETE BROWN and PIBLOKTO
CLIFF CHARLES and COLIN SMITH
CRAB NEBULA LIGHTS
D.J. ANDY DUNKLEY
ADMISSION 20/-
STUDENTS 16/- (on production of S.U. Cards only)
Enquiries: Please ring 01-734 7464

Don't be fooled by the Melody Maker date being after the concert. The papers were always dated for Saturday, but it was published on Thursday, the day before the show.

Carl's time with Atomic Rooster was short and sweet. From this first headlining gig at the Lyceum in August '69, a record deal was quickly secured. The album was recorded in December into January 1970 and released the following month.

Left to right: Vincent Crane, John Cann and Carl Palmer.

In early 1970 Palmer received a call from Keith Emerson to audition for a new group. He left Atomic Rooster in the summer of 1970, and the rest, as they say, is history.

Carl seems very happy to be photographed here with The Crazy World of Arthur Brown, despite Arthur's knitted suit.

Two very early shots of Keith and Greg together at home taken on 10th April, 1970. The Nice's last show had been less than two weeks before. For Greg, aside from his performance on *Top of the Pops* with King Crimson the previous month, early 1970 had been spent in the studio recording his second and last album with King Crimson, *In The Wake Of Poseidon*.

© Laurens van Houten (Frank White Photo Agency)

Together

ELP became known for the dramatic nature of some of their disagreements, with Emerson's musical interests often being geared more towards complex classically influenced music and Lake sometimes being more drawn to straightforward rock. Endearingly though, for all of their differences, there was also a tremendously strong creative rapport between Emerson, Lake and Palmer and as a result, from the early days, musical magic was certainly on the cards.

In *Melody Maker* in May 1970, Chris Welch reported on what was very early days for ELP; "Being witness to the birth of a band is always an exciting experience, and especially pleasing when the talents consist of three superb musicians like Keith Emerson, Greg Lake, and Carl Palmer. It was a privilege to hear the first tentative steps together of those who quit the security of three established bands — The Nice, King Crimson and Atomic Rooster — at a special preview at a London recording studio. The band had only played four times when I heard them at Island's half-built main studio in an old church in Notting Hill. Their representatives took pains to point out that they had only just started and were not entirely together. But the sounds that emerged were immediately startling and auger well for the future.

"Surprisingly, when one considers that they are already tipped as a major new force and have been under pressure to appear at this year's galaxy of festivals, the group have been having serious problems, the main one being a place to rehearse. There were several complaints about the noise as they thundered away — Carl 'The Basher' Palmer contributing one of his phenomenal drum solos, Greg buzzing his bass until the floor began to vibrate, and Keith tipping his organ around to obtain the frightening effects he made famous with The Nice.

"On bearding them in their lair, they were grappling with a piece of contemporary music by Béla Bartók, which sounded quite remarkable in their dextrous hands. They paused for deep conversation about the placing of accents, Keith peering across his grand piano to Carl concentrating furiously on drum patterns… They treated me to a fast and furious version of 'Rondo' with Carl disappearing in a blur of hair and drum sticks as he attacked his snare, bass and tom toms with brutal strength. 'And there's more where that came from', he gasped later. A version of '21st Century Schizoid Man' set my teeth on edge, aggravated by the vibration of the flooring, which in turn caused a stream of complaints from the studio below.

© Marka/ Press Holland/ (Alamy Stock Photo)

Plymouth Guildhall, 23rd August 1970
The first gig as captured by Tony Byers.

© Tony Byers (Alamy Stock Photo)

Plymouth Guildhall, 23rd August 1970.

"They have to work a lot on material and arrangements. But the raw resources are there and when they are ready to explode upon us – BAZONKA! Hey, that's not a bad name for a group."

As a footnote, Emerson played a version of *Pictures At An Exhibition* on the organ at Chris Welch's wedding on 4th December 1971. It was included among a choice of traditional hymns.

The band's first live gig took place on 23rd August 1970 at the Plymouth Guildhall. A local band by the name of Earth was the support act. It was reported in *New Musical Express* in August 1970; "Emerson, Lake and Palmer made their world debut on Sunday at Plymouth Guildhall. The group strolled on stage looking somewhat nervous, somewhat apprehensive. They'd been rehearsing for four months and this was the test. 'This is what we sound like', said Keith Emerson, and the group launched into 'Barbarian', a thundering wall of sound with Keith playing two Hammond organs at the same time and Greg Lake pumping at his fuzz bass. The music had a feeling of power, of indestructible strength and the capacity audience were unleashed. Then 'Take A Pebble', a more fragile number with Keith plucking at the piano strings and then Greg switching to acoustic guitar, his voice floating out smoothly with Keith now on electric harpsichord. Next, a forty-minute composition, aptly titled *Pictures At An Exhibition*, a series of musical paintings and musical modes. *Pictures* saw the debut of the Moog synthesiser, weird electric sounds, sometimes harsh and angry and sometimes soft and soothing. Throughout, Carl Palmer bent over his drums, sometimes smiling at Greg who stood solid like a three-hundred-year oak tree. Emerson's showmanship was exceptional as he attacked his instruments in an orgy of visual excitement. Suddenly *Pictures* was over and the group were walking off stage, sweating and happy. The audience wanted more, much more. E. L. and P. returned and 'Rondo' — tighter and more forceful than ever before — blasted out. Then another encore. 'Remember this?' said Keith, as he led into 'Nut Rocker' once more. As Keith, Greg and Carl finally

Plymouth Guildhall, 23rd August 1970.

© Tony Byers (Alamy Stock Photo)

walked off, shirtless and exhausted, the audience stood on their chairs shouting, clapping, whistling, stamping their feet. For a full quarter of an hour the hopeful shouts of 'more, more' filled the concert hall. Emerson, Lake and Palmer had arrived."

Palmer recalled, "Our first show was at the Plymouth Guildhall, ahead of the Isle of Wight Festival of August 1970. It only held about 430 people, so it was a pretty small venue. But we went down a storm and earned around £400."

It was still relatively humble beginnings though; ELP travelled to the gig in a transit van that had previously been owned by Yes. The logic behind playing in a small venue outside of London was to ensure that if things didn't go well on the night, embarrassment would be less public and ideally, minimised. Fortunately though, the gig went well.

From the sublime to the ridiculous, ELP's second gig was six days later on the 29th August at the Isle of Wight Festival. Emerson had put in a memorable performance there with The Nice the previous year and in some ways, the pressure was on. Lake asserted, "If you could imagine the problems that faced this band when we started. We had to live down The Nice for a start, which wasn't easy since we had the main element of The Nice with us. Then, we only had a few weeks to get an act on the road and an album made. It had to be unpretentious and it had to set a direction for all of us at the same time. Incredibly difficult, as you can imagine."

The scale of the Isle of Wight Festival was such that it drew a lot of attention to ELP. Lake said, "After that festival, the very next day ELP was on the front page of every music newspaper. It was indeed one of those overnight sensations."

Skilled showmen that they were and not ones to miss an opportunity, Emerson and Lake set off cannons at the end of *Pictures At An Exhibition*. Prior to the performance, Emerson had tested the cannons in a field close to Heathrow Airport. Lake enthused on how at "the very end of our experimental arrangement of *Pictures At An Exhibition*, when Keith and I triggered the two cannons on stage, it was an unbelievable once in a lifetime moment when the entire audience rose to their feet and gave the band a standing ovation."

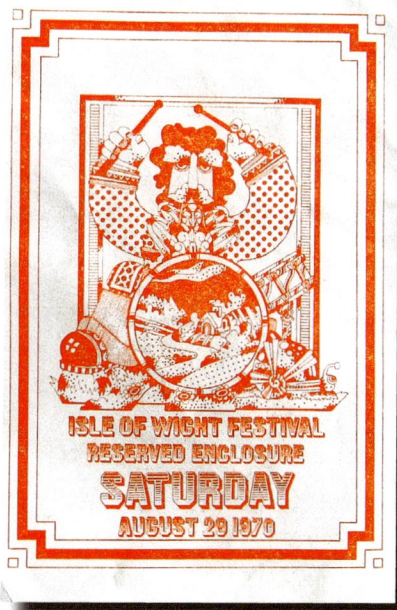

Only the band's second gig. The biggest ever concert to be held in the United Kingdom propelled ELP's career overnight.

Greg looking out at the sea of faces.

Keith doing his thing at the monumental Isle of
Wight Festival. An estimated audience of around
600,000 is thought to have descended on the tiny
island over the course of the weekend.

© Philippe Gras (Alamy Stock Photo)

Emerson, Lake and Palmer's eponymous debut studio album was released in the UK in November 1970 on Island Records. The album's initial North American release was several weeks later, in January 1971, on Atlantic Records' Cotillion Records subsidiary. Recording of the album began in July 1970 at Advision Studios when ELP were still yet to perform live. The performance at the Isle of Wight Festival and the subsequent touring through in September and October proved to be excellent promotion for their debut album. It went to number four in the UK and on the American Billboard 200 it got to number eighteen. The album got to number seventeen in Canada on three separate occasions, the first of which was 8th May — it stayed in the top one hundred for thirty-five weeks.

Released as a single in 1970, 'Lucky Man' charted in the US and in Canada. It got to number forty-eight on the Billboard Hot 100. It also got into the top twenty in the Netherlands. It was re-released in 1973 and charted again in the US and Canada. In 1971, Billboard described the song as being "loaded with programming appeal and should make its mark on the sales charts." Lake presented the song (the one that he had written when he was twelve years old) to Emerson and Palmer and the three of them improvised arrangements for it. ELP's treatment of the song showcases one of rock music's earliest uses of a Moog synthesiser solo.

For years to come, Lake would go on to explain the origins of 'Lucky Man' across a number of interviews. When his mother gave him his first guitar, the first chords he picked up were D, A minor, E minor, and G. He wrote 'Lucky Man' within the scope of his early knowledge of those chords, and here it was, used on ELP's debut album when the group were in need of one more song. When Lake first played the song to Emerson and Palmer, they were initially unimpressed. They were also unsure of whether the feel of it would be a good fit for the album overall. Lake then worked on the song in the studio with Palmer. He added multiple overdubs of bass, triple-tracked acoustic guitars, electric guitar, and harmony vocals until it sounded convincing. This particular recording of the song is featured on the deluxe edition of ELP's debut album. It also has a second electric guitar solo in place of where Emerson would later come in to overdub his Moog solo. Emerson's Moog synthesiser solo was recorded in one take. The solo begins as a low drone on D before it shoots up by two octaves and glides distinctively throughout.

'Lucky Man' still stood out as a unique component of ELP's eponymous album; unlike many of the songs that richly made use of a distorted fuzz bass, 'Lucky Man' is of a more acoustic nature overall. The lyrics tell the story of a man who had everything but died when he went to war.

Lake considered of the song; "I truly cannot remember everything about writing it other than I think it struck me as being a sort of minstrel type of event with these chords, G, D, E Minor and A Minor. 'Lucky Man' has kind of an almost medieval element tone to it. It is like a medieval folk song in a way.

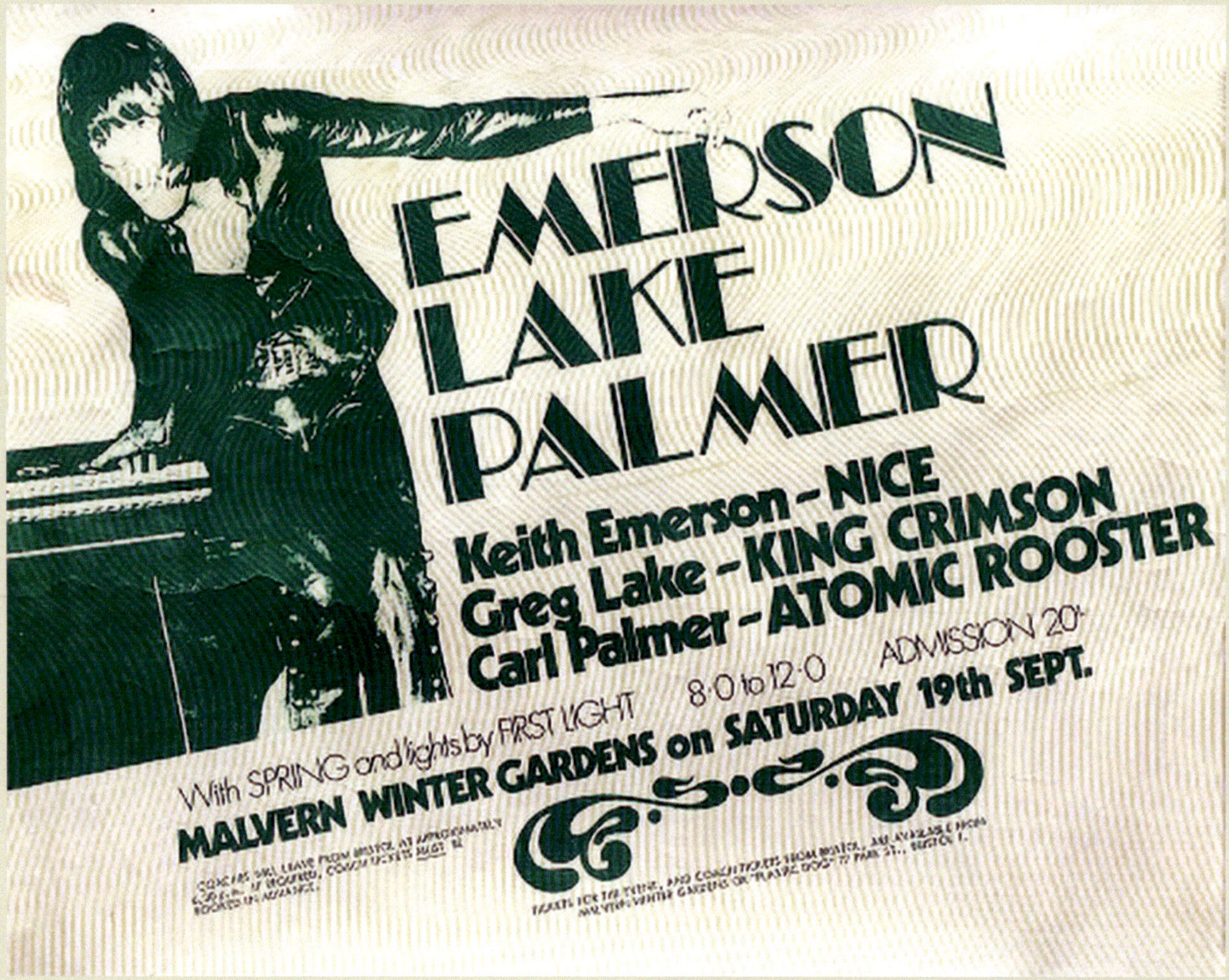
EMERSON
LAKE
PALMER
Keith Emerson - NICE
Greg Lake - KING CRIMSON
Carl Palmer - ATOMIC ROOSTER
With SPRING and lights by FIRST LIGHT
8·0 to 12·0
ADMISSION 20/-
MALVERN WINTER GARDENS on SATURDAY 19th SEPT.

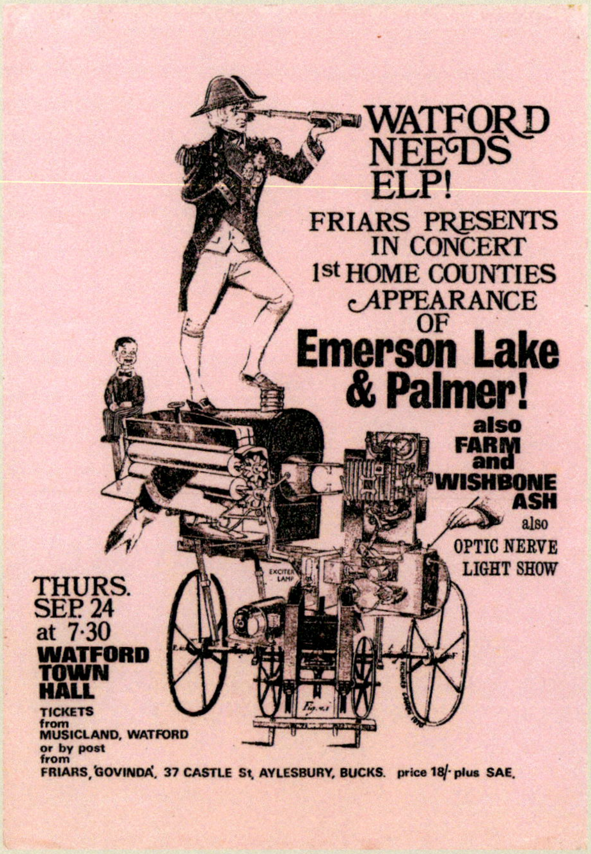
WATFORD NEEDS ELP!
FRIARS PRESENTS IN CONCERT
1st HOME COUNTIES APPEARANCE OF
Emerson Lake & Palmer!
also
FARM and WISHBONE ASH
also
OPTIC NERVE LIGHT SHOW
THURS. SEP. 24 at 7·30
WATFORD TOWN HALL
TICKETS from MUSICLAND, WATFORD or by post from FRIARS, 'GOVINDA', 37 CASTLE St, AYLESBURY, BUCKS. price 18/- plus SAE.

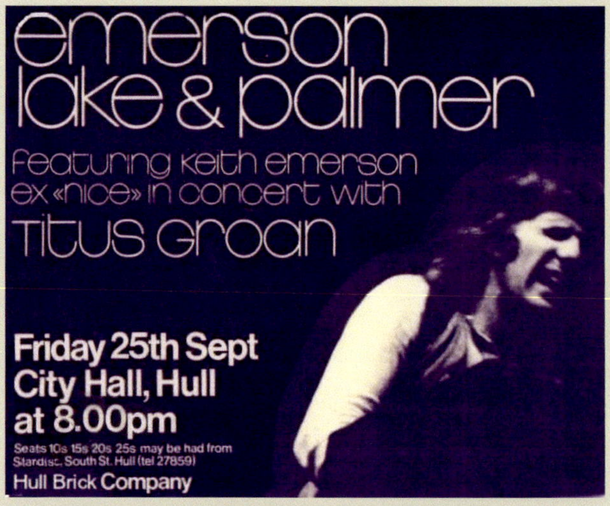
emerson
lake & palmer
featuring keith emerson
ex «nice» in concert with
TITUS GROAN
Friday 25th Sept
City Hall, Hull
at 8.00pm
Seats 10s 15s 20s 25s may be had from
Stardisc, South St. Hull (tel 27859)
Hull Brick Company

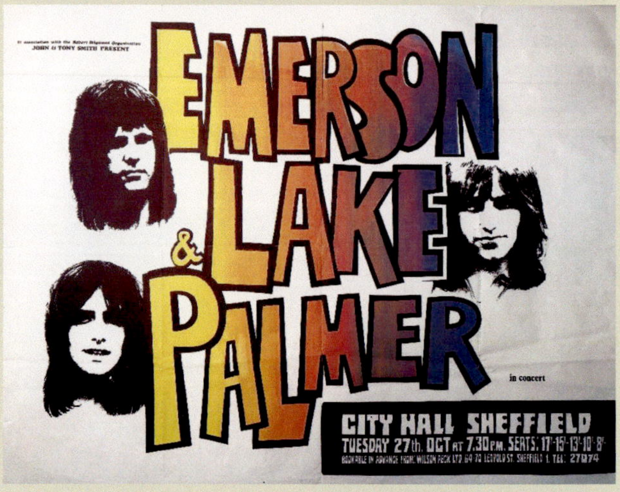
JOHN & TONY SMITH PRESENT
EMERSON
& LAKE
PALMER
in concert
CITY HALL SHEFFIELD
TUESDAY 27th. OCT AT 7.30 P.M. SEATS: 17/- 15/- 13/- 10/- 8/-
BOOKABLE IN ADVANCE FROM: WILSON PECK LTD. 64-70 LEOPOLD ST. SHEFFIELD 1. TEL: 27074

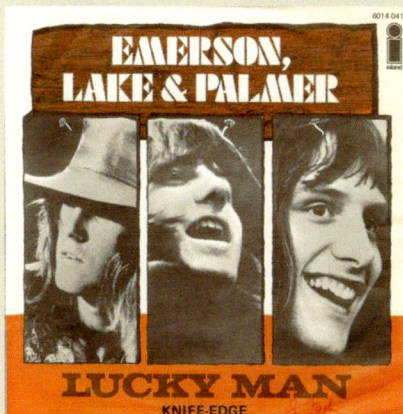

That was the essence of the idea. I wrote the song in its entirety and I finished it and I remembered it… You cannot disassociate the tune; the song has been very lucky for me. It came about because of a piece of good fortune, which was my mother giving me the guitar and it has been lucky for me ever since. I would say if I was going to be honest, I have been very lucky in life."

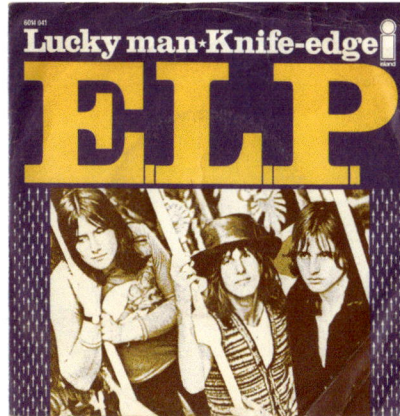

ELP began to work on their second studio album in January 1971. Following their 1970 European tour, the band returned to Advision Studios in London, to begin work on new material. ELP's second album, *Tarkus*, was released in June 1971 on Island Records. The album went to number one in the UK and to number nine in the US. It got to number twelve in Canada on two occasions that totalled four weeks.

Despite the album's success, it wasn't all plain sailing. Lake was frustrated that Emerson chose to play in keys that were not a good fit for his voice. Also, Lake wasn't happy with the album's title track. After a band meeting with management, he was persuaded to record the song but as a compromise, he contributed his original composition, 'Battlefield'. Such were the tensions of the 'Tarkus' suite that Lake nearly left the band over the whole thing. He eventually got on board with the project but evidently, even at a relatively early stage in their tenure, it is clear that ELP consisted of strong-minded individuals.

61

A rather unusual advertising poster for the show at Painters Mill Music Theatre, Owing Mills, Maryland

H & S PRODUCTIONS
AL HAYWARD & JOHN SCHER
PRESENTS IN CONCERT

EMERSON, LAKE & PALMER

plus

"Hog Heaven"

Friday MAY 7 8 PM
ONE PERFORMANCE... ONE NIGHT ONLY

at UPSALA COLLEGE
IN VIKING HALL ON CAMPUS
E. ORANGE, N.J.

TICKETS $5

TICKET INFORMATION
CALL 694-1347

Tensions aside, everyone got their heads together. *Tarkus* was a strong album commercially and musically and it didn't take too long to record either. Emerson said, "*Tarkus* was like a testing ground for us, I think, mainly because of the time changes and key changes. I think it was a good start for us to get into doing something that was really experimental. To that extent it means a lot to me."

Lake said, "It took six days to record *Tarkus*. I don't know whether that's because there are so few people in the band, but I'm sure that doing an album quickly helps to make it sound fresh. If you spend four days on one song you lose a lot, whereas you can maintain one hundred percent energy if you only do it for a day. There is a danger in becoming analytical. In some ways you score but in others you dip badly. If you take out a note because it's slightly flat you lose the rawness and aggression."

Side one of the album consists of the seven-part 'Tarkus' whilst side two features a collection of shorter tracks. As a suite in seven parts, 'Tarkus' is one of the earliest multipart progressive rock songs. It is almost twenty-one minutes long, The odd numbered sections are instrumentals, and the even numbered ones include vocals. It is a concept piece whereby not only is the overall idea embedded in the music and lyrics alone, but also from the album artwork and the section titles. That said, the concept and narrative is ambiguous and is certainly open to interpretation. The short songs on side two are unrelated to 'Tarkus' and indeed, each other.

The Melody Maker Awards, 16th September 1971. Is Greg looking down on the journalists?

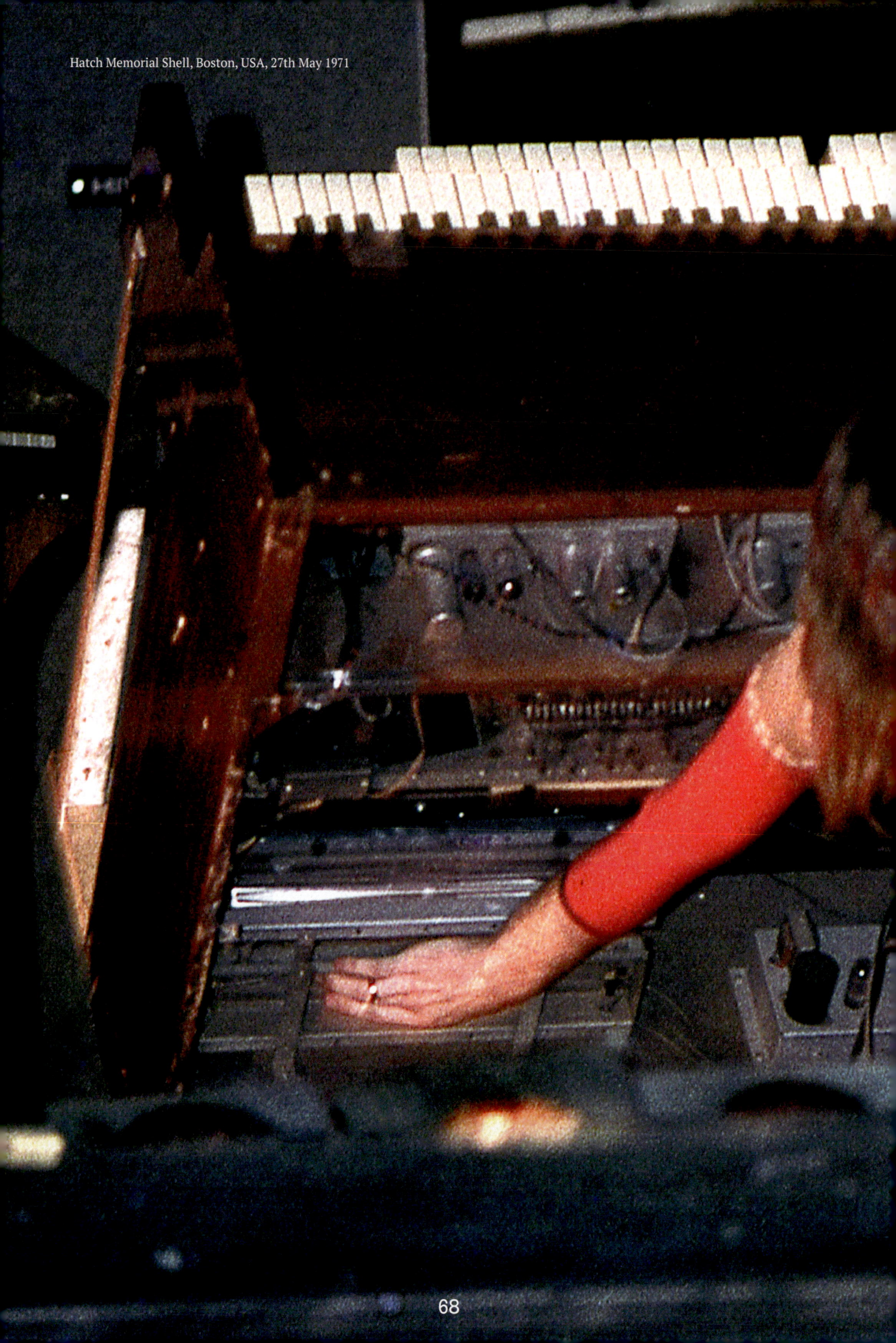

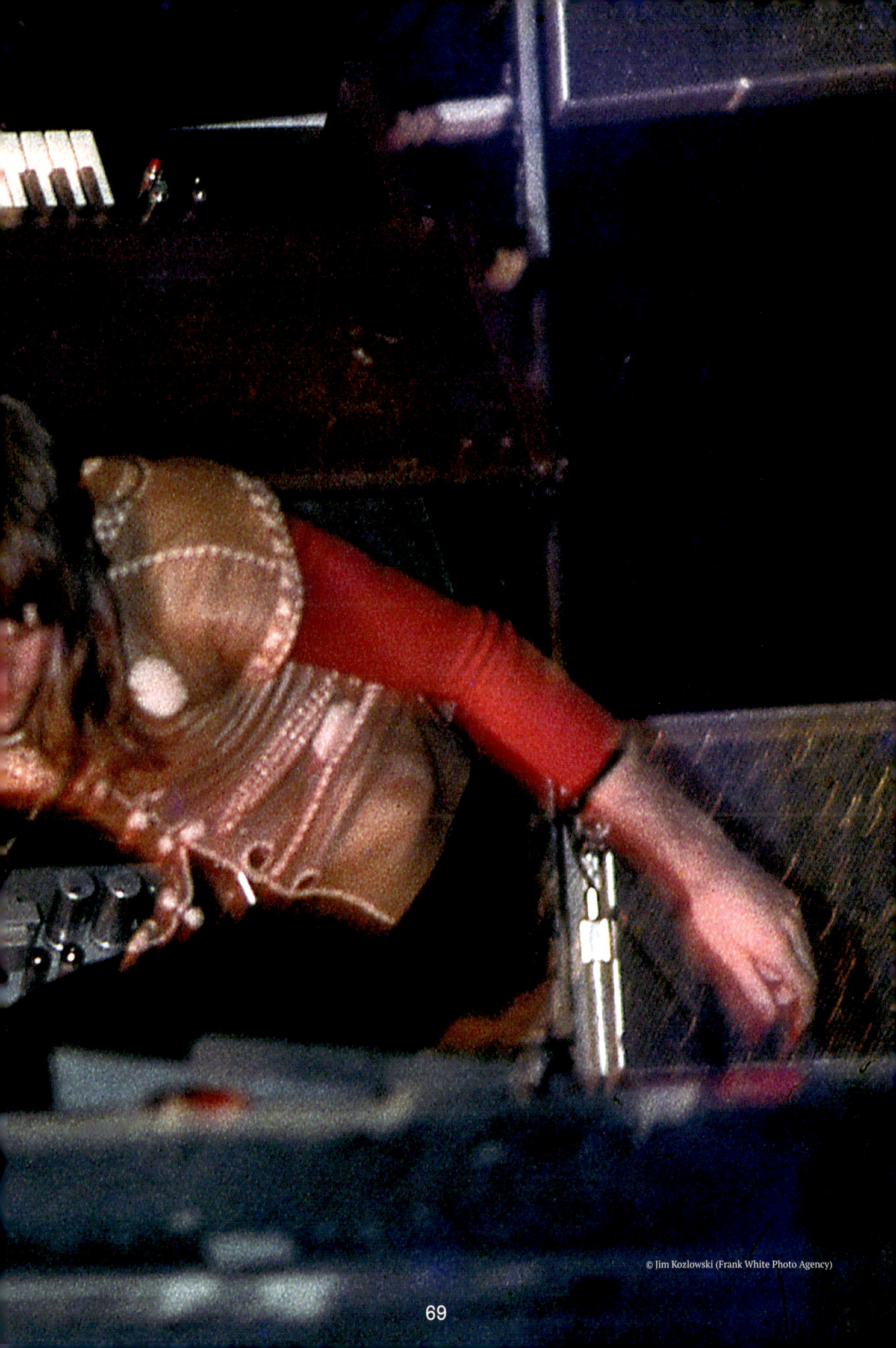

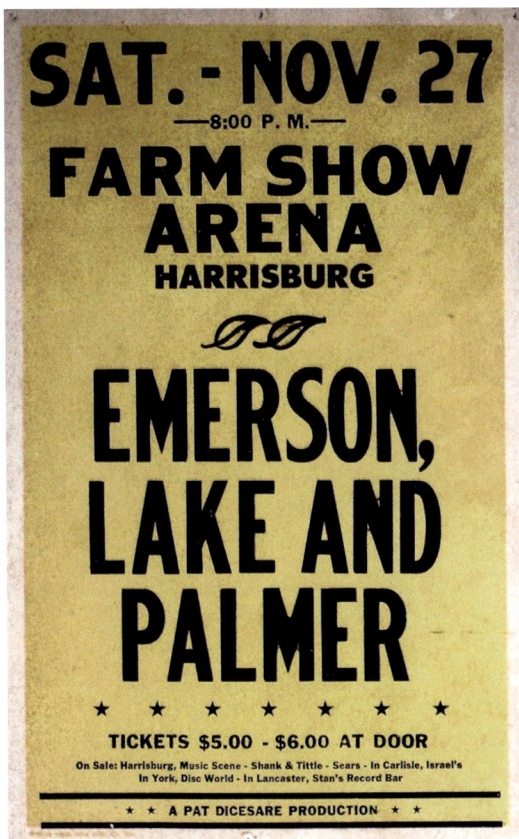

SAT. - NOV. 27
——8:00 P. M.——
FARM SHOW
ARENA
HARRISBURG

EMERSON,
LAKE AND
PALMER

★ ★ ★ ★ ★ ★ ★

TICKETS $5.00 - $6.00 AT DOOR

On Sale: Harrisburg, Music Scene - Shank & Tittle - Sears - In Carlisle, Israel's
In York, Disc World - In Lancaster, Stan's Record Bar

★ ★ A PAT DICESARE PRODUCTION ★ ★

ELP's next album was *Pictures At An Exhibition*. It was released in the UK in November 1971. It features their performance of Mussorgsky's composition that was recorded at Newcastle City Hall on 26th March 1971. As the full performance of the piece is barely half an hour long the encore of 'Nut Rocker' concluded the album. There was much uncertainty regarding how the recording should be released, if at all! There was initially an idea to release *Pictures At An Exhibition* as the second ELP album following the success of their eponymous debut album. However, it was felt that the length and classical nature of the piece was such that it would struggle to get radio play. There was also a feeling from ELP that to release *Pictures At An Exhibition* as their second album would be a risk to their reputation overall because they didn't want to be pigeonholed as a band whose main thing was classical music, hence why they decided to focus on *Tarkus* first.

Lake explained,"There was talk of releasing the Newcastle City Hall recording as ELP's second album, but the record company was not convinced that an interpretation of a whole classical suite was going to sell, despite how it had gone down at our live performances. The idea was shelved for the time being, but after the success of our second album and tour, it was released in November 1971, reaching number three in the UK album charts. As well as *Pictures*, the album included the live encore of 'Nut Rocker', inspired by Kim Fowley's version of the March from Tchaikovsky's ballet, *The Nutcracker.*"

ELP took a break from touring in September 1971 to record new material for what would be their third studio album. Emerson stated that he was pleased that the material was notably different to *Tarkus*. With *Tarkus* having confirmed ELP's position commercially in 1971 and with *Pictures At An Exhibition* being seen as something of a side project, in 1972, ELP's *Trilogy* album moved somewhat away from the group's use of classical music influences.

MAR Y SOL POP FESTIVAL

The First International Puerto Rico Pop Festival

April 1, 2, 3

appearing in concert

Alice Cooper
Allman Bros. Band
B. B. King
Black Sabbath
Bloodrock
Dave Brubeck
with
Gerry Mulligan
Dr. John
Emerson, Lake & Palmer

Faces with
Rod Stewart,
Ronnie Wood,
Ron Lane,
Ian McLagan,
Ken Jones

Fleetwood Mac
J. Geils Band
Goose Creek Symphony
Herbie Mann
Malo
Osibisa
Poco
Pot Liquor
Roberta Flack
Savoy Brown

A fiesta in Puerto Rico. Camping on 429 acres including over a mile of Caribbean beach.

Tickets **$15.00** (not including travel arrangements.)

TICKETRON Available from Ticketron Agencies in Atlanta, Boston, Chicago, New York, Philadelphia, Washington, and other major cities.

Complete Festival Package:
Including Round Trip Air Fare, Ground Transportation, Camping Facilities, and Tickets to the Festival.   **$149.**

Atlanta Price for Travel Package: $169.

In New York call: (212) 687-3500
In Boston call: (617) 884-6800
In Washington call: (202) 785-0744
In Miami call: (305) 358-6430
In Philadelphia call: (215) 985-0111

call: (404) 255-1215

A Presentation of Island Ventures, Inc.

EMERSON, LAKE & PALMER
with special guest stars
WEST, BRUCE & LAING

OHIO UNIVERSITY THURSDAY APRIL 20 8 P.M. CONVOCATION CENTER TICKETS: $3.50 $4 $4.50

ELP's one and only visit to Japan in the seventies wasn't exactly a tour. They played just two shows. Tokyo on the 22nd July and this gig at the Koshien Stadium in Osaka on the 24th. For both shows ELP was supported by fellow British rockers Free. Although Free was coming towards the end of its career (disbanding in February the following year), the big stadium shows were another example of ELP's meteoric rise that was still on the ascendancy.

ELP's third studio album *Trilogy* was released in July 1972 on Island Records. It got to number two in the UK and to number five on the Billboard 200. It appeared in the top ten in Denmark for four non-consecutive weeks (it peaked at number six there). Billboard advocated positively of the album on the basis of Emerson's "steady progression" on the Moog synthesiser.

Trilogy increased ELP's worldwide popularity. It included the track, 'Hoedown' — an arrangement of the Aaron Copland composition. It quickly became one of ELP's most popular songs live. With new material from the *Trilogy* album added into the setlist, ELP began to use less content from *Pictures At An Exhibition*. Material from the latter went on to become the stuff of ELP encores in later years. *Trilogy* went gold in the US and the song 'From The Beginning' made ELP's music accessible to a wider audience. It was released as a single and it got to number thirty-nine in the US. Lake said of writing the song, "I just felt an inspiration to do it, and it flowed through me in a natural way. My hands fell upon these very unusual chords... It was kind of a gift."

Hipgnosis did the artwork for *Trilogy*. The interior of the original gatefold sleeve features a photomontage of ELP in Epping Forest. The front cover was the first to feature their faces; Emerson asserted that this was a deliberate decision rather than a product of coincidence.

After the release of *Trilogy*, ELP toured Europe and the US, playing to sold-out venues. By the beginning of 1973, ELP had secured commercial success in both the UK and the US.

At the 1972 Melody Maker awards ceremony

© Marka / EPS (Alamy Stock Photo)

Rock At The Oval

1972 MELODY MAKER POLL AWARDS CONCERT

THIS SATURDAY
30 SEPT.
MIDDAY-9PM

EMERSON LAKE AND PALMER

Special Guest Stars

WISHBONE ASH
ARGENT
GENESIS · FOCUS

FOR LATEST DETAILS SEE THIS ISSUE OF MM

Special ticket prices:
£1.00 in advance, £1.25 on day

ALL THOSE GIVEN SPECIAL PASSES FOR CLEARING LITTER AT THE LAST OVAL CONCERT, MAY EXCHANGE THEM FOR FREE TICKETS AT HARLEQUIN, 66 GREAT TITCHFIELD ST., W.1

From All Branches Of Harlequin Record Shops The Oval & One Stop Records 97 Dean St W1.

record shops 01-636 1348

40 South Molton St W1. 2 The Square Richmond

CORNHILL 74 Cornhill	FLEET ST. 163 Fleet St.	BALHAM 108 High Rd.	WEST END 67 Gt Titchfield St
LUTON 12 Arndale centre	50 Fenchurch St.	OXFORD 12 George St.	OXFORD ST. 201 Oxford St
BOW LANE 4 Bow Lane	HIGH HOLBORN 36 High Holborn	CAMBRIDGE 4 Bridge St.	MARBLE ARCH 527 Oxford St
CANNON ST. 129 Cannon St.	BROMPTON RD Escalate 187	BEDFORD 97 High St	NEW BOND ST. 119 New Bond St.
LIVERPOOL ST. 41 Liverpool St.	MAIDENHEAD 7 Nicholson's Walk	EPSOM 16 High St.	BERWICK ST. 98 Berwick St.
MOORGATE 121 Moorgate	GUILDFORD 14 Tunsgate Square	CAMBERLEY 14 Princes Way	HAYMARKET 35½ Haymarket
CHEAPSIDE 116 Cheapside	READING 22 Union St.	CHELSEA Drug Store, 49 Kings Rd.	VICTORIA 28 Strutton Ground
FENCHURCH ST. 150 Fenchurch St.	57 The South Mall Butts Centre		

TICKETS BY POST FROM HARLEQUIN RECORDS 67 GT TITCHFIELD ST LONDON W1

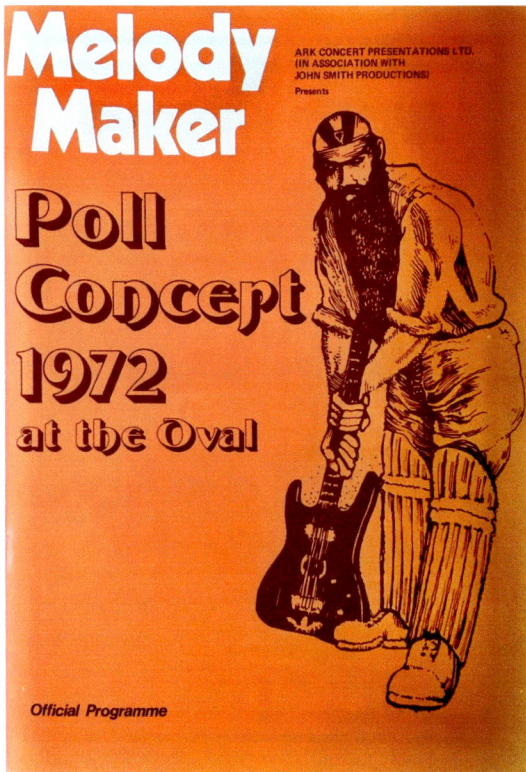

Melody Maker Poll Concert 1972 at the Oval

ARK CONCERT PRESENTATIONS LTD.
(IN ASSOCIATION WITH JOHN SMITH PRODUCTIONS)
Presents

Official Programme

ELP's performance at London's Oval cricket ground was reviewed in *Circus* in January 1973; "As the crowd roared their approval, the group raced from backstage, launching immediately into 'Hoedown', the upbeat, good-humoured number from their recent *Trilogy* LP, and the crowd was on its feet. Without hesitation, the group jumped immediately into 'Tarkus', and simultaneously pulled off the biggest feat in the history of rock wizardry. Two mammoth armadillo tanks appeared on both sides of the stage, bellowing replicas of the figures on the *Tarkus* cover. The metal dragons breathed clouds of smoke, and, as the show thundered to its climactic high point, the tanks thundered an ear-deafening barrage, driving fans into a wild frenzy of excitement and jubilation. Keith pounded the piano as 'Take A Pebble' echoed from the massive multi-toned speakers, and Greg Lake brought down the house with his excellent acoustic guitar work on 'Lucky Man'.

"But with the advent of *Pictures At An Exhibition*, off the LP of the same name, the crowd watched in absolute amazement as Carl Palmer's drum solo threatened to pop the sliver of sun out of the darkening sky. In a fury, Carl hurled himself at the drum kit, battering the cymbals and destroying the gongs. The *Tarkus* tanks belched forth their deafening roar as London's last great rock concert of the season shrieked to its end — and ELP proved once again that they remain the world's greatest rock band, upholding their title of Britain's Best Band, (the title they won last year) and taking on the title of World's Best Band as well. As the last fans wearily straggled home, ELP slowly unwound backstage, gathering the remains of their shattered instruments with them. Each clutched at their golden trophies: Top Group, British and International; Emerson's tribute as the top keyboard man; Palmer's trophy

as top drummer; Lake's souvenir as the world's most accomplished producer; ELP as the top pop arrangers; and finally the shared award, Keith Emerson and Greg Lake taking honours as the world's top composers."

JOHN & TONY SMITH PRESENT

EMERSON LAKE & PALMER
+ JIMMY STEVENS
in concert

CONCERT DATES:
Friday,   10th Nov. WINTER GARDENS, BOURNEMOUTH
Saturday,   11th Nov. GAUMONT, SOUTHAMPTON
Monday,   13th Nov. FREE TRADE HALL, MANCHESTER
Tuesday,   14th Nov. HARDROCK, MANCHESTER
Wednesday,   15th Nov. ST. GEORGE'S HALL, BRADFORD
Thursday,   16th Nov. ODEON, NEWCASTLE
Friday,   17th Nov. GREEN'S PLAYHOUSE, GLASGOW

Saturday,   18th Nov. GUILDHALL, PRESTON
Sunday,   19th Nov. TRENTHAM GARDENS, STOKE ON TRENT
Tuesday,   21st Nov. DE MONTFORT HALL, LEICESTER
Wednesday,   22nd Nov. TOP RANK SUITE, LIVERPOOL
Thursday,   23rd Nov. THE CAPITAL, CARDIFF
Friday,   24th Nov. ODEON, BIRMINGHAM
Saturday,   25th Nov. CITY HALL, SHEFFIELD
Sunday,   26th Nov. ODEON, HAMMERSMITH
Monday,   27th Nov. THE DOME, BRIGHTON

After doing the tour to support *Trilogy*, ELP began work on new material that would once again blend classical and rock influences. With their commercial profile growing ever higher, it made sense to take more control from a business perspective.

ELP had become frustrated with Atlantic Records. It was felt that they were not getting involved enough when and where it mattered. In March 1973, along with their manager Stewart Young, ELP decided to form their own record company. Collectively, they purchased an abandoned ABC cinema in Fulham, West London. They converted it into a rehearsal room and a company headquarters, which they later named as Manticore Records. Lake explained "We set up Manticore to try and make the entire record process as good as it could be. We were also aware of a number of artists who we knew were having problems getting their music released and getting a record deal."

In April 1973, Atlantic promoter, Mario Medious, who had worked with ELP since their first album, was brought in to serve as the president of Manticore. The decision was made on the basis that ELP didn't have the time to do the job themselves. Atlantic handled distribution duties.

Brain Salad Surgery was recorded from June to September at Olympic and Advision Studios. It was mixed in October 1973 at AIR Studios in London. As was the case with all of ELP's previous albums, their fourth was produced by Lake. It was released on 19th November 1973, their first on Manticore.

The album cover was designed by H. R. Giger. *Brain Salad Surgery* continued to support ELP's commercial success. It got to number two in the UK

Greg and Carl relaxing on tour.

and to number eleven in the US, eventually going gold in both countries. To support the album, ELP embarked on their largest world tour thus far — the one that included a headlining spot at the California Jam Festival in 1974.

ELP had started work on new material towards the end of 1972. Lake explained in an interview, that *Trilogy* had been recorded via the use of 24-track machines and, as a result, featured too many overdubs that made the music very difficult to recreate well for live performance. A decision was therefore made to make an album that could comfortably be performed on stage. With the rehearsal facilities being a former cinema it allowed ELP to alternate between playing live and then writing more material after assessing how it all played out. It was during the writing sessions in late 1972 / early 1973 that the first two tracks for the fourth album began to take shape. One of them was the first movement of the epic 'Karn Evil 9'. The other was an adaptation of the fourth movement from Alberto Ginastera's 1st Piano Concerto.

When completed the three movements 'Karn Evil 9' ran for nearly half an hour. Originally, the first movement had to be split into two parts across sides one and two of the vinyl record. Although the original Atlantic CD remained loyal to the division of the suite, later releases have presented it as a cohesive piece. Written by Emerson, it combines inspiration from both rock and classical music. In terms of structure, the first and third movements are split up by a distinctive instrumental passage.

'Karn Evil 9' was initially intended as an instrumental piece. This ultimately didn't emerge to be the case though. Lake wrote lyrics for the first movement. To assist him he brought in lyricist Peter Sinfield who he had worked with in King Crimson. Sinfield recalled, "I was halfway through making a solo album when Greg called me to say that Manticore wanted to release it. The catch was that he wanted me to collaborate on lyrics for a long piece that had begun to take shape."

Sinfield felt that the music Emerson had written reminded him of a carnival and he came up with the title 'Karn Evil 9' on that basis. The second part of the first movement of 'Karn Evil 9' features the famous lyric "Welcome back, my friends, to the show that never ends..." The line eventually being used as the title for ELP's second live album.

The sped-up and altered voice in the second movement and the "computer" voice in the third movement were made by Emerson — they were his only vocal contribution to the trio's repertoire. In order to create the "computer" voice, Emerson ran his voice through the Moog's ring modulator.

As far back as 1971, Emerson had been thinking about recording an adaptation of the 4th Movement ('Toccata concertata') of Ginastera's 1st Piano Concerto. He was still a member of The Nice when he had first heard the piece and it had stayed with him since. It wasn't until Palmer suggested adding a drum solo to the trio's repertoire that Emerson began to weigh up the prospect of how the piece

It was at these shows where Keith said he first tried out the revolving piano stunt.

could be executed by ELP. Lake and Palmer were up for it but it required some thought when it came to designing an arrangement that would work with everyone's strengths in mind.

Emerson got in touch with Ginastera's publishers. In their response, they insisted that it would be unlikely that the composer would allow any of his works to be adapted. Despite this, they did advise Emerson that he should talk with Ginastera face to face. Consequently, Emerson flew to Geneva to talk to the composer. Upon playing the new arrangement to him, Emerson was granted the permission to proceed. Emerson recalled of the meeting; "He played our recording of 'Toccata' on a tape recorder. After a few bars he stopped the tape... and exclaimed 'Diabolic!' I thought he said 'diabolical' and expected him to show us the door. He had been listening to the tape in mono and our recording was in stereo. I jumped up and switched the machine to stereo hoping he would listen again. It transpired that he wasn't concerned about that at all. He listened again and declared 'Terrible!' which actually was a compliment. 'You've captured the essence of my music like no one else has before,' the great maestro said."

Both 'Karn Evil 9: 1st Impression' and 'Toccata' were used as part of the setlist for a series of concerts that took place across Europe beginning in late March 1973. It was around the same time that a new song was introduced to the repertoire. 'Still... You Turn Me On' was written by Lake. The semi-acoustic number brought a mellow balance to a set that was dominated by more abrasive numbers.

The recording sessions were prolific with three tracks recorded that weren't included on the album. 'When The Apple Blossoms Bloom In The Windmills Of Your Mind I'll Be Your Valentine' was the b-side of the single 'Jerusalem' and bizarrely the title song was released in conjunction with the *New Musical Express* as a flexi single in October '73. The third track, 'Tiger In A Spotlight' didn't see the light of day for another four years.

With the exception of his drum solo in 'Toccata', *Brain Salad Surgery* was the first ELP album where Palmer had no song writing credits. Despite this, over the years, he has still said that the album is a favourite of his.

Brain Salad Surgery took nine months to complete. Lake considered, "It's certainly taken longer to write and put together than others, but after you've made four albums people expect a certain thing from you and it's harder to come up with something that'll surprise them. A lot of bands go into solo ventures to avoid the monotony of playing the same style of music. Although we'll get into solo albums ourselves one day, the real answer for us is just to work harder and longer within the band. So when we do make solo albums it won't be through frustration."

In October 1973, it wasn't long after the recording sessions had finished that the tracks for *Brain Salad Surgery* were mixed. Following this and of course, rehearsals, ELP embarked on a world tour

© Jim Kozlowski (Frank White Photo Agency)

© Jim Kozlowski (Frank White Photo Agency)

17th January 1974. Norman St John-Stevas, Minister
for the Arts, presenting Keith with a gold disc to mark
100,000 sales of *Brain Salad Surgery*. A week later
ELP began yet another American tour at the Omni in
Atlanta, Georgia.

from 14th November 1973 that continued through to 21st August 1974. In all there would be close to one hundred and fifty live performances.

On 2nd February 1974, in the main arena at the Anaheim Convention Centre in California, ELP's performance was recorded. It was released as a three-disc anthology — *Welcome Back, My Friends, To The Show That Never Ends* — *Ladies And Gentlemen* — on 19th August 1974. An amount of the same material was broadcast on the *King Biscuit Flower Hour*. The live album got to number six in the UK chart and to number four on the Billboard 200. It was the highest US chart position ever achieved by ELP.

Exciting and innovative as ever, ELP's live shows blended skilled musicianship with spellbinding theatrics, some of which included Emerson playing a grand piano while it revolved in mid-air. His knife abuse on the Hammond organ continued, as did throwing it around the stage and letting it feedback. Meanwhile, Palmer would play on a revolving drum kit. By this stage in their tenure, ELP carried almost forty tons of equipment. It typically took five hours to unpack and set up. This included a thirty-channel board discrete quadraphonic public address sound system that had been provided by International Entertainers Service. In addition to this, there was a state-of-the-art lighting system. It had been designed by Judy Rasmussen to include large ladders at each corner of the stage and two arches installed above the centre stage.

© Marka / EPS (Alamy Stock Photo)

Welcome back EMERSON, LAKE & PALMER for the 2nd half of your triumphant U.S. Tour.

EMERSON, LAKE & PALMER ON TOUR

Jan. 24-Omni, Atlanta/Jan. 25-University of Alabama, Tuscaloosa, Alabama/Jan. 26-Barton Coliseum, Little Rock
Jan. 28-Coliseum, Denver/Jan. 30-Salt Palace, Salt Lake City/Feb. 1 & 2-Anaheim Convention Center, Anaheim, California
Feb. 3-Long Beach Arena, Long Beach, California/Feb. 9-Swing Auditorium, San Bernadino, California/Feb. 11-Arena, Seattle
Feb. 12-Coliseum, Spokane, Washington/Feb. 13-Coliseum, Portland, Oregon/Feb. 14-Coliseum, Vancouver
Feb. 15-Washington State University, Pullman, Washington/Feb. 17 & 18-Civic Auditorium, San Francisco
Feb. 20-Selland Arena, Fresno, California/Feb. 21-Sports Arena, San Diego/Feb. 22-Convention Center, Tucson, Arizona
Feb. 24-University of New Mexico, Albuquerque/Feb. 26-Municipal Auditorium, San Antonio/Feb. 27-Convention Center, Dallas
Feb. 28-Coliseum, Houston/Mar. 1-Louisiana State University, Baton Rouge

Latest album, "Brain Salad Surgery."   MC 66669

Manticore

ON MANTICORE RECORDS AND TAPES
DISTRIBUTED BY ATLANTIC RECORDS

89

EMERSON LAKE & PALMER
WEDNESDAY, FEB. 20 8PM
SELLAND ARENA

ADVANCE TICKETS $5.50 AT THE CONVENTION CENTER BOX OFFICE, SUN STEREO, SEARS CUSTOMER SERVICE, GOTTSCHALKS—MERCED & VISALIA, PLUS ALL THE USUAL LOCATIONS.

PACIFIC PRESENTATIONS

NORTHWEST RELEASING PRESENTS...

EMERSON LAKE & PALMER
with special guest
BACK DOOR

MEMORIAL COLISEUM
WED., FEBRUARY 13-8:00PM

Tickets: $5.00 Advance $6.00 Day of Show
Tickets on sale at Lipman's, Stevens & Son, Lincoln Savings, Everybody's Records, Pacific First Federal (in Vancouver) and Coliseum.

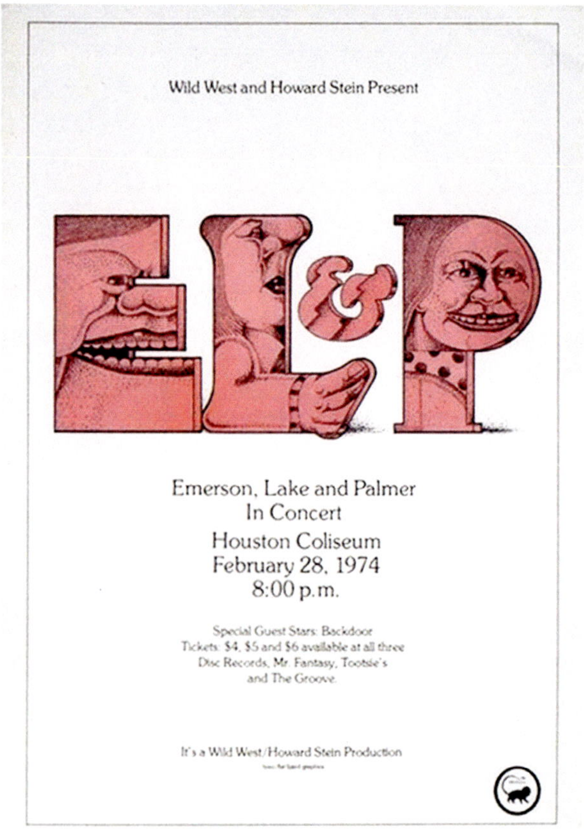

Wild West and Howard Stein Present

EL&P

Emerson, Lake and Palmer
In Concert
Houston Coliseum
February 28, 1974
8:00 p.m.

Special Guest Stars: Backdoor
Tickets: $4, $5 and $6 available at all three
Disc Records, Mr. Fantasy, Tootsie's
and The Groove.

It's a Wild West/Howard Stein Production

MID-SOUTH CONCERTS PRESENTS

Emerson Lake & Palmer

MARCH 31 • SUNDAY • 8:00 P.M.
MID-SOUTH COLISEUM
Reserved Seats
$6, $5, $4 (Obstructed View)

Ticket Locations
Coliseum Box Office • Goldsmith's Central Ticket Office (Downtown and Oak Court)
Raleigh Springs Mall Information Counter • Budget Tapes & Records
Pop's • Lafayette Radio (Southbrook Mall) • Village Records (Parkway Village)

90

Emerson Lake & Palmer

FRIDAY, FEBRUARY 15 • 8:00 P.M. • WSU PERFORMING ARTS COLISEUM

TICKETS:
$4.00 & $5.00
Doors open at 6:30
for $5.00 tickets;
7:15 for $4.00 tickets
Tickets at the door, $5.00

FESTIVAL SEATING

Tickets go on sale
Thursday, February 7th
at the CUB listening lounge
and U of I SUB.

AN ASWSU PERFORMING ARTS CONCERT...DEFINITELY!

It was on 6th April 1974, when ELP co-headlined with Deep Purple at the famous California Jam Festival. Held at the Ontario Motor Speedway, there were 350,000 paying fans in attendance. ELP's performance was broadcast by the ABC television network — it was they who sponsored the festival. The audio recording of the performance first appeared on the 1998 album, *Then And Now*.

At the time, the California Jam set records for the loudest amplification system ever installed, the highest paid attendance, and highest grossing concert. The event has gone down in history for a number of reasons, both economic and entertaining.

Deep Purple was given the choice of when they would go on stage to perform. Their guitarist, Ritchie Blackmore, was particularly explicit about the fact that he wanted to be on stage after sunset. Such decision resulted in ELP being scheduled for the last performance. Deep Purple's performance at the California Jam was one of their first with their third line-up of David Coverdale on vocals and Glenn Hughes on bass and additional vocals.

When it was time for Deep Purple to perform their set, sunset had not yet arrived. As a result, Blackmore locked himself in his trailer in protest. Eventually, after much to-ing and fro-ing, Deep Purple finally graced the stage just as it was starting to get dark but as fans were about to witness, Blackmore wasn't happy by this point. The result was a TV camera being obliterated as he furiously jabbed his guitar into it.

Not ones to have their thunder stolen, ELP's set featured Emerson's usual theatrics with extended synthesiser frenzies and playing the Hammond organ upside down.

It was so much more than that though. Emerson had opted to float in the air on a piano — not only

91

© Pictorial Press Ltd / Alamy Stock Photo

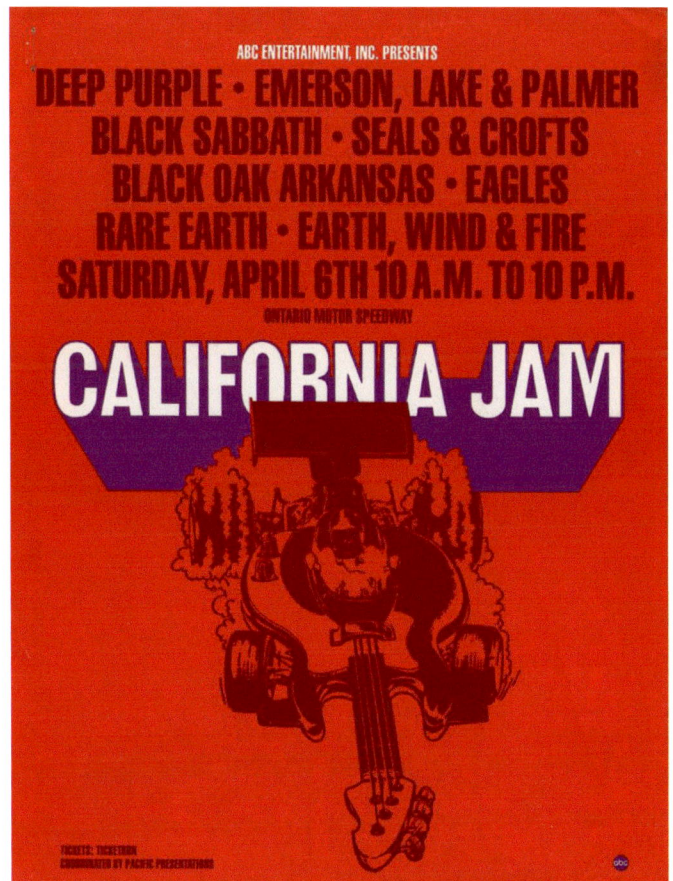

that, but he threw in a number of somersaults too. The stunt was everything that an ELP fan could hope for and more. A sight to behold, caught on tape and in front of an immensely large audience. Fantastic!

Keith explained how the stunt came to be; "I think having a pilot's licence helped a little bit. One of my road crew said we found this guy that used to work in the circus and he does a lot of things for TV and special effects and he's made something that might interest you, it's a piano that spins round, and I immediately responded, 'oh that sounds interesting.' I happened to be within the New York area and I was driven over to Long Island to a guy called Bob McCarthy, and there in the background he had this piano situated. So he called his wife down from upstairs and said, 'darling could you demonstrate this for Keith?' I looked on — I wasn't quite sure what to expect. His wife comes down and sits on the seat and up she goes in the air and proceeds to spin around. I thought, 'well that's great!' Then Bob asked me, 'do you want to have a go at it?'... 'Yeah, okay.' You need to understand, below the keyboard there's an inverted-tee, like a bar. You wrap your legs around the down pipe and put your heels under the inverted-tee. Then you go up in the air and try and do your best to play. It was a little difficult to play at first because of the centrifugal force, so it wasn't easy. I think we actually used it for the first time at Madison Square Garden, it was a Christmas concert. People in the audience were so astounded they couldn't quite believe what they were seeing.

"Later on that coming year the California Jam came up and I said we have to do that there. Bob drove the whole contraption down to the California Jam and there was very little space to set it up. There

HARVEY GOLDSMITH FOR JOHN SMITH ENTERTAINMENTS IN ASSOCIATION WITH MANTICORE PRESENTS

EMERSON, LAKE & PALMER

EMERSON, LAKE & PALMER

BRITISH TOUR 1974

APRIL 18, 19, 20 & 21. EMPIRE POOL WEMBLEY

were loads of bands up on that stage, all having to do their set and then getting their equipment off. Now, with the Moog, the Hammonds, Carl's gongs and everything, it was hard enough to just get that on stage. We had the spinning piano and everything that went along with it and we tried to find a place to situate it. It ended up going just at the end of the stage, so when the piano went up it was literally over the heads of the audience. After that, every TV show I did came the question, 'Keith, how do you spin around on that piano?' I'd say 'what about my music?' When I had the honour of meeting the great jazz pianist Dave Brubeck just before he died, he said, 'Keith you've got to tell me how do you spin around on that piano?' Dave Brubeck was ninety years old then and I said, 'Dave, don't try it!'"

Years later, Lake explained, "It was a Steinway piano. The idea was that Keith would sit in it — he would be strapped in. There would be a lot of smoke, and the piano would start to rise up into the air. It would get about fifteen, twenty feet in the air, and then it would start to spin. With him on it!"

Injuries and the ergonomic demands of the stunt were such that sadly, it came with a shelf life. Lake added, "He'd be playing while all of this was going on. You had this spinning piano, and there would be more smoke and more smoke until the piano was spinning in smoke — and then there'd be a huge explosion, and it would disappear. Now, I can't tell you how it was made to disappear. But that's what happened… There was a few times that Keith actually hurt himself doing it. So, we had to stop it. But for a while it was very impressive."

© Pictorial Press Ltd / Alamy Stock Photo

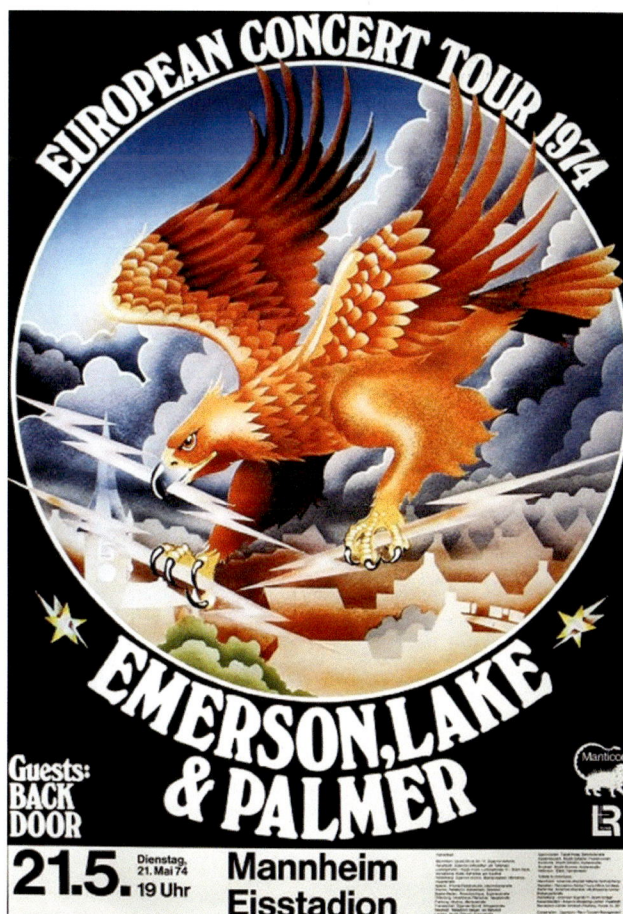

Practising backstage during the 1974 tour.

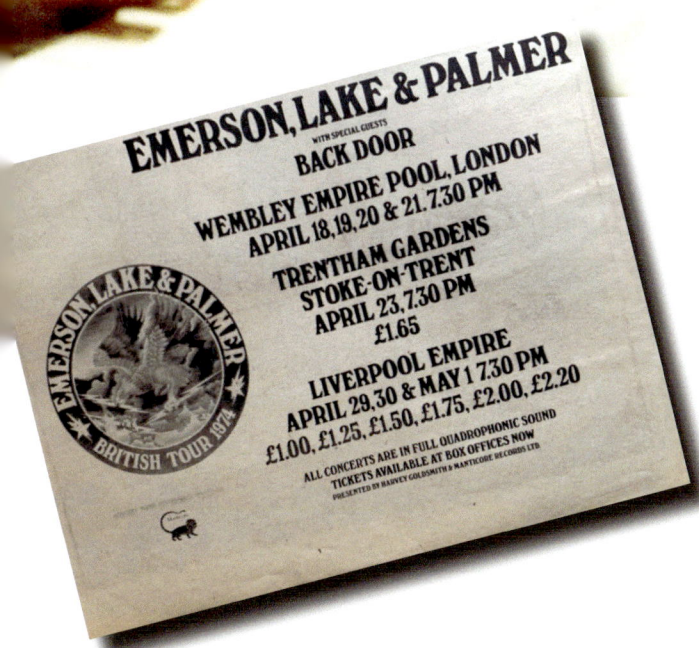

Towards the end of 1974, ELP decided that it was time for a break. Lake took the opportunity to catch up with family life and to travel. He continued to write and release music though. By this time, ELP were tax exiles relocated to Switzerland, France, Canada and the Bahamas. It meant that they were restricted to only two months' stay in England per year. Palmer spoke to *Melody Maker* about the tax situation, "England is like stealing my pension when you have to pay 83% income tax."

The extended break was certainly needed; by that point, ELP had been recording and touring every year since their formation in 1970. Emerson said that at this stage in their career, their musical direction had been "milked dry". Everyone agreed that time out was needed in order to consider what direction to go in next.

It was in 1975 and whilst still officially a member of ELP that Lake had a hit single with 'I Believe In Father Christmas'. Lake said of writing the song, "I wrote it in my house in west London. I'd tuned the bottom string on my guitar from E down to D and got this cascading riff that you hear on the record." Co-writer Sinfield said, "Some of it was based on an actual thing in my life when I was eight years old and came downstairs to see this wonderful Christmas tree that my mother had done. I was that little boy. Then it goes from there into a wider thing about how people are brainwashed into stuff. Then I thought, 'This is getting a bit depressing. I'd better have a hopeful, cheerful verse at the end.' That's the bit where me and Greg would've sat together and done it. And then I twisted the whole thing with the last line, 'The Christmas you get, you deserve', which was a play on 'The government you get, you deserve.' I didn't necessarily explain all the politics or the thoughts behind it. It's not anti-religious. It's a humanist thing, I suppose. It's not an atheist Christmas song, as some have said."

'I Believe In Father Christmas' got to number two in the UK and has been a seasonal staple ever since. Upon its release, the single sold at least 13,000 copies over just two days. Queen's 'Bohemian Rhapsody' claimed the number one spot that year. Lake said, "I got beaten by one of the greatest records ever made. I would've been pissed off if I'd been beaten by Cliff."

Emerson released a single called 'Honky Tonk Train Blues' in 1976.

Having struck up a rapport with the jazz rock trio Back Door when touring, Palmer produced their fourth album that was released in 1976 — *Activate*. Saxophonist Ron Aspery and bassist Colin Hodgkinson, co-wrote the song 'Bullfrog' with Palmer. It features on *Works Volume 2*.

Back from a break and refreshed for new innovations, in 1976, ELP began working on what would be their fifth studio album.

ELP released *Works Volume 1* in March 1977. A double album where each member of the trio had one side of an LP for solo music, with the fourth side reserved for a collective effort.

With lyrical assistance from Sinfield, Lake wrote

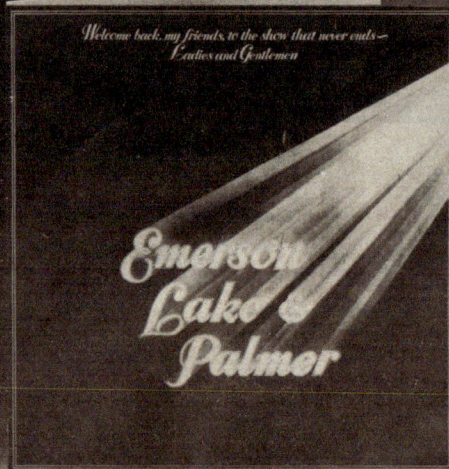

102

ELP took a break from touring in 1975 & '76.' At least Keith had other interests to occupy his time. His passion for bikes and cars is well known.

KEITH EMERSON

AV N

© Marka/ Press Holland/ (Alamy Stock Photo)

five songs. He specifically wanted to avoid doing "just ballads" in favour of embracing a wider range of musical styles. As part of this, he incorporated orchestral overdubs to the songs. One of his songs, 'C'est la Vie', was released as a single. Sadly though, Lake called the album the "beginning of the end" of ELP on the basis that on future albums, he was no longer the producer. He also felt that despite their best efforts, *Works Volume 1* was not a "really innovative record."

Carl Palmer's contribution to the album was also musically diverse. He confirmed, "My stuff on *Works* was quite eclectic, I must confess. I'm still like that, if you came to my house and looked through my record collection. It's pretty weird, if I'm honest. It's hard to listen to one genre of music for too long. Last night I was listening to Buddy Guy, a new album of his called *Sweet Tea*, and I've never been a Buddy Guy fan but I heard one track and it was just fantastic. It's just whatever gets me at the time. I've always listened to all kinds of different music."

Works Volume 1 got to number nine in the UK and to number twelve on the US Billboard 200 chart. It went gold in both countries. The track 'Fanfare For The Common Man', was Emerson's adaptation of the 1942 composition by Aaron Copland. ELP released their version as a single in May 1977. It went to number two in the UK to become ELP's highest charting single there.

Emerson explained some of the changes he made to Copland's original piece; "It needed transposing, so I did that first. I wanted to improvise in a key that was sort of bluesy. It ended up in E. The rest of it was straightforward, really. You know, in order to get the shuffle sound, the timing had to be changed, but it was common sense." Lake said, "It was just wonderful how it came about: We were recording in Montreux, Switzerland, in 1976, and Keith was playing it as a piece of classical music. I played this shuffle bass line behind him and all of a sudden it started to connect. Then Carl came in and we three started to play it. Luckily, the engineer had a two-track running, and that is what's on the record — the first time we played through the piece."

Manager Stewart Young recalled, "We had to get the permission of Aaron Copland, the composer. The publishing house said forget it. So I got Mr Copland's home number, called him up and he was very friendly on the phone. And he says 'Send it to me, let me listen.' And he loved it. He called me and said 'This is brilliant, this is fantastic. This is doing something to my music'."

The last track on *Works Volume 1* is 'Pirates' — a prog epic that Lake admitted wasn't without its challenges technically, but certainly something that made for an incredible performance when played live. Palmer considered with hindsight, "'Pirates' was the last of the big ones. It's a terrific piece of music. Pete Sinfield, who was absolutely exceptional, came up with the idea, the whole concept, and I thought it all married up exceptionally well. It was recorded in Switzerland, Montreux, in Mountain Studios right on Lake Lucerne. I can't remember much of the

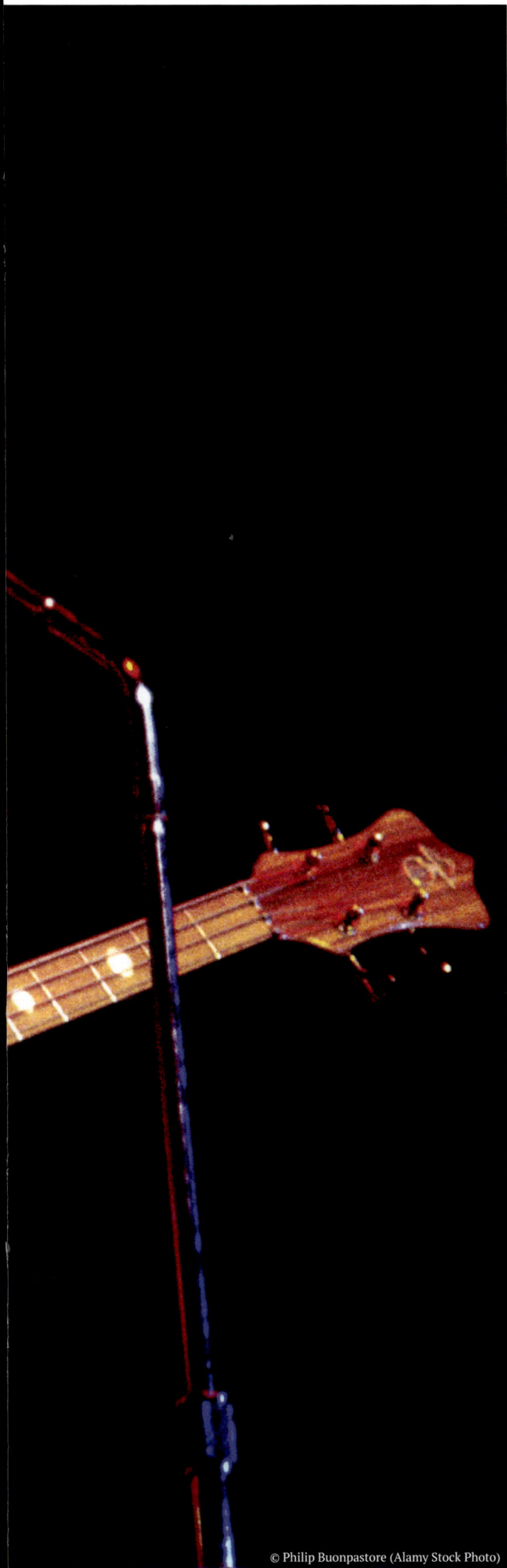

105

Carolina Coliseum, Columbia, South Carolina, 30th June 1977

recording, but it was all analogue so it was done in segments and there was probably a lot of editing. We could never play that stuff straight off. If you look at the master tape for *Tarkus*, for instance, it's got seventeen edits on it, all cut with a razorblade."

Additional material that was recorded in 1976, in addition to songs from previous studio sessions, were released as *Works Volume 2* in November 1977. Both *Works* albums were supported with a tour. Spanning dates across 1977–1978, it featured the band playing with an orchestra on stage for some early shows. Touring with an orchestra was a short-lived prospect due to the financial demands of such extravagance.

© Philip Buonpastore (Alamy Stock Photo)

© Philip Buonpastore (Alamy Stock Photo)

PISTOLS · KISS · SUPERTRAMP

sounds

ELP

WOULD YOU PAY TWO MILLION DOLLARS
TO SEE THESE MEN ?

FIC: NEAL PRESTON

KEITH EMERSON sits in a Detroit French restaurant wearing traditional black leather trousers and a very large grin. He's telling a reporter from *Rolling Stone* that champagne is rock 'n' roll mouthwash. To prove the point, Greg Lake proceeds to spit some bubbly on the floor.

Emerson, Lake and Palmer are in exceptionally fine spirits. An hour before they triumphantly walked off the stage of Cobo Hall, cheered on by a tumultuous reception. Detroit was the fifth concert on their first tour in three years and it was crucial. Could the city that bore Alice Cooper, thrilled to Kiss, and hysterically reacted to Ted Nugent, warm to ELP accompanied by their 70-piece orchestra?

With a JBL PA designed by the Montreal 1976 Olympics sound company, an album entitled 'Works Volume One' and a 70-piece orchestra, one could easily expect massive overkill.

What made me most doubtful was the orchestra. Always dabbling with the classics, would rock 'n' roll totally disappear? Besides, most experiments with rock band and orchestra were embarrassing shambles of misunderstood musical mediums. Van Morrison used a string quartet successfully, the Faces used a small orchestra with mixed results, 'Tommy' became musakal punctuated by strings.

But ELP have actually done the impossible. And it took me four concerts in three cities to finally believe this was true.

For starters, the orchestra are young accomplished musicians who enthusiastically tap feet in time when not playing during the show.

Visually the stage looks incredible, with the orchestra circling above the band in Stanley Kubrick type silver enclosures. They all wear t-shirts that say ELP in bold silver lettering. Conductor Godfrey Salmon towers above them, moving his baton and occasionally shaking ass.

The set is divided into two parts although the band is still experimenting with various running orders and pacing. The orchestra ceremoniously kick things off with 'Bolero' before ELP bound onstage and launch into the grits of the tune. During 'Hoedown', Emerson

briefly bumps and grinds with his infamous ribbon controller, but this visual trick is an appetiser. Music is the main course.

Onstage ELP all wear black and white apparel. But their music is technicolour fantasy, given new life and fire by the orchestra. Each individual is given ample spotlight attention in the two hour show.

Carl Palmer is featured first in 'Enemy God' based round a Prokofiev composition. Dressed in Karate-style clothes, Palmer looks like a youthful Bruce Lee on a revolving drum kit with Chinese painted cymbals. Nightly his drum solo earns a standing ovation.

Greg Lake is featured frequently, and impressively. A reworked 'From The Beginning' is sophisticated and elegant as Palmer adds congas and Lake contributes an excellent electric guitar solo. 'Welcome Back My Friends' shows how ELP rock, with Lake flaunting an aggressive vocal. Even better is the newer 'C'est La Vie' which smacks of instant hit single success. On stage Emerson adds some streets-of-Venice accordion. And, there is

Continues next page

**Welcome back my friends to the show that
costs $2,000,000 and takes Barbara Charone
back to the early days of . . .**

E ★ L ★ P

PICTURES   BY   NEAL   PRESTON

E★L★P

From previous page

'Lucky Man', done simply on a 12 string electric, sung superbly.

Keith Emerson is taking the biggest chance. The sixth number of the set is his piano concerto, and I'm sure some of the audience are still adjusting to that foreign thing called an orchestra. Onstage the concerto falls easily into place, as the music paints pictures that evoke Disney's animated film 'Fantasia'. Emerson cuts an ironic figure playing delicate music dressed in black leathers.

Nightly I expected shouts of 'BOOGIE' or 'ROCK 'N' ROLL' but not a trace of hostility was present. Unexpectedly, the ELP audience seem willing to follow them into their well documented brave new musical world.

"I almost expect a firework to be thrown," Keith laughs, thinking of the tension during his lengthy concerto. "I know I look like two opposites. Sometimes I get the feeling that the audience is a bit dumbfounded and that's why they don't react overtly aggressively."

Greg Lake instantly agreed that Emerson, though treading on thin ice, was getting stronger every day. "It's all a risk," Greg said of the entire show. "I'm sure if someone screamed 'boogie' Keith would probably break into a quick 12 bar to keep them amused, cast a sly glance in their direction and continue. We're not beyond a sense of humour."

When Carl Palmer dubs the band 'cheeky', what he means is that they take chances. And because they're taking chances *again*, a good degree of integrity and excitement has been put *back* into the music. I haven't enjoyed ELP live as much since they first exploded seven years ago.

Lake flatly admits that ELP would have broken up without the addition of the orchestra onstage and on record, bringing with them new excitement and a challenge that had been previously missing.

"In the past I've been involved with so much electronic music. Why shouldn't I work with an orchestra?" he demands passionately. "Do you have to be a certain age? Frank Sinatra works with an orchestra and nobody questions it."

"The stunt now is the music," Greg says with a wide, self satisfied smirk. "There comes a time when you must ask yourself, should the music be allowed to come out like one card trick following another? Artistically, music shouldn't be that processed or controlled. You can't come up with continual unique stunts.

"Already people are asking us what we're gonna do to follow this. I mean fuckin' hell," Lake spits out. "Cut me some slack Jack."

IN REALITY, their next musical endeavour is already being planned. 'Works Volume Two' is due out this fall, a single album stuffed with shorter pieces, more rock oriented, both group and solo. Some of these orchestral concerts will be recorded for a possible live album. And ELP will follow this extravaganza with another extreme — the return of the trio.

"We didn't want to come slipping back with the same old show," Palmer mused. "An orchestra seemed like a natural progression. It was the only way we could reappear after 2½ years. But it's not a permanent musical direction.

"It *all* works but ELP would work without the orchestra. The orchestra just puts the cream on top of the cake. Actually just the cherry right in the middle.

"Say Keith would have released a solo album," Palmer says hypothetically. "Later perhaps I'd release an album. But what happens is you blow each other out, steal each other's sales. You lose group unity.

"See, the public like unity. If they see 3, 4, 5 guys playing together for X amount of years, they see unity. It's like a family, right? If you start splitting up it gets disjointed. If you present it like we've done it, there's more unity. Then it's stimulating for the individuals."

And less frustrating. This ELP project gave the band another shot at longevity, preserving their past and preparing their uncharted future.

Keith Emerson provides group contrast to Carl Palmer, but then the crux of ELP has always revolved around contradiction and personality differences. When asked if it was important for Emerson personally to keep the band together, he took time thinking about it before committing himself.

"Yeah it's important," he said without much passion. "I certainly wouldn't form any other band. I wouldn't go through all that shit again," he laughed at the memories. "That's too much of a drag. While we're all thinking along the same directions which we are at the moment, it's certainly worth keeping together."

"Yeah it's important," he said without much passion. "I certainly wouldn't form any other band. I wouldn't go through all that shit again," he laughed at the memories. "That's too much of a drag. While we're all thinking along the same directions which we are at the moment, it's certainly worth keeping together."

Had the band's new direction not been orchestral, Keith Emerson would have undoubtedly quit the group.

"Sure Greg's right. I'd have definitely done it on my own cause that's what I was into. I didn't want to go back on the road unless there was an orchestra. I wouldn't go with anything less. After three years I didn't want to go back with the same set-up," Emerson says adamantly. "I needed a change, a new challenge.

"It was either stay everything down to the basics like no 13 keyboards but just possibly piano, bass and drums. Go that route or one step further than what we've ever been before. I chose to go one step further. Everybody laughed when I mentioned it. Said you're crazy, it'll never pay. They've been proved right so far," he laughs. "It hasn't paid. But it's working."

Cheap it's not. Palmer says the entire thing works to the tune of $2 million and ELP aren't laughing all the way to the bank. The 70-piece orchestra receive scaled union salaries, equipment is carried by 8 articulated trucks, there's mixers and submixers. Their outdoor show in Chicago to 65,000 people paid for the rest of the week. After one week on the road, ELP broke even.

But like Keith Emerson admits, it's working. "I'm actually broke," Carl Palmer says. "This is purely an artistic thing. After six years on the road we figured it was time to rethink our musical policy. It's quite an organic thing actually. We had to leave England for artistic reasons which is quite unusual. A lot of groups leave England for financial gain. We left so we'd have money to plow back into the band. We wanted that extra money to put back in the show.

"Still there's only so much money you can plow back in," Carl rationalized seriously. "After seven years of being together we really don't want to end up broke. And this kind of project can actually do that to you. We want to better music as much as we can. I like to be a pioneer as much as my pocket will let me."

PALMER HAS good reason to be concerned with ELP finances. As he quickly learned absence does not make the heart grow fonder.

"Our record sales haven't been as big as they should be," Palmer said honestly. "We kinda figured when we came back we'd be bigger than when we left. In actual fact the double album price is expensive, ticket prices are quite high and our overheads are astronomical. We've got everything against us.

"None of this is easy for us. There's no way to make money right?" he looks up sheepishly. "And I'm quite an enterprising lad. I know how valuable ELP is musically and economically. When something is that valuable you want to treasure every aspect 'cause ya never know how long it's gonna last."

"It's like this," Greg Lake says with authority. "Everyone criticises ELP. They say the band have made too much fuckin' money. What we do is reinvest it back into ourselves as entertainment. Anyone who had anything to do with the financing thought we were crazy. If one thing goes wrong one day it costs us arms and legs. Our back is against the wall to make it work faultlessly."

"Our heads are on the block. It's not the first time and probably won't be the last. I'm glad. It's great fun. It gives everyone something to promote. It's not just a question of another rock show hitting Pittsburgh. It's a question of presenting a *show* again, one *magic* night."

Where Greg Lake exhibits an infectious, cocky self confidence in himself and the band, Keith Emerson is more reserved, modest and humble. Only when prodded will the shy composer display self-assurance.

"Yes, I am being a pioneer," he reluctantly admitted. "There's no sense being modest about it because nobody's done this before on this level. Way back in '68 I did it together with Jon Lord and Deep Purple. We were the first to use an orchestra. A week after playing a festival Jon recorded his concerto for orchestra at the Royal Albert Hall.

"After that I recorded the Five Bridges Suite with the Nice. But technology wasn't what it is today, miking up every individual member of the orchestra. Back in those days it was 8 channel mixers, overhead mikes and a tremendous amount of overspill. The whole thing was a big battle where electronics drowned out orchestra."

Although the balance is acoustically proper, there's no question who is in charge. While the orchestra are an integral part of the show, ELP are most definitely the main attraction.

"We don't make *any* compromises," Lake said arrogantly. "The orchestra follow the band or get lost. I can promise you if I was a beat in front of them at the beginning, I'd be a beat in front of them at the end. In a way it's pulling more out of us musically. Instead of having a guy play with two hands you've got 70 people. Ya know what I mean?"

CARL PALMER knows just what Greg means. While the orchestra add power and majesty to the ELP sound, timing has to be as perfect as a metronome. The group rehearsed prior to the tour for two months alone, the orchestra rehearsed alone for one week, and for six long days they merged.

"I'm right in the middle," Palmer explained. "They all listen to me. I could do without it to a certain extent but I enjoy the challenge. What's frustrating is that you find string players always play behind the time. Brass players and woodwinds always hit it right on the nut, but your strings always drag. And if ya sit right in the middle like I do, there's an air of confusion. But you have to expect that when there's over 70 people blowing away."

ELP aren't the only ones enjoying this collaboration. The youthful orchestra is having a grand time tasting an unorthodox dose of rock 'n' roll living.

"For the orchestra it's the greatest experience ever," Palmer believes. "They go to Juilliard or Berkeley, get a Bachelor's or Master's degree and end up playing the standards for years, ya know Beethoven Brahms, Mussorgsky, and they don't play anything new. This is like a golden handshake for them."

"Anyone who writes music would love to hear it played by an orchestra. It's everyone's dream," Lake believes. "And it hasn't worked yet. The show will develop into something fantastic if we can survive economically. There are lots of reasons for us to tour with orchestra; not just to be smart and say 'we toured with an orchestra'. We *need* to and we *have* to try."

"We're there to entertain the kids but in actual fact we're educating them," Palmer says

---

with uninhibited pride. "Obviously seeing an orchestra with a rock group on that level might widen their interests. When we released 'Pictures At An Exhibition', classical record sales of that work picked up, especially in London."

Obviously the band are eager to help rock fans broaden their musical horizons.

"That's a good thing about the show," Lake enthuses. "It's like if you've never been to an opera before. Now I by sheer coincidence happen to have been to an opera. It's a beautiful experience the first time, not being pompous or weird about it. We'll get a lot of that on this tour.

"People who haven't been subjected to an orchestra before will focus on it. We're nailing them I can see it down front. There's a bit of shock but that's ok," Greg laughs. "It's tense. The show has good drama value."

Much of the drama and spectacle normally associated with ELP has been channelled into the music. Initially disappointed, fans are quickly seeing another dimension of the band more impressive than flashy visuals or clever gimmicks. As all of ELP are quick to stress, substance is in music.

"A few people have criticised us, saying what the hell am I doing, taking a back seat. But I'm doing a hell of a lot we there," says Emerson defiantly. "It's only because I'm not going up in the air on the piano and spinning round into the audience or using flamethrowers."

Emerson actually tried to incorporate more visuals but so far this hasn't been possible. He tried using a flame thrower on his ribbon controller opening night in Louisville and almost lost his hand. That was ruled out as too dangerous. Then they had two gigantic cannons built especially for 'Pirates' but these old ships cannons proved unsafe. Still they promise effects will gradually be added to several older numbers like 'Tarkus'.

Keith Emerson is trying to adjust the balance between showman and musician.

"More than anything else visuals stay imprinted on one's mind," Keith says softly in a limousine speeding towards Milwaukee. "This is a big change of image. It's the same as if Townshend stops smashing guitars or things similar to that. I'm more known as a showman. Well, I have been in the past. But I can't see why. When you are a showman it kinda overshadows the other things."

Yet Emerson insists that this was not a motivating factor in his piano concerto surfacing on the album. In fact, he was quite hesitant to place the work on any ELP album.

"I've done work before that involves electronic things with orchestra but this time I decided to write a straight work. I was very dubious about putting it on an ELP album because I thought it might be lost with the rest of the rock 'n' roll stuff. I'm quite relieved it isn't.

"It's being played on classical radio stations," Emerson says with a grin. "Lots of people are regarding it very seriously. The reaction is better than what I would have hoped for. It's not just the concerto that worries me. 'Enemy God' is even more outrageous. There's lots of things that needed work in the show."

But they do. And what works best are the more commercially orientated songs mostly written and sung by Greg Lake. Since their first 'Lucky Man' top ten hit, ELP have been branded with Lake's sound. They're hoping to change this situation with the group instrumental adaptation of Copland's 'Fanfare For The Common Man.'

Yet a song from Lake's solo side, 'C'est La Vie' stands excellent chances of capturing a top ten position if released. And if released it will be released as a Greg Lake song, not ELP.

"That's the whole idea of making a solo album," Lake laughs. Lake's songs have always tended to be the 'hits'. And when he performs 'C'est La Vie' and 'Lucky Man' back to back onstage, the reception from the audience is overwhelming. Lake humbly mumbles 'thank you's', while actually exuding total confidence.

"I know what I like," Greg says stubbornly. "I'd be a liar to tell you different. But that's cool cause it's the only way we can keep our own identity. When we come back together we're prepared to fight," Palmer says, like a true punk. "I mean we argue like fuck. For us to do an advert is monumental. It's like a company conference. Individuality is still in the band. I think that's fabulous."

"We could quite easily make a rock 'n' roll album at any time and enjoy it and get artistic rewards from it. Real ones. But when we stopped touring three years ago that wasn't a possible alternative. We could now."

If this tour works, I suggest, *anything* is possible.

"That's right," Greg Lake says with a sly grin. "That's right."

EMERSON, LAKE and Palmer have always had a strange collective group camaraderie. They still have separate dressing rooms, often travel independently to concerts, have personal roadies and private tastes. Yet they seem to respect personality differences in each other and try to positively exploit them. While some groups might be closer friends, ELP have less musical frustrations.

"Socially we lead different lives so when we meet up we've got something different to talk about, fresh ideas," Palmer enthuses. "If we were together on a day to day basis, conversation would become stale and I don't like to see that happen. Now when we meet it's stimulating."

While Keith Emerson takes a fairly platonic attitude to critical reception, Carl Palmer is

"The band policy is like this: If I was in a band and didn't get on offstage with the guys as well as musically it wouldn't bother me. If when we played together there was something musically wrong then I'd knock it on the head immediately. Musically it's got to work 99%. If it only worked 80% musically then forget it.

"Sure there are evenings that it doesn't work. I'd be a liar to tell you different. But that's cool cause it's the only way we can keep our own identity. When we come back together we're prepared to fight," Palmer says, like a true punk. "I mean we argue like fuck. For us to do an advert is monumental. It's like a company conference. Individuality is still in the band. I think that's fabulous."

The band are not the only ones who 'argue like fuck'. ELP have attracted severe criticisms, often hostile, from the very start of their inception. Yet their new show seems specially designed to prove the critics wrong. The band's sterile, technocrat image has now been replaced by more human emotion with the addition of the orchestra.

And without all the effects and stagy gimmicks, it's not so easy to scream "PRETENTIOUS". I mean you can't get more pretentious than having a flying pig like Pink Floyd. And you can't get more self indulgent than Led Zeppelin's overly long drum and moog solos.

"The critics will still find something," Greg Lake said, more amused than upset. "Roccoco ridiculousness' it's all healthy shit Knockin' us proves there's solidity there."

animated and agitated, trying to right the media wrongs.

"I'm sure people thought we were trying to be pretentious but it doesn't matter," Palmer said stubbornly. "When we came out with all those big lights and things blowing up, we *were* pretentious. Suddenly all your David Bowie's did the same things only bigger and better but they weren't pretentious. If someone says we're being pretentious I'll say yes but we invented our money in the music."

If expense allows, ELP would like to bring this latest orchestral extravaganza to Britain. But that all depends on the next couple of months touring America with their transportable but extremely expensive production.

"Tell ya what," Palmer continues, growing increasingly excited. "I been playin' since I was 11 and now I'm 27. I never get nervous. But when I'm in England I actually worry. I don't want any mistakes Cause I know someone will pick it up and write about it like it was Pearl Harbour, the biggest disaster in history. But I love to play to the British public."

Right now ELP and their portable orchestra are playing in the heart of the American midwest. Places where live rock groups dare venture. Unexciting locales like Des Moines, Iowa or Madison, Wisconsin. Don't expect any excitement or decadence in Terre Haute, Indiana.

Excitement or the complicated staging, Greg Lake has a portable TV monitor in front of his mike stand to flash urgent changes of plan. Sometimes the messages say enticing things like 'knock 'em dead' or 'far out'. And there's the occasional song lyric.

"I must confess that I have a slight look at the lyrics now and again," Greg laughs. "But the TV isn't in colour. And I can't turn on Kojak halfway through 'Pictures At An Exhibition'. None of that for me."

Other journeys through the past include 'Knife Edge', and for encores there is a magnificent rendition of 'Fanfare For The Common Man' that always adds a touch of drama. In Detroit there was a tremendous rush to the front of the stage just when the piece kicks off with that haunting, percussive jolt. While in Chicago Keith Emerson stuck in a refrain from 'Chicago That Wonderful Town' in the middle of his solo.

"Just the other night as I watched Carl disappear down the piano chute I thought to myself just how humorous this band is," Lake laughs. "Which tragedy do you want to know about?"

What I really wanted to know about were all the vices. All the decadence. Real News of the World Stuff. After all, Greg Lake has quite a few video cassettes on his coach. One night after the gig he showed a pretty mediocre porn film with the intriguing title 'The Hungry Hypnotist'.

"Not the 'Hungry Hypnotist' *again*," Emerson sighed restlessly.

And there were occasional parties in Lake's suite. These affairs were usually the same with plenty of champagne around and even some music. "I feel like some music tonight," Lake said digging through countless cassettes including the Wailers and Bob Dylan. "Fancy a bit of Beethoven?"

But what about all the decadence then?

"Vices to me honey," Greg Lake said laughing, "are things you put metal in and then turn the handle."

GULF ARTISTS PRODUCTIONS
PRESENTS
IN CONCERT

KEITH EMERSON

GREG LAKE

CARL PALMER

ELP

ONLY FLORIDA APPEARANCE

EMERSON, LAKE & PALMER
WITH
65 PIECE ORCHESTRA
OTHER GROUPS TO BE ANNOUNCED

Saturday night, July 2, 1977
6:00 P.M.

Tampa Stadium
TAMPA, FLORIDA

TICKETS: $10.00 Advance plus service fee—$12.00 day of show

AVAILABLE IN CENTRAL AND NORTHERN FLORIDA AT:

Regency Square Ticket Agency, Jacksonville
Chapter 3 Records, Gainesville and Temple Terrace
Music Box, Daytona Mall, Daytona Beach
B & K Music, Cocoa Beach
Tape Deck, Satellite Beach and Melbourne

Fashion Square, Altamonte Mall, Winter Park Mall Ticket Agencies and Infinite Mushroom in Orlando
Stagg Shop, Winter Haven Mall
Gems n Junk, Lakeland Mall
Brandon's Odyssey, Brandon
Budget Tapes, Tampa and Largo
Men's Room, Tampa Bay Center

Stereorama, Clearwater and Port Richey
Music Smith, Gateway Mall, St. Pete
Asylum Records, St Pete and Sarasota
Out of Sight Shop, St. Pete Beach
Surfing World West, Bradenton
Happy Note, Fort Myers
Powell's Audiotronics, Naples
Tampa Stadium Box Office

AVAILABLE IN SOUTHERN FLORIDA AT:

Record Grove, Vero Beach
Rock of Ages, Boca Raton

Jeans Etc., North Palm, West Palm and Stuart
Sid's East and West, Fort Lauderdale

Tapesville, Hialeah and Miracle Mile, Miami
Sounds Good, North Miami Beach

RAIN OR SHINE—TICKETS AVAILABLE DAY OF SHOW—TAMPA STADIUM BOX OFFICE ONLY

Originally scheduled with the orchestra this show was rearranged for 28th November and would have been the penultimate show of 1977 but ultimately was cancelled.

ELP: 'Show me the way to go home'

'Works' pt. two: ELP due in soon

EMERSON LAKE AND PALMER release the second volume of 'Works' next month. A single album, it will contain 12 tracks of old and new material, which includes Keith Emerson's 'Honky Tonk Train Blues' and a remixed version of Greg Lake's 'I Believe In Father Christmas'.

ELP have compiled the album as an extension to 'Works Volume One'. Among the new material is Keith Emerson's arrangement of Scott Joplin's 'Maple Leaf Rag' recorded with the London Symphony Orchestra, a Greg Lake/Pete Sinfield composition called 'Watching Over You' which was recorded recently in Paris, Carl Palmer's 'Bullfrog', and an interpretation of 'Show Me The Way To Go Home'.

The band have just begun the second leg of their American tour and are finalising plans for British and European dates. The British concerts are likely to be around Christmas and will comprise several dates at a major London venue. It is not sure whether ELP will be backed by a full orchestra, as they were for the first few dates of their American tour.

Emerson explained, "I've never been one to check on how much it would cost or how long it would last. Obviously I had a feeling that we couldn't afford to last out the tour with the orchestra. But it came as a bit of a shock when our manager walked in the dressing room one night before the show and said we had to stop the orchestra. We had to go out as a three piece, there was no other choice. We had our manager with a shotgun behind us saying, 'Look, if you don't play as a three piece, forget it, you'll be bankrupt'… I know what I like. Any artist knows their taste. We play rock 'n' roll really well. But we were at a stage in our career where just to play rock 'n' roll would have been very enjoyable but not serious enough. We enjoy rock 'n' roll. We could quite easily make a rock 'n' roll album at any time and enjoy it and get artistic rewards from it. Real ones. But when we stopped touring three years ago that wasn't a possible alternative. We could now."

Love Beach was ELP's final studio album released prior to their split the following year. By the end of their 1977–1978 North American tour, dynamics within the band were already strained. However, they were still under contractual obligation to make one more album. Retreating to Nassau in the Bahamas as tax exiles, ELP recorded *Love Beach* with lyricist Peter Sinfield — he is credited as a co-writer on each track. Once Lake and Palmer had finished recording their parts for the album, they left the island; Emerson was left to finish the album himself.

ELP had made it clear that they wanted to rest but they were encouraged by Atlantic Records President Ahmet Ertegun to record a new album. Ertegun didn't hesitate to remind the group that they had to deliver one more album. Emerson recalled a meeting with Ertegun and his suggestion for the group to make "a commercial album".

From the very start, Emerson was reluctant about the idea. Lake recalled that Ertegun threatened to decline the band the prospect of solo albums if they refused to work together. With little say in the matter, ELP complied. Working on a commercial album suited Lake's method of song writing. Having already written 'Lucky Man', he wasn't out of his comfort zone in that regard. Emerson however, admitted that he "eased up on my opinions to an extent, bit my nails, and gave him the freedom he kept asking for on side one."

Recording took place in 1978 at Compass Point Studios without a dedicated producer. Despite Lake having produced ELP's previous albums, when the recording of *Love Beach* began, nobody had been assigned to the role. Early pressings of the album didn't even express a producer's credit but the mixing had largely been done by Emerson on the basis that he was the last of the trio to remain with the project when Lake and Palmer had left. The pressure was on; Emerson's increasing drug use had started to impair his ability to work well as part of a team.

Peter Sinfield had been asked by ELP's manager, Stewart Young, to join them in Nassau to assist Lake in writing the lyrics. Sinfield committed to the role but reluctantly so. He had his own frictions with Lake to the

A still from the TV broadcast of 'Tiger In A Spotlight' from the German show *Pop Rock* in early 1978. It catches Carl looking rather concerned by the tiger. Despite the beast being chained up, as the performance progressed it ended up lying at Greg's feet. Ever the professional he performed without apparent concern but did take a couple of steps away once the song had finished.

© KPA (United Archives GmbH / Alamy Stock Photo)

An Evening With
EMERSON LAKE & PALMER

FEB. 22   8:00 P.M.

AMARILLO
CIVIC CENTER COLISEUM
TICKETS: $7.00 ADV., 8.00 DAY OF SHOW
TICKETS ON SALE AT THESE LOCATIONS...
The Coliseum box office and all HASTINGS locations.

point that he insisted on being able to work alone.

Emerson was particularly unhappy with the album's title. It had been chosen by Atlantic Records — it had been taken from one of the album's songs by Lake and Sinfield that had been named after a stretch of beach on Nassau. The front cover photo was taken on an island off Salt Cay, the second largest of the Turks Islands.

Such was Emerson's uncertainty about the album that he organised a booth at Chicago's O'Hare International Airport to conduct a questionnaire on the public's opinion of it. When Emerson reported back to Atlantic Records that many who took part in the survey were not impressed, the company still insisted on doing it their way and nothing was changed despite Emerson's research.

Love Beach was released in November 1978. Although Palmer spent two months trying to arrange a farewell tour, the ongoing tensions within ELP at the time determined that it wasn't to be.

The album was reviewed in *Rolling Stone*; "*Love Beach* isn't simply bad; it's downright pathetic. Stale and full of ennui, this album makes washing the dishes seem a more creative act by comparison." Emerson later called the album "an embarrassment against everything I've worked for."

Years later, Palmer said of the album, "To write a prog album, you've got to sit in traffic jams and go through a lot of shit before you get to the studio, and then you come up with the goods. When you're living in the Bahamas and you've got the beach and the sea and you've all got boats, what are you going to get? You're going to get *Love Beach*. But I will say that it does have 'Canario' by (Joaquin) Rodrigo, which was an idea of Keith's, and that's a fantastic piece of music."

In addition to negative reviews, *Love Beach* only got to number forty-eight in the UK and to number fifty-eight on the US Billboard 200 (it still went gold in the US by January 1979 though). It spawned one single released in the UK, Lake and Sinfield's track 'All I Want Is You'. With *Love Beach* not being supported by a tour, in early 1979, ELP disbanded.

Apart

Following the break-up in 1979, Lake began to write new songs in preparation for his first solo album. He had "put down a tremendous amount of material." He travelled to Los Angeles to work with session musicians in order to further develop his songs. He was disappointed to find that, through no fault of the session musicians, the material lacked the spark that he was hoping for. This caused Lake to reconsider his approach; he concluded that he worked best as part of a committed group. As a result, he formed the Greg Lake Band.

The resulting album, *Greg Lake*, was released in September on Chrysalis Records. In both the UK and the US, the album only got to number sixty-two. The group's debut concert for the tour to promote the album was at the Reading Festival in the August of 1981. The line-up consisted of Gary Moore on guitar, Ted McKenna on drums, Tommy Eyre on keyboards, and Tristram Margetts on bass. A performance that took place at the Hammersmith Odeon in 1981 was broadcast live on the *King Biscuit Flower Hour* and was released as a live album in 1995.

© Alan Perry Concert Photography

Greg performing at the
Reading Festival on 30th
August 1981. His first gig
since ELP disbanded.

© Alan Perry Concert Photography

Following the one-off performance at Reading, the Greg Lake Band toured from October through to December. The two shots here (one with Gary Moore) are from the Capitol Theatre, Passaic, New Jersey, 3rd December 1981. The tour gave Greg the opportunity to also revisit King Crimson with performances of '21st Century Schizoid Man' and 'In The Court Of The Crimson King'.

© Frank White

The short-lived PM, Carl's first venture after ELP failed to garner the level of success he was accustomed to.

In 1980, Palmer formed a band by the name of PM with Texas blues rock guitarist John Nitzinger. PM made one album prior to Palmer teaming up with John Wetton and Steve Howe in early 1981. The aim was to form a new supergroup. Enter one Geoff Downes and then Asia was born. The band was nominated at the 25th Annual Grammy Awards for Best New Artist. They were the second and last progressive rock band to achieve this accolade. Also, Palmer was only the second artist to be nominated twice for the award (David Crosby was the first).

Asia: A record company accountant's dream. A coming together of former members of Yes, King Crimson and of course ELP.

From left to right: Steve Howe, Carl Palmer, John Wetton and Geoff Downes.

Carl on stage with Asia on the first tour at Capitol Theater, Passaic, New Jersey, 30th April 1982

126

In 1991, Palmer would leave Asia in order to reunite with Emerson and Lake. After numerous personnel changes over the years, the four founding members of Asia, Palmer included, would get back together in 2006.

In 1981, Emerson released his solo album, *Honky*. He recorded it in the Bahamas with local musicians. It marked a strong deviation from Emerson's usual style in how it showcased material that was calypso and reggae inspired. Commercially, the album didn't go down well. Thereafter, Emerson's solo releases were few and far between.

He did however, proceed to write and perform music for films. His classical style and use of orchestras made him well suited to film work. He excelled in that field rather than aiming for the new wave dominated pop/rock market. Emerson contributed soundtrack music to a number of films including: Dario Argento's *Inferno* (1980), *Nighthawks* (1981), *Best Revenge* (1984), Lucio Fulci's *Murderock* (1984), and Michele Soavi's *The Church* (also known as *La Chiesa*) (1989). He also composed for the briefly running 1994 US animated television series, *Iron Man*.

Emerson's sporadic solo releases thereafter included a Christmas album in 1988, and the album *Changing States*. It was recorded in 1989 but it wasn't released until 1995 after a number of the songs had already been re-recorded and released as different versions on ELP's 1992 comeback album, *Black Moon*. *Changing States* features an orchestral remake of the ELP song 'Abaddon's Bolero' – it was recorded with the London Philharmonic Orchestra. Emerson had originally written the track, 'The Church', for the 1989 Michele Soavi horror film of the same name.

Manoeuvres, Lake's second solo album, was released in July 1983. He disbanded his group not long after completing it. He didn't promote or tour for the album. He also split from the record company.

In November 1983, Palmer invited Lake to briefly join Asia as a replacement for fellow King Crimson alumnus, John Wetton. Palmed needed Lake for four scheduled concerts in Japan. Lake agreed and spent three weeks learning Asia's songs. It culminated in his performance in the Asia In Asia concert at the Nippon Budokan Hall in Tokyo. It took place on 6th December 1983 and was the first concert to be broadcast over satellite to MTV in the US. The footage was soon released on home video. Lake left the group after the tour on the basis that he had only joined as a favour just to help with the Japanese concerts.

In 1985, Emerson and Lake decided that it was time to reform Emerson, Lake and Palmer to record another album. However, Palmer was already committed to Asia. As a result, Emerson and Lake proceeded to audition other drummers. They found that they had a good rapport with drummer Cozy Powell, who had excelled in his work with Rainbow and had a fantastic reputation as a very capable and heavy drummer by then.

Emerson, Lake and Powell is sometimes abbreviated to ELPowell or ELP2. Emerson, Lake

and Powell released one eponymous studio album in 1986. The debut single from the album, 'Touch And Go', peaked at number sixty on the Billboard charts on 19th July of the same year.

A number of drummers had been auditioned before Powell was. Powell had been friends with Emerson for a long time so getting in touch to invite him to audition for the band was not difficult. The band always stipulated that Cozy's surname conveniently beginning with the letter P was coincidental rather than what qualified him to drum for the band.

Powell spoke highly of what it was to work with Emerson and Lake; "I've had to work hard with them, learning a lot of the old stuff. It's not just a three minute twelve-bar blues you have to learn. It's been interesting working out on *Tarkus*. It's opened up my musical vocabulary. They are clever pieces of music and Keith isn't exactly a three-chord wonder. He comes up with some very clever stuff, and Greg as well. I've had to learn 'Pirates' (from *Works Volume 1*) which runs for fourteen minutes. They are also playing *Pictures At An Exhibition*, it's not three choruses, verse and fade out. To play this stuff you need a lot of experience and confidence. It's not beginner's music, that's for sure. It's been a real challenge and it's brought me out from being a backing drummer, which I was in Michael Schenker Group and Whitesnake. I can express myself now and play a solo as well! So I've been practising hard and I've even stopped drinking, which a lot of people can't believe. I am determined to make this successful, I'm going to give it my best shot because the band is worthy of a good crack."

Keith recalled of ELP2's early days; "I remember Cozy being in my barn in Sussex. He set up his impressive drum rig, then realised he had no drumsticks! He considered using some fallen branches from by the orchard until a local farmer drove into town to get some proper ones. They weren't the correct weight but were sufficient when he held then upside down using the fat end. Then he'd do his drum solo and it would be like world war three had broken out."

The band's tour began on the 15th August 1986 in El Paso, Texas and initially, sixty-five dates were set up for as far as late October. Disappointingly, Emerson, Lake and Powell's live tour was impaired by disagreements with the management. It resulted in the band firing them. The difficulties snowballed from there and ultimately, the band broke up.

130

131

In 1988, Emerson and Palmer then teamed up with Robert Berry to form the band 3. Their album, *To The Power Of Three*, was released the same year and a North American tour was also carried out in April and May including a prestigious gig at The Fillmore. Emerson had played at the original Fillmore twenty years previously with The Nice.

Liebe Festivalbesucher,

Im Laufe des gestrigen Tages erreichte uns eine sehr traurige Nachricht. KEITH EMERSON verunglückte auf dem Weg von den Proben der Band ELP für die "OUT IN THE GREEN " - Festivals nach Hause mit dem Motorrad so unglücklich, dass er auf Anweisung seines Arztes (siehe umseitiges ärztliches Attest) unter keinen Umständen bei den "OUT IN THE GREEN " Festivals auftreten kann.

Schweren Herzens musste deshalb die Gruppe ELP ihre Auftritte, für die sie mehrere Monate im Studio geprobt hatten absagen.

Die Gruppe ELP sowie die Veranstalter der Festivals entschuldigen sich auf diesem Wege bei Euch allen für diesen unglücklichen Umstand. Trotz Allem möchten wir aber betonen, dass niemand für einen derartigen, tragischen Vorgang eine Schuld zugewiesen werden kann.

Wir versichern Euch an dieser Stelle, dass die Gruppe ELP durch diese Vorgänge am Meisten betroffen ist, da diese Festivals als Startschuss für das Comeback weltweite Aufmerksamkeit erregen sollten.

Die Gruppe ELP hat uns mitgeteilt, dass sie zum frühest möglichen Zeitpunkt ihre Auftritte im Rahmen einer Tournee nachholen werden und möchten hier allen Besuchern der "OUT IN THE GREEN " Festivals folgendes Angebot unterbreiten:

Jeder Besucher, der seine Eintrittskarte für die Festivals bei der kommenden ELP Tournee vorlegt, erhält eine Ermässigung auf den Eintrittspreis von DM 5.--

Trotz des sicherlich vorhandenen Ärgers bei allen Beteiligten, wünschen wir hiermit KEITH EMERSON schnelle Genesung und eine umso erfolgreichere Tournee.

Obwohl die Zeit sehr kurz war, gelang es uns, die Gruppe BAD COMPANY dazu zu bewegen, für ELP einzuspringen. Wir bedanken uns hiermit herzlich bei BAD COMPANY, die extra um dies zu ermöglichen eine Amerikatournee unterbrochen haben und nach Deutschland eingeflogen sind.

Wir sind der festen Überzeugung, dass uns mit der Verpflichtung von BAD COMPANY ein Ersatz gelungen ist, der durchaus adäquat zu ELP ist. Wir können Euch an dieser Stelle nur noch einmal unser Bedauern ausdrücken, und Euch ein genau so tolles und friedliches " OUT IN THE GREEN " Festival wie im Vorjahr wünschen.

Die Veranstalter

MUSIK SERVICE GMBH
HANSEL CONCERTE GMBH
ARGO CONCERTE GMBH

Martin Sourr, MRCP, MRCGP 2a Pennant Mews, London W8 5JM
Jane Roffell, MBBS

July 8, 1987.

MEDICAL CERTIFICATE.

RE: Mr. Keith Emerson.

This is to certify that Mr. Keith Emerson is under my care. He suffered a road traffic accident on a motorcycle on the 30th June, and was seen on the 1st July for attention to the injury of his wrist. There has been no fracture, but he certainly has a serious sprain in the form of soft tissue injury. I reviewed the matter on the 7th July, and although he has improved it will be three to four weeks before he has full function.

Signed,

Martin Sourr, MRCP, MRCGP.

NEUE RUNNING ORDER:

11.15 h - 11.45 h	MCH
12.15 h - 13.00 h	NILS LOFGREN
13.30 h - 14.15 h	BLUE OYSTER CULT
14.45 h - 15.45 h	BAD COMPANY
16.30 h - 17.30 h	MEAT LOAF
18.00 h - 19.00 h	STATUS QUO
20.15 h - 22.00 h	BARCLAY JAMES HARVEST

//
DRINGENDE FESTIVALINFORMATION - DRINGENDE FESTIVALINFORMATION - DRINGENDE
//

Dear Festival Visitors,

In the course of the day yesterday a very sad message reached us. Keith Emerson had a very unfortunate accident with his motorcycle on the way to his home from rehearsals with ELP, for the "Out in the Green Festivals" and he cannot play, under any circumstances, on instruction of his physician (see medical certificate) at these festivals.
With a heavy heart ELP announced their appearance as off, for which they had rehearsed several months in the studio. ELP and the organisers of the Festivals apologise in this way to you all for this unfortunate circumstance. Despite everything, we would like to stress however that nobody can be blamed for such a tragedy. We ensure you here, that ELP is most concerned by this, since these festivals should excite world-wide attention as a starting signal for their comeback. ELP communicated to us the fact that they will reschedule their appearances at the earliest possible time in the context of a tour, and would like to submit to all visitors of the Festivals the following offer: Each visitor who submits a Festival ticket while attending the coming ELP tour, receives a reduction on the admission fee by 5 Deutsche Marks. In spite of the unfortunate circumstances with all involved, we hereby wish Keith Emerson a fast recovery and a very successful tour. Although the time was very short, we managed to procure the group Bad Company to replace ELP. We hereby cordially thank Bad Company, who interrupted an American tour especially to make this possible and flew immediately to Germany. We are convinced that, with the appearance of Bad Company, a suitable replacement was found in lieu of ELP. We can only again express to you our regrets and wish you just as great and peaceful a festival as in the previous year.

The Festival Team

As is clearly evident here, although the band was finally reunited in 1991, the original plan had been to get back together in 1987.

Together
again

Whilst Emerson was working on a film score in 1991 for former Atlantic employee, Phil Carson, he brought in Lake and Palmer to assist him. Although Palmer was still working on something with Asia at the time, but when John Wetton quit Carl followed suit. With Lake back in the fold as well, ELP began rehearsals by playing 'Tarkus' "just to get back into shape." Carson signed ELP to his new label, Victory Records.

However, we should mention that an initial reunion was planned in 1987. ELP were scheduled to play at the Out In The Green Festivals. The dates were for 12th July at Grosse Allmend, Frauenfeld in Switzerland and for 18th and 19th July at Germany's Paderborn Schloss Neuhaus, and St Wendel Bosenbachstadion respectively. Sadly though, the band had to cancel owing to the fact that Keith was unable to play. The festival organisers were issued with a medical certificate to confirm. Keen to be honest with those looking forward to seeing ELP, the festival organisers released a statement as shown opposite.

It wasn't long before the word got out that ELP were going to make a comeback and soon afterwards, it was confirmed with the release of *Black Moon* in May 1992. The album's title track was released as a single. The whole album remained true to ELP's original sound and didn't go for the easier option of a more commercial style. New advances in technology expanded the scope of what was musically possible, but it was essentially the ELP sound that fans had grown to love decades ago. The album was produced by Mark Mancina.

Palmer said of ELP's intentions with the album, "I think what we hope to bring back into the music industry is the sound of a group. People actually playing their instruments, a real positive side of music — unlike a lot of music that came out in the eighties which was computer-driven with a lot of button pushing — and I think it's now time to get that identifiable sound of a band actually playing together. We were always a live band. We designed the music to be played in a live situation and then transferred it to record. Also, now with the technology that is available to us, which we didn't have in the seventies, it is a very positive time for a progressive band to come back."

"I don't think we're gonna do the flyin' piano. Everything we do in terms of visual production is always linked to the music. So you will not be seeing things like Vari-lites, none of that. It'll be a very dark show, very theatrical — It might be more related to a ballet or an opera. Very musical, very dramatic, and intense. One of the things that ELP is, is intense."

Greg Lake, in an interview with Steve Newton, published in *The Georgia Straight*, 27th August 1992

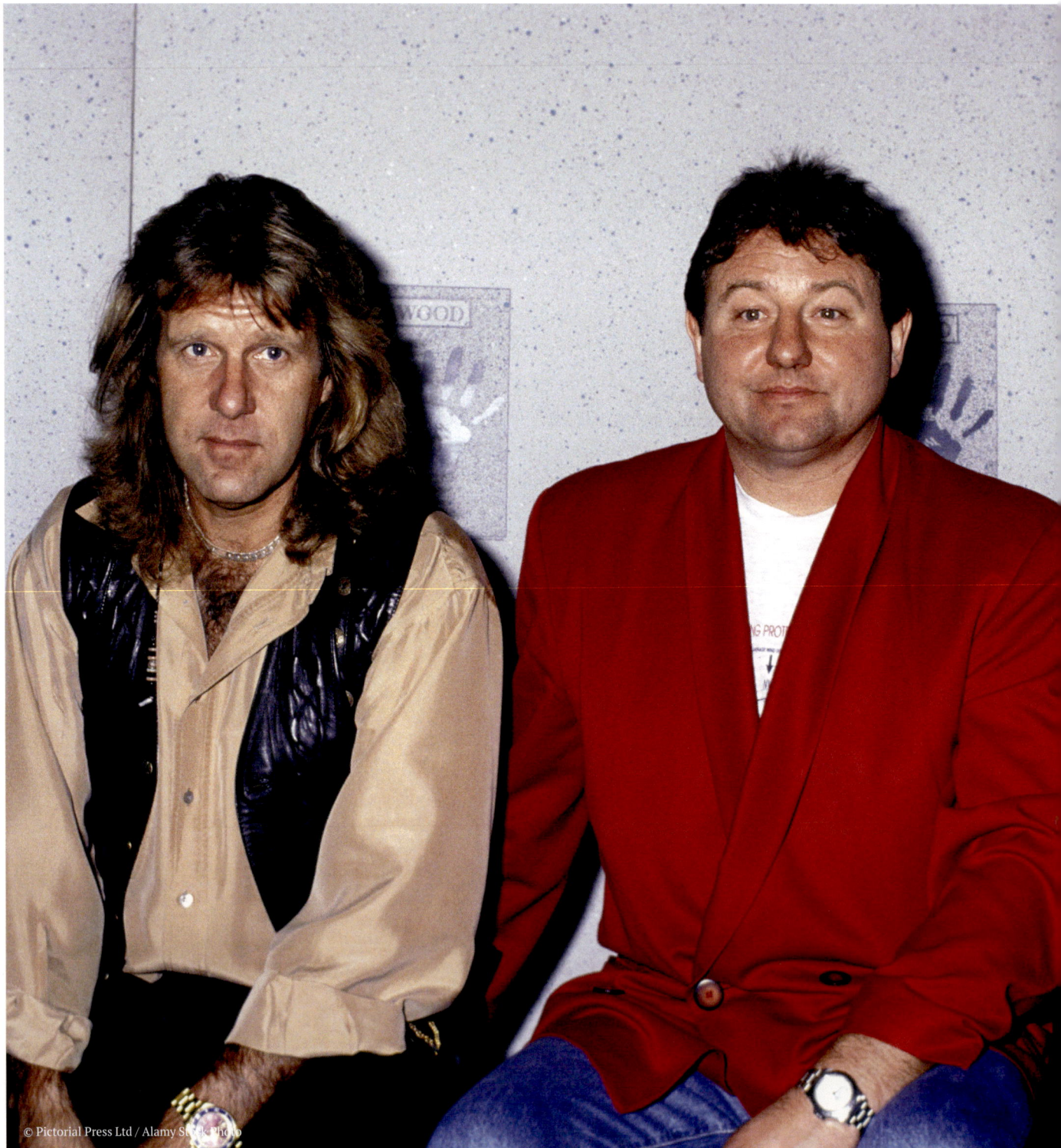

Having got back together after a break, Lake considered, "There was a thrill, and a genuine feeling that we could make a great record. I think we all heard something none of us had heard for many years. So many bands today seem to have no recognisable sound or personality. Well, we do, and we're not going to apologise for that." Chris Welch advocated that 'Footprints In The Snow' was "the final rebuke for those who see ELP solely as some sort of bombastic machine."

Palmer enthused, "In the early seventies when we started, we never realised the chemistry that existed. We made an album every fourteen months, toured virtually every year, so time went very quickly and we just never realised what it was. Then coming back and playing together we thought 'wow! This is just like we played yesterday' — it just happened, a bit like putting on an old pair of shoes, and I think what we've grown to appreciate individually and collectively is the contribution we've made to this situation — not just musically, but to the ambience of the whole thing. We're older and wiser, and thus appreciate each other more."

Black Moon showcased Lake's skills as a lyricist regarding contemporary issues. He explained that "a lot of the album was written during the Gulf crisis. 'Black Moon' came when I saw the oil wells burning in Kuwait. I was watching television one day and I saw a report about all these oil fields being set alight, and this picture had the sun blacked out by all this smoke, but you could still see it and it looked like a moon, and then a black moon, and that started me thinking."

The most classical sounding piece on *Black Moon* is inevitably, ELP's version of 'Dance Of The Knights' from Prokofiev's *Romeo And Juliet*. Emerson explained, "What struck me about this particular music was the similarity between it and the way that Jimi Hendrix started 'Purple Haze'. The rhythm was so similar that I was sure I could make it work with the Prokofiev. Amazingly, you don't have to force too many changes to make it happen. It works quite naturally, the same as the shuffle rhythm works with 'Fanfare For The Common Man'."

CONCERTS

Miller Genuine Draft

EMERSON LAKE & PALMER

SPECIAL GUEST

BONHAM

TUESDAY
SEPTEMBER 1

CAL EXPO AMPHITHEATRE • 7:30PM

TICKETS AT BASS

EMERSON, LAKE & PALMER

WORLD TOUR 1992

ELP's world tour began on 24th July 1992. This date marked their first live performance together in over fourteen years. Such was the success of the tour that extra dates were added. Emerson admitted, "We certainly hadn't anticipated this sort of response to the tour — not in the UK anyway. The reaction of the audiences in America has been fantastic. Nothing seems to have changed with regards to audience reaction. We're a little different, of course. There's no room for partying after the show as we may have done in the seventies. Things like that you've got to be aware of. We're older and wiser now, and we keep ourselves in pretty good shape."

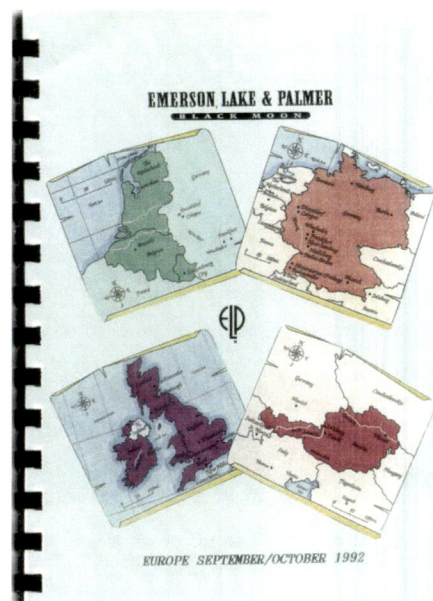

EMERSON, LAKE & PALMER
BLACK MOON

EUROPE SEPTEMBER/OCTOBER 1992

— The Return of the Legendary —
EMERSON, LAKE & PALMER

ELP

OCTOBER
GLR	ROYAL ALBERT HALL	FRI 2/SAT 3/MON 26	071 589 8212
PICCADILLY RADIO	MANCHESTER APOLLO	SUN 25	061 236 9922

NOVEMBER
GOLD	BOURNEMOUTH INT. CENTRE	WED 25	0202 297297
METRO fm	NEWCASTLE CITY HALL	THUR 26	091 261 2606
BRMB	BIRMINGHAM SYMPHONY HALL	FRI 27	021 212 3333
GWR GOLD	BRISTOL COLSTON HALL	SAT 28	0272 223686

All tickets £15 and £13 except Royal Albert Hall £17.50, £15 and £12.50
CREDIT CARDS ACCEPTED (may be subject to booking fee)
New single 'Affairs of the Heart' out now taken from the new album 'Black Moon'

The reunion tour included three nights at the Royal Albert Hall. The first time that ELP had played the prestigious London venue. Presumably the ban imposed on Keith with The Nice back in 1968 had been lifted. Or maybe overlooked?

142

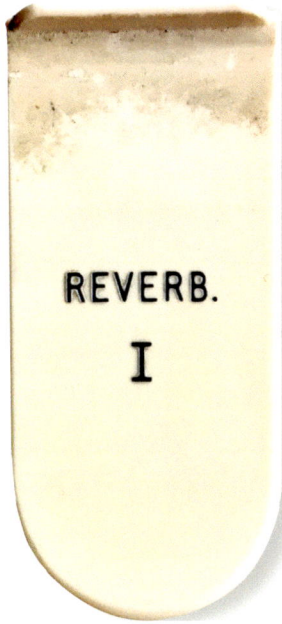

A nice memento from the Manchester show on 25th October from photographer Lee Millward who says, "The Reverb 1 key broke off the Hammond in Keith's hand as he was torturing it during the encore of 'Rondo' and he threw it over his shoulder. I was the lucky one who caught it."

REVERB.
I

EMERSON LAKE & PALMER

CONCERT '92

Sonntag, 18.10.1992 · 18.00 Uhr

18.10. ESSEN Grugahalle

RONNIE PRODUCTIONS PRESENTE:

EMERSON, LAKE & PALMER

JEUDI 5 NOVEMBRE 1992
à 20 h 00

Carl in Hollywood, 27th September 1993.

EMERSON, LAKE & PALMER

WORLD TOUR
1992/3

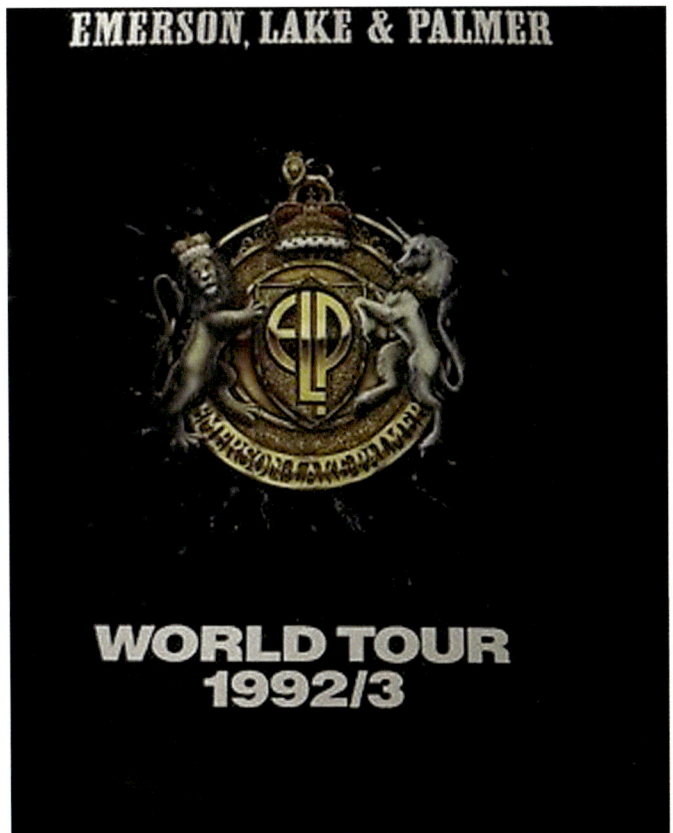

In January 1993, ELP continued the world tour, returning to the lucrative North American market as well as playing South America for the first time. The box set, *The Return Of The Manticore* was released that year.

BRANDY
PRESIDENTE
PRESENTA

EMERSON, LAKE & PALMER

PRESIDENTE

19 y 20 de Marzo

AUDITORIO
NACIONAL

Reunited in the nineties. After an intensive bout of touring in 1992 and 1993, ELP toured again in 1996, firstly as special guests to Jethro Tull throughout America, followed by a ten-date headlining tour of Japan.

A tri-fold flyer for a brace of shows in Buenos Aires, Argentina on 8th and 9th August 1997.

Things were looking good for ELP and they went straight into the studio to work on their next album. It was initially going to be called *The Best Seat In The House* — the idea came from Dolby's advertising campaign for their TVs at the time. Eventually though, it was decided that the album would be called *In The Hot Seat*. All was not well though. Victory records were having financial problems and it resulted in ELP being put under pressure to go in a more commercial direction than they had done with *Black Moon*.

Palmer said of the *In The Hot Seat* recording sessions; "We are not totally committed to any one direction. We have about six tracks recorded and another three we are looking at. We're not dealing with any long conceptual pieces, but we do have songs which are about seven minutes. There is nothing in the twenty-minute area as of yet, but that could change tomorrow. We have some ideas we'd like to try but it depends on how the writing comes along. We have four or five tracks recorded that are four to five minutes long, but whether or not we are going to tie them together in any way really depends on how the lyrics turn out. It's too early to say."

In The Hot Seat was the first instance in which ELP covered a Bob Dylan song, 'The Man In The Long Black Coat'. Interestingly, each of the trio had covered Dylan songs with their previous bands. Lake had covered 'Love You Too Much' on his first solo album whilst the Nice had covered 'She Belongs To Me', 'My Back Pages' and 'Country Pie'. When Palmer was in the short-lived band Qango (a spin-off from Asia), they played 'All Along The Watchtower'. It features on their album, *Live In The Hood* — a recording of the band's second show that took place in February 2000.

Once again, Lake's writing dealt with contemporary issues on ELP's second studio album of the nineties. Lake wrote 'Daddy' after having seen a feature on *America's Most Wanted* regarding Sarah Ann Wood who had disappeared from home and was presumed dead. He explained, "I wrote the song originally just to get it out of my system. Not intending to record it because I thought it was a very morbid thing to do. It was a very disturbing story, but what really hit me was when Robert Wood, Sarah's father, began to talk about Sarah's loss and the fact that he wanted to be close to her and he believed she wanted to be close to him."

When working on *In The Hot Seat*, Emerson was recovering from an operation in relation to a blockage around his radial nerve and problems with the ulna nerve in his right arm. Not only was this difficult for him physically but also, mentally; he feared that the best of his days as a musician were behind him. Emerson wasn't the only one having trouble with his hands though. Palmer had developed carpel tunnel syndrome by this point. He eventually had to have surgery for it. Famous hands indeed though — on 23rd November, ELP were inducted into the Hollywood Rock Wall on Sunset Boulevard. They put their handprints and signatures into the cement there.

The recording sessions continued into 1994.

147

DEEP PURPLE

with special guest

EMERSON, LAKE & PALMER

and

DREAM THEATER

THE WARFIELD
FRIDAY, AUGUST 28
doors 7/show 8

TIX AT ALL BASS OUTLETS INCLUDING WHEREHOUSE & TOWER RECORDS PLUS SERVICE FEE. ADVANCE TIX WITH NO SERVICE FEE FOR WARFIELD SHOWS AVAILABLE SUNDAYS 10-4 AT THE FILLMORE BOX OFFICE. CASH, VISA, MC, AMEX & ATM ACCEPTED. SIX TIX LIMIT. VERY LIMITED MAIN FLOOR SEATING. ALL AGES WELCOME. DISABLED SEATING AVAILABLE AT ALL TICKET CENTERS.

CHARGE BY PHONE: 510/762-BASS • 408/998-BASS   BASS TICKETS

982 MARKET STREET, SAN FRANCISCO • INFO: (415)775-7722

LIVE IN CONCERT

Emerson, Lake & Palmer

ELP

"...See THE Show"

On Sale Thursday July 2 10am

August 2nd · 8pm

Flynn Theatre, Burlington

Tickets: Flynn Theatre Box Office, Burlington   UVM Campus Ticket Store, Burlington
New England Video, Essex   Peacock Music, Plattsburgh   Sound Source, Middlebury
Limited Gold Circle seating available

Charge by phone (802) 86-FLYNN

Tax and applicable service charges on tickets. Date and time subject to change.
Presented by All Points Booking and Metropolitan Entertainment Group. Co-sponsored by

WIZN

Just before *In The Hot Seat* was released in the September of that year, it was announced that ELP's tour of the US and Japan had been cancelled. Without a tour to promote the album, it wasn't even given many reviews. Years later, Emerson said of the album, "The sun has shone a little more for me in the past." Lake considered, "I didn't really like the album very much in the end."

By early 1995, ELP had nothing in the pipeline and the early discussions of whether or not to do a 25th anniversary tour were put aside. In the spring though, Emerson released *Changing States*. Meanwhile, Palmer began work on a new project with John Wetton and the guitarist Misha Calvin. The band went by the name of K2 and although they did have a little bit of interest, they ultimately didn't manage to strike up a record deal.

With other irons in the fire, Palmer started to prepare to offer drum clinics (he still runs them to this very day — they include continuing professional development for fellow musicians as well as work with schools and learners with special education needs). Lake had already began working on songs for a solo album. Towards the end of the year, ELP were in the process of trying to change record companies. Victory's back catalogue was taken on by Rhino Records.

In 1996, talks of touring with Yes had fallen through but it was announced that ELP would be touring the States and Japan as the support act for Jethro Tull. Tull's frontman Ian Anderson spoke of how ELP were "thoroughly nice people to work with." Emerson recalled, "The tour with Jethro Tull eliminated a lot of possible pressures that I anticipated after not having played on stage for such a long time and having gone through surgery, it actually gave me the confidence to go to Japan."

In June 1998, some of the original T-Bones had a reunion. There was also a reunion of the Nice not long after. All reunions consisted of sporadic live performances. August 1998 saw ELP embark on what would be their last ever tour together. They co-headlined with Deep Purple and Dream Theater. By late 1998, an ELP tour was booked for the following spring by Jim Davidson (yep, the comedian has also worked as a promoter). It fell through though; by December, ELP had split up.

Touring continued in 1997 and 1998, the latter as guests to Deep Purple, that saw Keith once again hooking up with his old friend Jon Lord. Although the '98 tour saw ELP as special guests to Deep Purple, with Dream Theater also on the bill, ELP played a few shows on their own prior to the first show with Purple on 6th August. Likewise the very last show in San Diego on 31st August was an ELP only gig with a slightly longer show that consisted of: 'Crossing The Rubicon', 'Karn Evil 9', 'Hoedown', 'The Sheriff', 'Knife Edge', 'Piano Concerto 3rd Movement', 'C'est la Vie', 'Lucky Man', 'A Time And A Place', 'Tarkus', '21st Century Schizoid Man', 'Fanfare For The Common Man' and 'Rondo'.

149

Apart
again

Still prolific as individuals, in the same year, Emerson recorded a live album with Glenn Hughes and Marc Bonilla where they did their own version of 'Tarkus'. Emerson said that it "really cooked."

After an Asia reunion fell through in 1999, for a while, Palmer played in a band named after himself: Palmer. It featured Shaun Baxter on guitar and Dave Marks on bass. The group played ELP instrumental pieces.

As part of Ringo Starr's All-Starr Band, Lake began a tour of the US in July 2001. Consisting of twenty-eight dates, the line-up included Mott The Hoople's Ian Hunter, Supertramp's Roger Hodgson and Howard Jones. As well as playing Ringo's material, the band played some of their own songs too. Lake's were 'Lucky Man', 'Karn Evil 9' and 'In The Court Of The Crimson King'. He said, "Touring and performing with Ringo Starr was a great experience. Aside from being one of my musical heroes, Ringo was just a terrific person to be around. I absolutely fell in love with the band. They are all such wonderful people and enormously talented musicians. We were all from different styles of music but somehow there was a spiritual connection. Ringo brought the whole band together and after only ten days of rehearsal we were performing a two and a half hour show, which, when bearing in mind the complexity of some of the material and the fact that it was the first time that any of us had ever played together, it was a pretty remarkable achievement. After spending nearly two months playing with Ringo, I came to see a deeper picture of just how important he was to the creative power and ultimate success of The Beatles. Not only is he a great rock drummer and a dedicated musician, but he also has an impressive sense of realism and humility. He was, I have to say, a total pro in every respect."

Greg performing with Ringo Starr And His All-Starr Band at Chastain Park Amphitheatre in Atlanta, Georgia on 13th August 2001.

KEITH EMERSON
+ THE NICE

Keith Emerson of Emerson, Lake and Palmer
Plus The Nice featuring original members Lee Jackson and Brian Davidson.

Wednesday 2nd October - Civic Hall - Wolverhampton

Tickets £19.50 from Midland Box Office on
01902 55 21 21
Lines open Monday - Saturday, 10 am - 6 pm. Tickets also available online @
www.wolvescivic.co.uk

Following the one-off gig at London's 100 Club in April, The Nice played a handful of shows in October kicking off with this gig in Wolverhampton.

The reformed Nice: With Lee Jackson at the Derngate, Northampton, England, 10th October 2003.

© Alan Perry Concert Photog

In January 2002 Emerson took part in a BBC 2 Radio series called *Live From The Stables* where he played with Johnny Dankworth and Cleo Laine. In the same year, the Nice also got together to play a live show at The 100 Club on Oxford Street. Despite his initial reluctance to release a piano album, in May 2002, *Emerson Plays Emerson* was released on the EMI Classical label.

To address the continued talk and rumours regarding whether or not another ELP reunion was on the cards, Lake posted a message on his official website in August 2002. He stated; "I really do have very fond memories of some great times playing with ELP. It was an extraordinary band. However, the beauty of some things is that they happen in a particular way and at a particular moment in time and, because they cannot be easily duplicated, they become unique and special. For me, both the music of ELP and, for that matter, the music of King Crimson fall into that category. It isn't just a question of the three guys getting back together for old times' sake. So many factors went into making those early albums as creatively successful as they were. I'm not honestly sure, even with the good will of all those concerned, if the same degree of innovative creativity could be replicated in the same way today. Onward and upward."

2003 was a busy year for Emerson. He had his own radio show; a weekly half an hour called *Emo's Memos.* In the July, his autobiography was published. In October 2003, the Nice did a twelve-date tour of the UK.

In the same year, Lake revealed that he was close to finishing an album of new recordings of some of his most prominent songs. It wasn't released until 2013 though. The thought that went into the project was substantial, Lake said, "I always wondered what it would be like if we could have had today's technology back in the days when these songs were originally cut."

2003 saw Palmer release his album, *Working Live, Volume 1*. It features a live recording of his band playing at The Robin in Bilston from July 2001. In 2004, *Working Live, Volume 2* was released.

The reformed Nice: With Lee Jackson at the Derngate, Northampton, England, 10th October 2003.

As photographer Alan Perry recalls: "The first half of the concert comprised Nice music with original members Keith Emerson, Brian 'Binky' Davison and Lee Jackson, augmented by Dave Kilminster. Keith Emerson and ELP tracks were played in the second half, with all of the players appearing for the encore. Keith Emerson and ELP tracks were played in the second half, and all of the players combined for the encore."

Set-list: 'America Rondo', 'Tantalizing Maggie', 'Little Arabella', 'Brandenburger', 'Hang On To A Dream', 'Country Pie', 'Intermezzo From The Karelia Suite', 'Just Crazy' (Dave solo), (Keith Solo), 'A Blade Of Grass', 'A Cajun Alley', 'Creole Dance', 'Tarkus, Epitaph', 'Hoedown, Touch And Go', 'Fanfare For The Common Man', 'Honky Tonk Train Blues'.

Keith with the reformed Nice at De Montfort Hall, Leicester, England, 16th October 2003.

GOFF
Professional

155

De Montfort Hall, Leicester, England, 16th October 2003.

© Alan Perry Concert Photography

157

De Montfort Hall, Leicester, England,
16th October 2003.

Alan Perry: "The set was the same as at Northampton a week
earlier. I met Lee Jackson in the bar at the interval, and he invited
me backstage for the 'meet & greet' session after the concert.
Keith Emerson was obviously suffering with problems with his
right hand because he was shaking everyone's hand left-handed."

Carl performing at the Robin 2, Bilston, England, 2nd November 2002. The previous year he had recorded his *Working Live, Volume 1* at the same venue.

© Alan Perry Concert Photography

Robin 2, Bilston, England, 8th May 2003.

© Alan Perry Concert Photography

Robin 2, Bilston, England, 8th May 2003.

© Alan Perry Concert Photography

165

Robin 2, Bilston, England, 20th May 2004.

© Alan Perry Concert Photography

With bassist Dave Marks. Robin 2, Bilston, England, 20th May 2004.

Keith at the third annual Moogfest at B.B. King Blues Club & Grill, Times Square, Manhattan, New York, 22nd June 2005. Sadly Bob Moog died two months after this event.

Greg performing at the Royal Theatre Nottingham, 3rd November 2005. Greg took most of his material for this solo tour from his ELP days.

The Set-list was: 'In The Court Of The Crimson King', 'Paper Blood', 'Touch And Go', 'From The Beginning', 'Footprints In The Snow', 'Take A Pebble', 'I Believe In Father Christmas', 'Farewell To Arms', [Interval], 'Fanfare For The Common Man', 'I Love You Too Much', 'Hang On To A Dream', 'Lucky Man', '21st Century Schizoid Man', 'Pictures At An Exhibition', [Encore] 'Welcome Back My Friends'.

Photographer Alan Perry says, "I first saw ELP at Wembley in 1974, then again in 1992. Greg signed autographs in the foyer of the Royal Theatre after the show."

In fact the photo here shows Greg signing Alan's photo taken twenty-four years earlier at Reading Festival which can be seen on page 118.

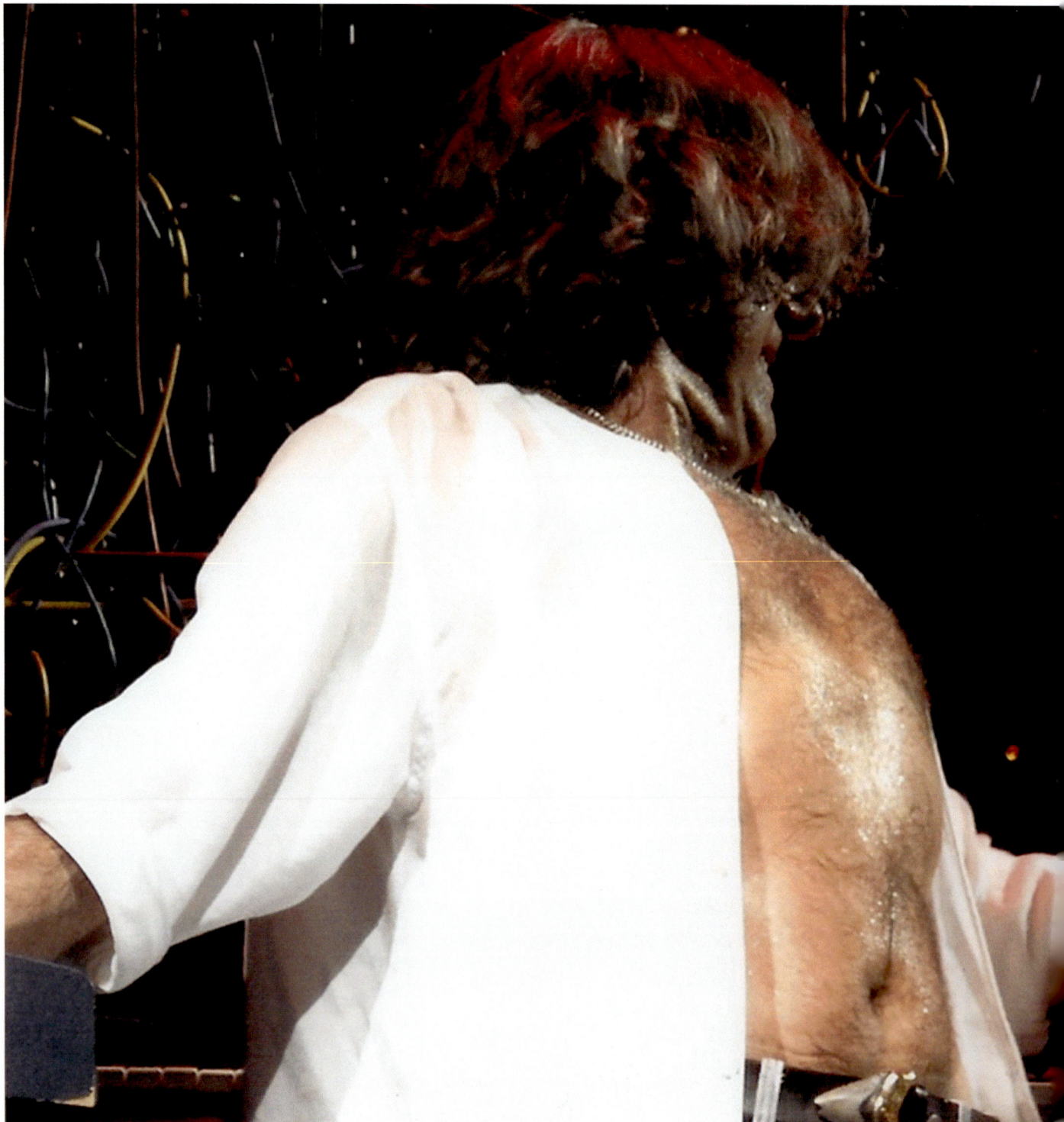

In 2005, a 35th anniversary DVD was released in celebration of ELP's career. Lake said "there's stuff on there which I didn't even realise had been filmed. It's astonishing when you see the footage. You think, 'however did that get filmed? I never saw any cameras!'" The release of the DVD fuelled speculation regarding the prospect of another ELP reunion. By this time though, Emerson had commitments with the Nice; they had begun touring in late 2004 as the support group for Scorpions.

The reunion didn't happen and Lake began working with The Who. He was asked by Roger Daltrey to take part in a benefit concert for the National Teenage Cancer trust. The show went so well that Lake was invited to do further sessions with the band.

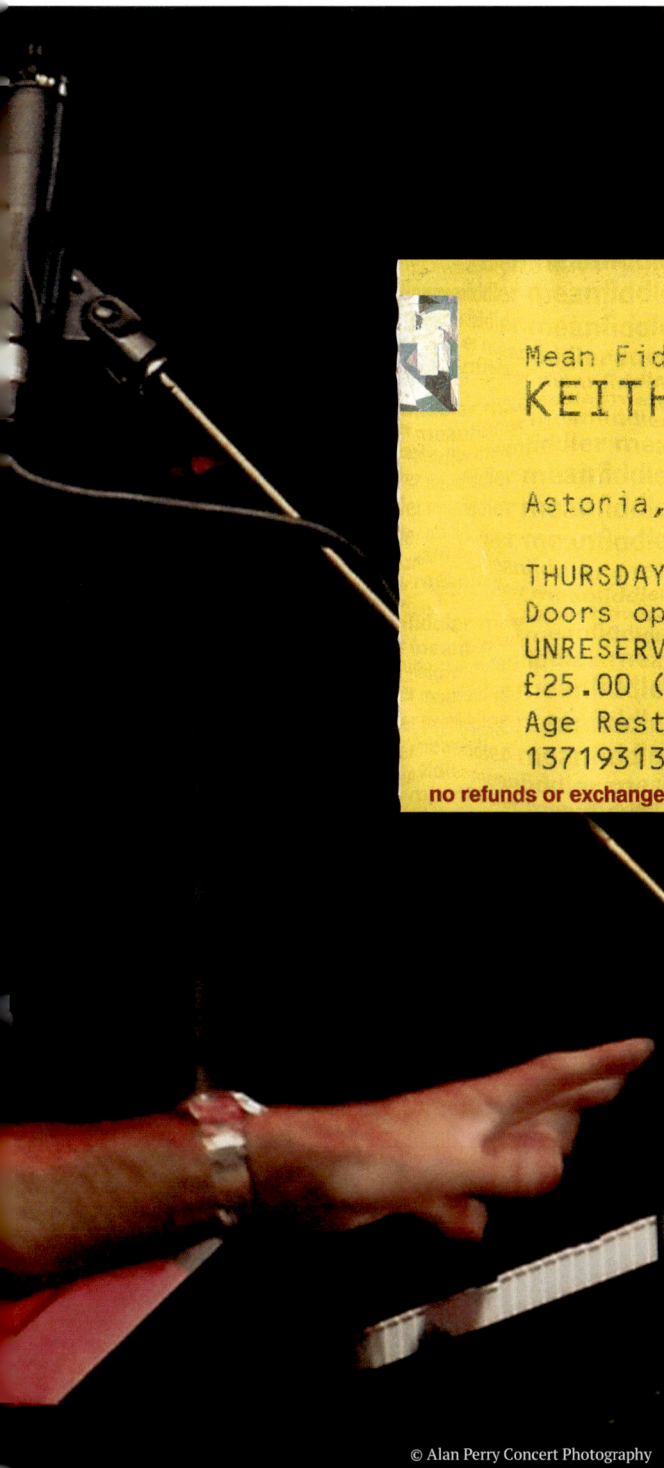

© Alan Perry Concert Photography

Mean Fiddler Presents
KEITH EMERSON

Astoria, London

THURSDAY 20 JULY 2006
Doors open 19.00
UNRESERVED SEATING
£25.00 (Subject to booking fee)
Age Restrictions Apply
13719313 PERRY   147

no refunds or exchanges   0870 060 3777 24hrs 7 days a week

meanfiddler.com

13042844

mf

After the brief time with The Nice, Keith toured with his band in 2006. The last show of the tour was the one and only UK concert at the Astoria in London on 20th July

177

WELCOME BACK
PIANO CONCERTO
LIVING SIN
BITCHES CRYSTAL

HOEDOWN
WHITE NOISE
COUNTRY PIE

NEW ORLEANS
FROM THE BEGINNING

LUCKY MAN
KARELIA SUITE
TOUCH & GO
AMERICA / RONDO

TARKUS

FANFARE
NUTROCKER

© Alan Perry Concert Photography

179

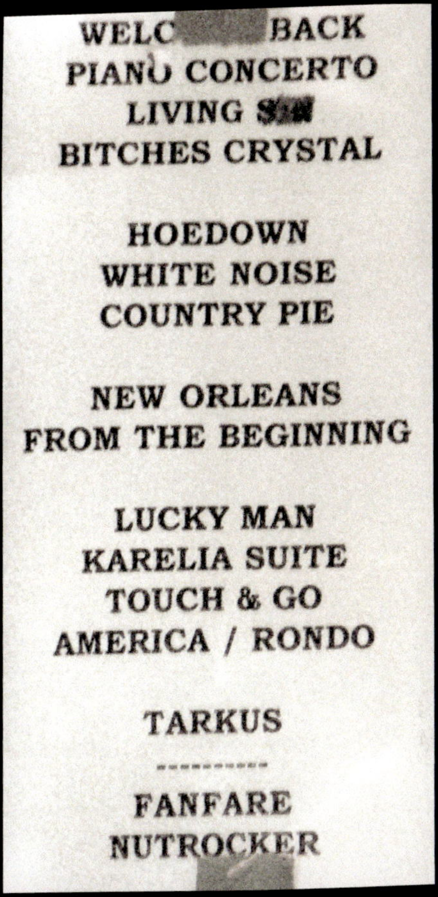

WELC   BACK
PIANO CONCERTO
LIVING S
BITCHES CRYSTAL

HOEDOWN
WHITE NOISE
COUNTRY PIE

NEW ORLEANS
FROM THE BEGINNING

LUCKY MAN
KARELIA SUITE
TOUCH & GO
AMERICA / RONDO

TARKUS

FANFARE
NUTROCKER

© Lee Millward

The Final
Farewell

Emerson, Lake and Palmer continued with their individual projects until it was announced that they would be headlining *Classic Rock*'s High Voltage Festival in July 2010 at Victoria Park. It was initially believed that the gig would be the only reunion but in January 2010, it was announced that Emerson and Lake would tour the US doing a few small acoustic shows. Palmer was unable to commit due to his work with Asia. As a result, anticipation was high for the trio's reunion at the High Voltage Festival. Getting all three musicians on stage together was a big deal by that time, but it was certainly worth it.

Although Emerson had been keen to bring back his spinning piano again for the High Voltage Festival, he wasn't allowed to on the basis that the local authority insisted the plan did not meet health and safety standards. Still though, ELP played through their old classics and it was a beautiful way to celebrate forty years of phenomenal music. However, Emerson said "It's very unlikely that we'll ever play together again so I think Greg, Carl and I should leave the stage on a positive note and not make the mistake of returning to sour the memory."

Palmer confessed later, "It was a good time to wrap things up. I felt we weren't cutting edge anymore. I told the others that was it for me, it's over." Four days after the High Voltage Festival, Palmer was back on tour with Asia.

© Lee Millward

Photographer Lee Millward explains: "An advert for Sadowsky Guitars featuring a shot of mine from High Voltage. Roger Sadowsky asked me if it was okay to use the image and sent me some merch for accepting."

In 2012, Lake went on the road with his show, Songs Of A Lifetime. Performing as a one-man band occasionally joined by guests, he played ELP songs as well as others he was fond of by other artists.

Pocklington Arts Centre 13th November 2012. Following the cancellation of Greg's 2006 tour, he returned to the stage as a solo performer in 2012.

© Lee Millward

© Lee Millward

Interestingly the two dates at the Pocklington Arts Centre for 12th / 13th are not included as they were classed as warm up gigs.

Lee Millward's treasured possession: "Greg sent this note along with some of my High Voltage shots that he kindly signed."

Dear Lee,

I wonder if you would be so kind as to send me a set of these pix for my own collection.

Many thanks

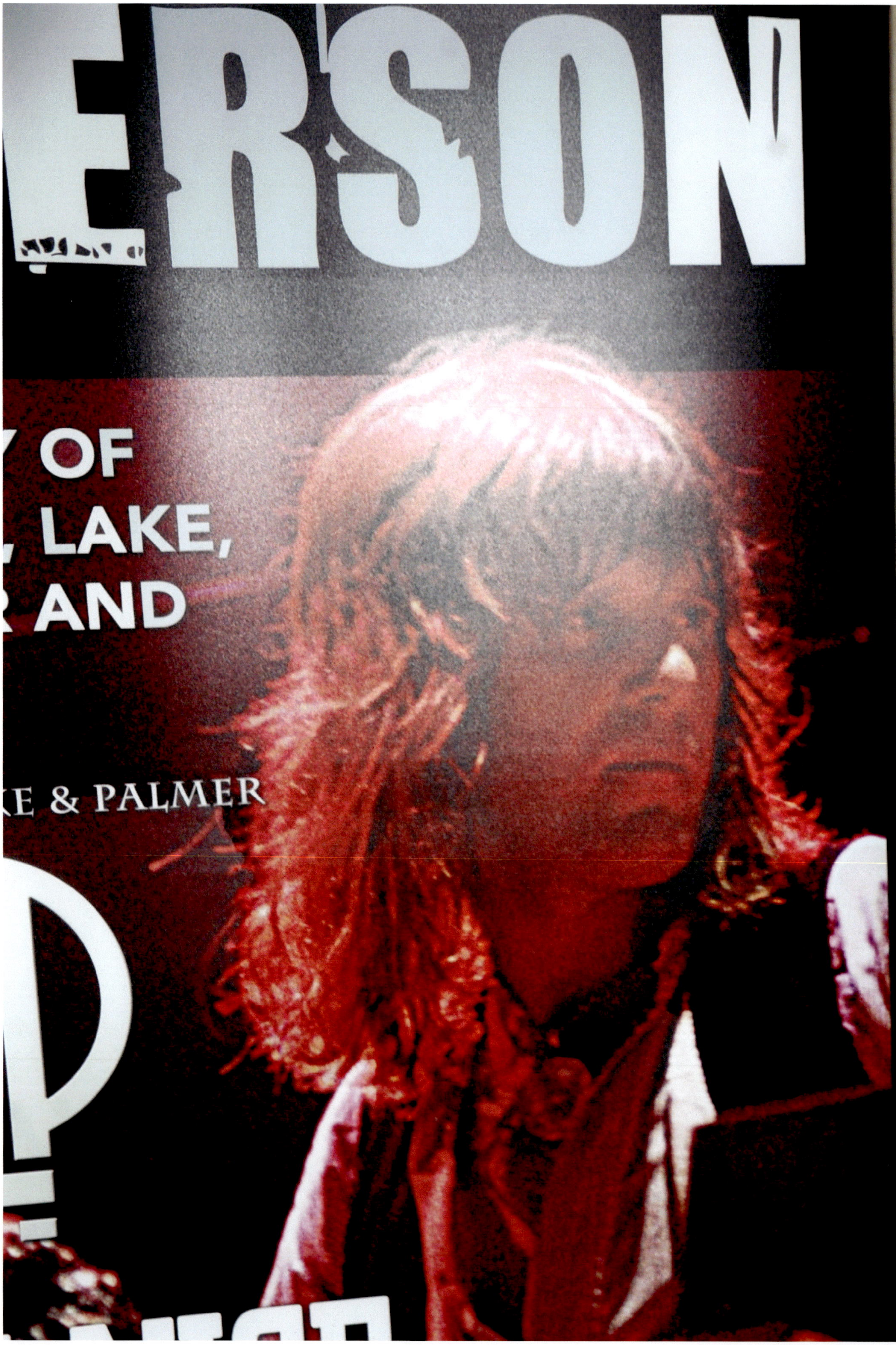
ERSON
OF
LAKE,
AND
& PALMER

Keith at the Sheraton Hotel, Parsippany, New Jersey. October 26th, 2013.

© Frank White

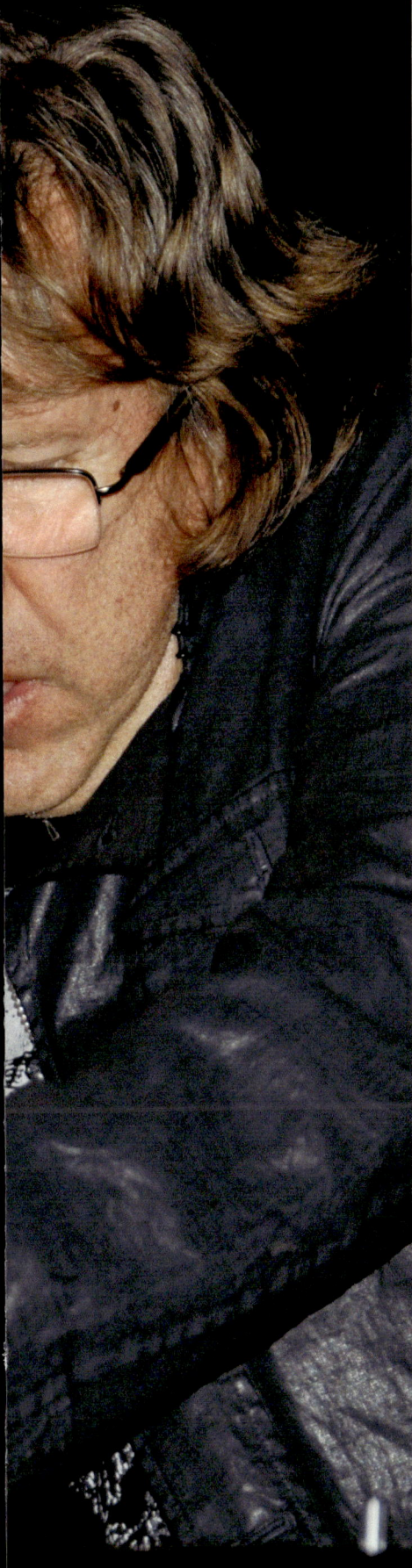

Palmer went on a world tour in 2013 with guitarist Paul Bielatowicz and bassist Simon Fitzpatrick. He then embarked on the 2014 Rhythm Of Light tour in the November of that year. He undertook an ELP Legacy tour in 2016, and again in 2017. On 2nd April 2019, it was announced that Palmer would play with both Asia and his ELP Legacy band during The Royal Affair tour with Yes and John Lodge. Arthur Brown was announced as a guest vocalist part way through the tour.

Emerson made his conducting debut in September 2013 in Bowling Green with Orchestra Kentucky. He conducted the South Shore Symphony at his 70th birthday tribute concert at Molloy College in Rockville Centre, New York in October 2014. The performance included the premiere of his three string quartets, as well as his version of 'Piano Concerto No. 1' by Jeffrey Biegel.

A nice gesture from Carl as he gives a speech at the Blue Plaque unveiling
ceremony in Cirencester on 7th January 2016 in
commemoration of Cozy Powell. Also in the photo are
Suzi Quatro, Brian May of Queen and Tony Iommi of Black Sabbath.

On 9th January 2016, Lake was awarded an honorary degree in music and lyrics composition from Conservatorio Nicolini in Piacenza, Italy. He had spent several years writing his autobiography and it was originally planned to be released in 2012. Poignantly though, it was released posthumously in June 2017.

In 2021, along with Bielatowicz and Fitzpatrick, Palmer returned to performing after the COVID-19 pandemic. The ELP Legacy Tour celebrated the fiftieth anniversary of ELP.

© John Spreadbury (Alamy Stock Photo)

For Immediate Release
Thursday, March 24th 2016

Carl Palmer

**CARL PALMER'S ELP LEGACY
ANNOUNCES 9TH TOUR OF NORTH AMERICA.
"REMEMBERING KEITH AND THE MUSIC OF
EMERSON LAKE & PALMER."
SPECIAL TRIBUTE SHOW TO KEITH EMERSON
TO BE PRESENTED IN MIAMI, FL ON JUNE 24TH.**
Exciting show features the instrumental rock clas
EMERSON LAKE & PALMER, in final leg of worl

Carl Palmer, among the most renowned drummers in rock
founding member of both ELP and ASIA, is returning to the Unite
Canada for a tour he has decided to name: THE 2016 REMEMBE
AND THE MUSIC OF EMERSON LAKE & PALMER TOUR. Origin
to be a celebration of Palmer's 50th year in music, the focus and
tour was changed in light of the tragic death of Keith Emerson o

"I will deeply miss Keith and I want you all to know I will
the ELP banner and playing the great music with my band for r
come," said Palmer, in a statement. "We have lost a very talen
musician but this great music will continue for a long, long tim

To honor his late friend and former band mate, Palmer
with Audio One, will present a special show: **"Pictures At An
Tribute To Keith Emerson"** which will feature music by Car
Legacy band with special guests, cinematic images, and pe
Center For Contemporary Dance, who will interpret the mus
& Palmer in contemporary dance segments combined with
and his band. The tribute show, which will also include oth
yet to be announced, will be staged one nigh
Miami, Florida's historic
this link

to approach the music of ELP. I didn't want to have a singer trying to sound like
Greg Lake. ELP did so much instrumental music, this format made sense to me.
The idea was to re-invent the music; there will be several new classic ELP tunes
this time around."

The tour will also include special art events designed to benefit regional
charities which will exhibit and sell canvases from Palmer's two acclaimed
collections: *The Rhythm of Light (2014)* and *A Twist Of The Wrist (2013)*. The
images in these collections are the result of collaboration between Palmer and
the acclaimed Los Angeles Art Team, Scene Four and feature a series of signed
and numbered prints of stunning visual images constructed by capturing
rhythm. The images combine motion, color, and lighting into some of the most
compelling fine art visuals ever created. These very limited Palmer art
collections are available at www.CarlPalmerArt.com.

Carl Palmer's ELP Legacy enthusiasts can expect an evening of compelling percussive skills, from the man
who brought the drum set to the forefront of rock n roll music.

http://www.carlpalmer.com

CARL PALMER'S ELP LEGACY
"REMEMBERING KEITH" -THE MUSIC OF EMERSON LAKE & PALMER TOUR

DATE	VENUE	CITY
Thur Jun 2 BUY TICKETS HERE	BB King Blues Club,	New York, NY
Fri June 3 BUY TICKETS HERE	Sellersville Theatre 1894	Sellersville, PA
Sat June 4	Private Art Event	
Sun June 5 BUY TICKETS HERE	Tupelo Music Hall	New York, NY
Mon June 6 BUY TICKETS HERE	World Café	Londonderry, NH
Tues June 7 BUY TICKETS HERE	Regent Theatre	Wilmington, DE
Wed June 8 BUY TICKETS HERE	Studio in Hamilton Canada	Arlington, MA / Hamilton Ontario Canada

CARL PALMER'S ELP LEGACY
PICTURES AT AN EXHIBITION – A TRIBUTE TO KEITH EMERSON
Celebrating The Music Of
Emerson Lake & Palmer
Interpreted In Contemporary Dance

With special guests to be announced!
ONE NIGHT ONLY
FRIDAY, JUNE 24TH, 2016
8:00pm

Adds Palmer: "I hope this is somethin
will all want to come along and see to help
marry the music of ELP with a contempora
while. Originally, this event had been sche
year in music and I had invited Keith to c
special events that had been planned in
sadly, fate intercepted these plans. I felt it we
into a tribute to him and the music we made together.

The "Remembering Keith" tour features his popular ELP Legacy
will also highlight his collection of fine art, recently done in conjunction with
California's Scene Four Art Studios.

Carl Palmer's ELP Legacy returns after a successful run of shows this
past June, November and December. Palmer will present bold, new
arrangements of the best-loved instrumental music of ELP, and other
composers. A multi-media experience combining music and video projection,
the show promises to be among the most musically compelling tours of the
year. Carl Palmer ELP Legacy is a red-hot power trio that features Palmer on
drums and percussion; guitarist **Paul Bielatowicz** and bassist **Simon
Fitzpatrick.**

"Since 2001, I have been playing with my own power trio, replacing the
keyboards with electric guitar," says Palmer. "I felt that was the only honest way

Carl during his Remembering Keith & The Music of ELP Tour held at the Molson Canadian Studio at Hamilton Place, Hamilton, Ontario, 8th June 2016.

On the 11th August 2017 Carl's ELP Legacy took part in the "Yestival" at the Ford Ampitheatre on Coney Island, New York along with Yes and Todd Rundgren. A photo was posted on Carl's official Facebook page of him backstage with fellow drummers Prarie Prince, Carmine Appice, Alan White and Dylan Howe. With the exception of Appice they all performed at the event.

© Frank White

214

Keith Emerson died on 11th March 2016 of a self-inflicted gunshot wound to the head. His body was found at his Santa Monica home in California. The medical examiner who carried out his autopsy ruled that Emerson had died of suicide in relation to depression associated with alcohol. Emerson's girlfriend, Mari Kawaguchi, revealed how he had become "depressed, nervous and anxious" due to having nerve damage that compromised his playing. In particular, she expressed that Emerson was worried that he wouldn't perform well at upcoming concerts in Japan; he was anxious that he would disappoint his fans.

Emerson was buried at Lancing and Sompting Cemetery in West Sussex on 1st April 2016. Palmer and Lake both issued statements on his death. Palmer said, "Keith was a gentle soul whose love for music and passion for his performance as a keyboard player will remain unmatched for many years to come." Lake said, "As sad and tragic as Keith's death is, I would not want this to be the lasting memory people take away with them. What I will always remember about Keith Emerson was his remarkable talent as a musician and composer and his gift and passion to entertain. Music was his life and despite some of the difficulties he encountered I am sure that the music he created will live on forever."

Greg Lake died later that same year on 7th December after suffering from cancer. When his manager announced the news on Twitter, he described Lake's battle with the illness as having been "long and stubborn". Many fellow musicians paid tribute, including Rick Wakeman, Steve Hackett, Ringo Starr, John Wetton and indeed, Carl Palmer, who is of course, the last surviving member of ELP.

DISCOGRAPHY

Emerson, Lake & Palmer's Studio Albums

Emerson, Lake & Palmer (1970)

Tarkus (1971)

Trilogy (1972)

Brain Salad Surgery (1973)

Works Volume 1 (1977)

Works Volume 2 (1977)

Love Beach (1978)

Black Moon (1992)

In The Hot Seat (1994)

Emerson, Lake & Palmer's Live Albums

Pictures At An Exhibition (1971)

Welcome Back, My Friends, To The Show That Never Ends – Ladies And Gentlemen, Emerson, Lake & Palmer (1974)

In Concert (1979)

Live At The Royal Albert Hall (1993)

Works Live (1993)

Live At The Isle Of Wight Festival (1997)

Live In Poland (1997)

King Biscuit Flower Hour – Greatest Hits Live (1997)

Then And Now (1998)

The Original Bootleg Series From The Manitcore Vaults – Volume 1 (2001)

The Original Bootleg Series From The Manitcore Vaults – Volume 2 (2001)

The Original Bootleg Series From The Manitcore Vaults – Volume 3 (2002)

The Original Bootleg Series From The Manitcore Vaults – Volume 4 (2006)

A Time And A Place (2010)

Live At Nassau Coliseum '78 (2011)

Live At The Mar Y Sol Festival '72 (2011)

Live In California '74 (2012)

Live In Montreal 1977 (2013)

Once Upon A Time – Live In South America 1997 (2015)

Live At Montreux 1997 (2015)

Masters From The Vaults (2017)

Live At Pocono International Raceway, USA, 8th July 1972 (2019)

(Emerson & Lake sans Palmer) Live From Manticore Hall 2010 (2014)

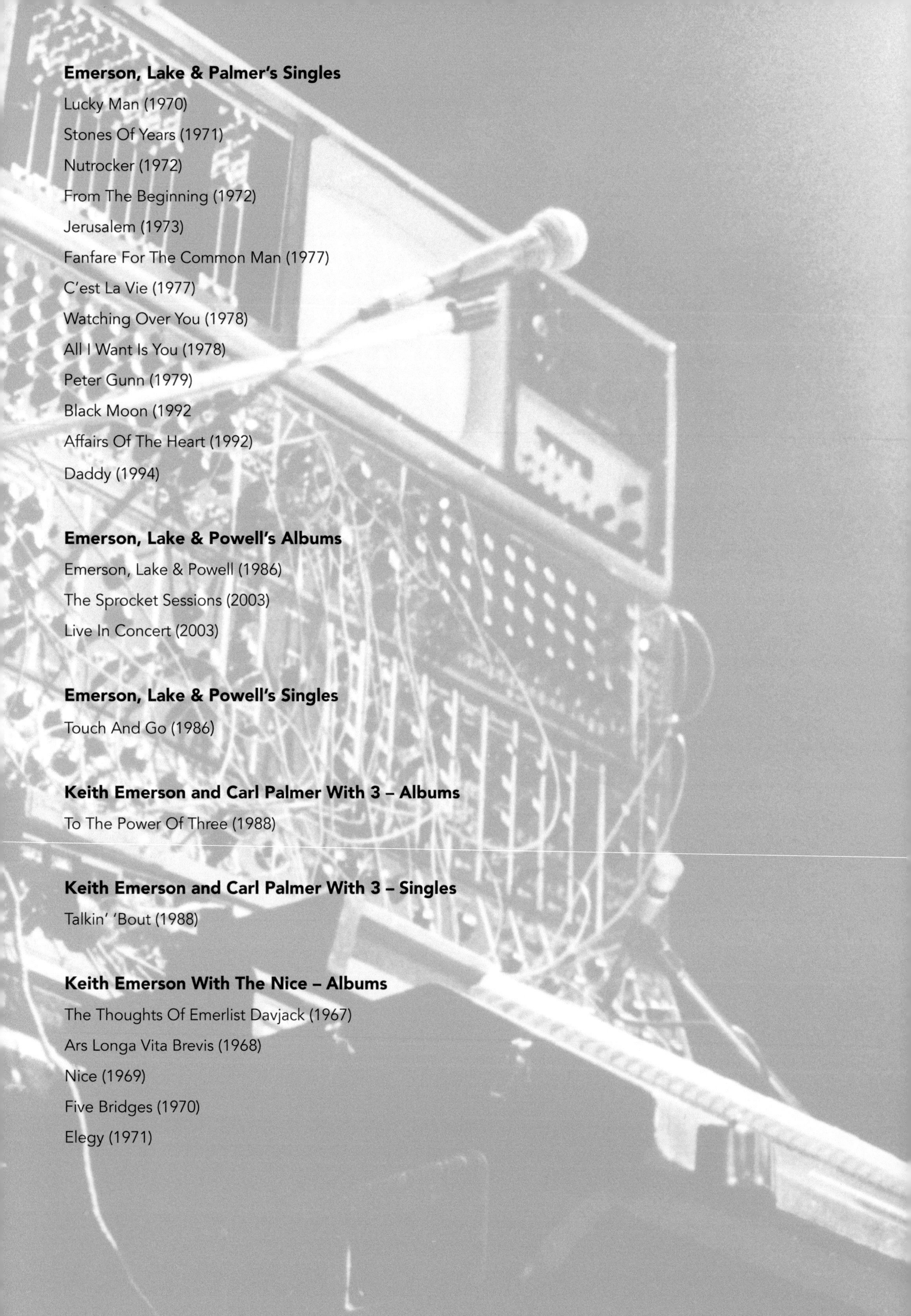

Emerson, Lake & Palmer's Singles

Lucky Man (1970)

Stones Of Years (1971)

Nutrocker (1972)

From The Beginning (1972)

Jerusalem (1973)

Fanfare For The Common Man (1977)

C'est La Vie (1977)

Watching Over You (1978)

All I Want Is You (1978)

Peter Gunn (1979)

Black Moon (1992

Affairs Of The Heart (1992)

Daddy (1994)

Emerson, Lake & Powell's Albums

Emerson, Lake & Powell (1986)

The Sprocket Sessions (2003)

Live In Concert (2003)

Emerson, Lake & Powell's Singles

Touch And Go (1986)

Keith Emerson and Carl Palmer With 3 – Albums

To The Power Of Three (1988)

Keith Emerson and Carl Palmer With 3 – Singles

Talkin' 'Bout (1988)

Keith Emerson With The Nice – Albums

The Thoughts Of Emerlist Davjack (1967)

Ars Longa Vita Brevis (1968)

Nice (1969)

Five Bridges (1970)

Elegy (1971)

Keith Emerson With The Nice – Singles

The Thoughts Of Emerlist Davjack (1967)

America (1968)

Brandenburger (1968)

She Belongs To Me (1969)

Country Pie (1970)

Keith Emerson's Solo Albums

Inferno (1980)

Nighthawks (1981)

Honky (1981)

Harmageddon (1983)

Murderock (1984)

Best Revenge (1984)

La Chiesa (The Church) (1989)

The Christmas Album (1989)

Changing States (1995)

America – The BBC Sessions (1996)

Iron Man Volume 1 (2001)

The Swedish Radio Sessions (2001)

BBC Sessions (2002)

Emerson Plays Emerson (2002)

Vivacitas Box Set (2003)

At The Movies Box Set (2005)

Off The Shelf (2006)

The Keith Emerson Band Featuring Marc Bonilla (2008)

Live At The Fillmore East – December 1969 (2009)

The Diamond Hard Blue Apples Of The Moon (2010)

Moscow Live (2011)

The Three Fates Project (2012)

Keith Emerson's Singles

Honky Tonk Train Blues (1976)

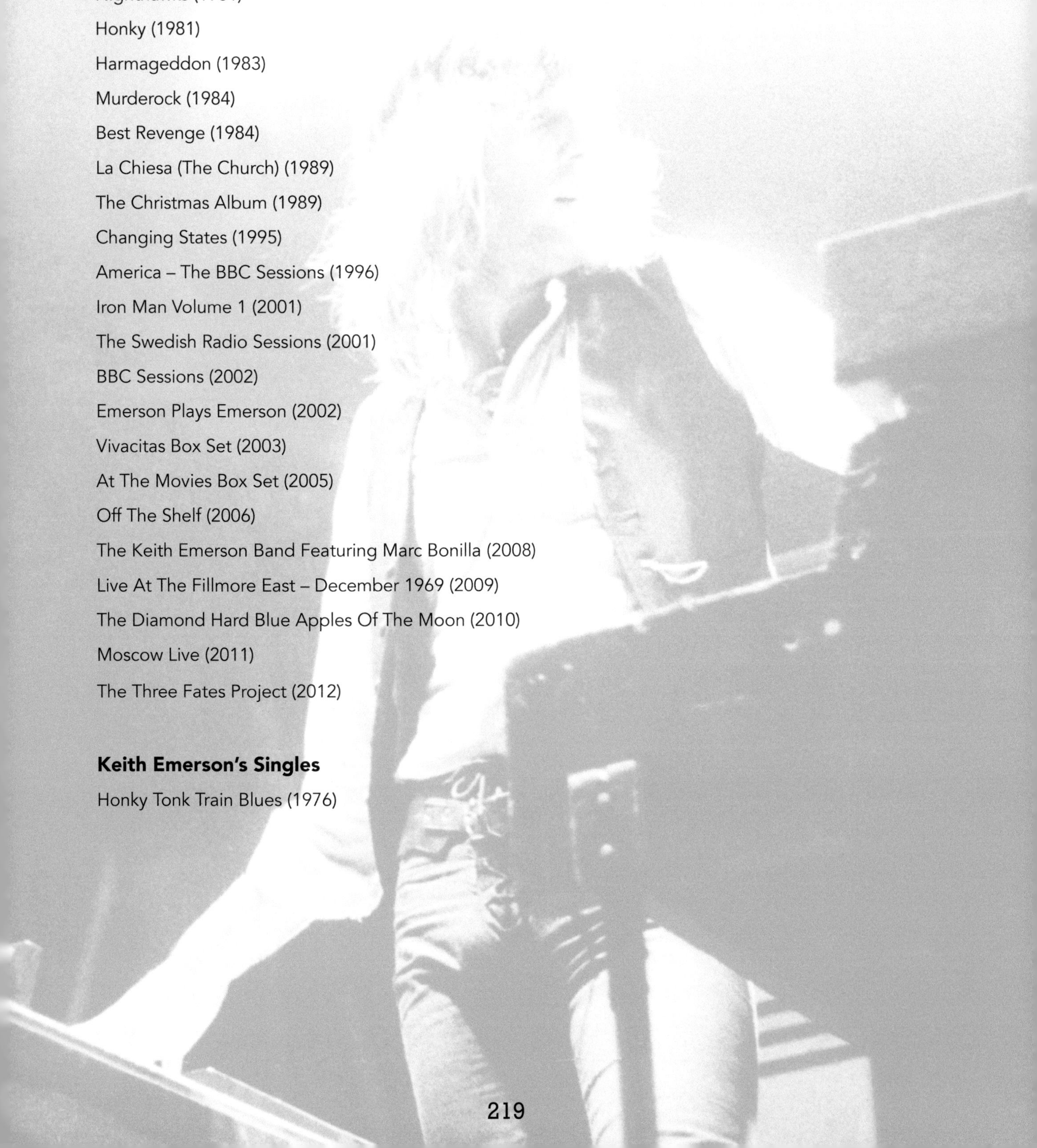

Keith Emerson's Soundtrack Albums

Inferno (1980)

Nighthawks (1981)

Best Revenge (1985)

Murderock (1984)

Harmageddon/China Free Fall (1987)

(A split album with Derek Austin. Emerson did the *Harmageddon* soundtrack whilst Austin did the *China Free Fall* soundtrack.)

La Chiesa (2002)

(Music from the 1989 horror film *The Church*, also known as *La chiesa*. The album also contains material by Fabio Pignatelli and Goblin.)

Godzilla: Final Wars (2004)

Keith Emerson's Contributions

'In The Flesh?' (two versions) and 'Waiting For The Worms' on the Pink Floyd tribute album, *Back Against The Wall* (2005)

'Black Dog' on the Led Zeppelin tribute album *Led Box: The Ultimate Led Zeppelin Tribute* (2008)

Spinal Tap – 'Heavy Duty' on *Back From The Dead* (2009)

Boys Club – Live From California (with Glenn Hughes, Marc Bonilla) (2009)

Ayreon – 'Progressive Waves' on *The Theory Of Everything* (2013)

Greg Lake With The Shame – Singles

Don't Go Away Little Girl (1967)

Greg Lake With The Shy Limbs – Singles

Reputation (1968)

Greg Lake With King Crimson – Albums

In The Court Of The Crimson King (1969)

In The Wake Of Poseidon (1970)

Epitaph (1997)

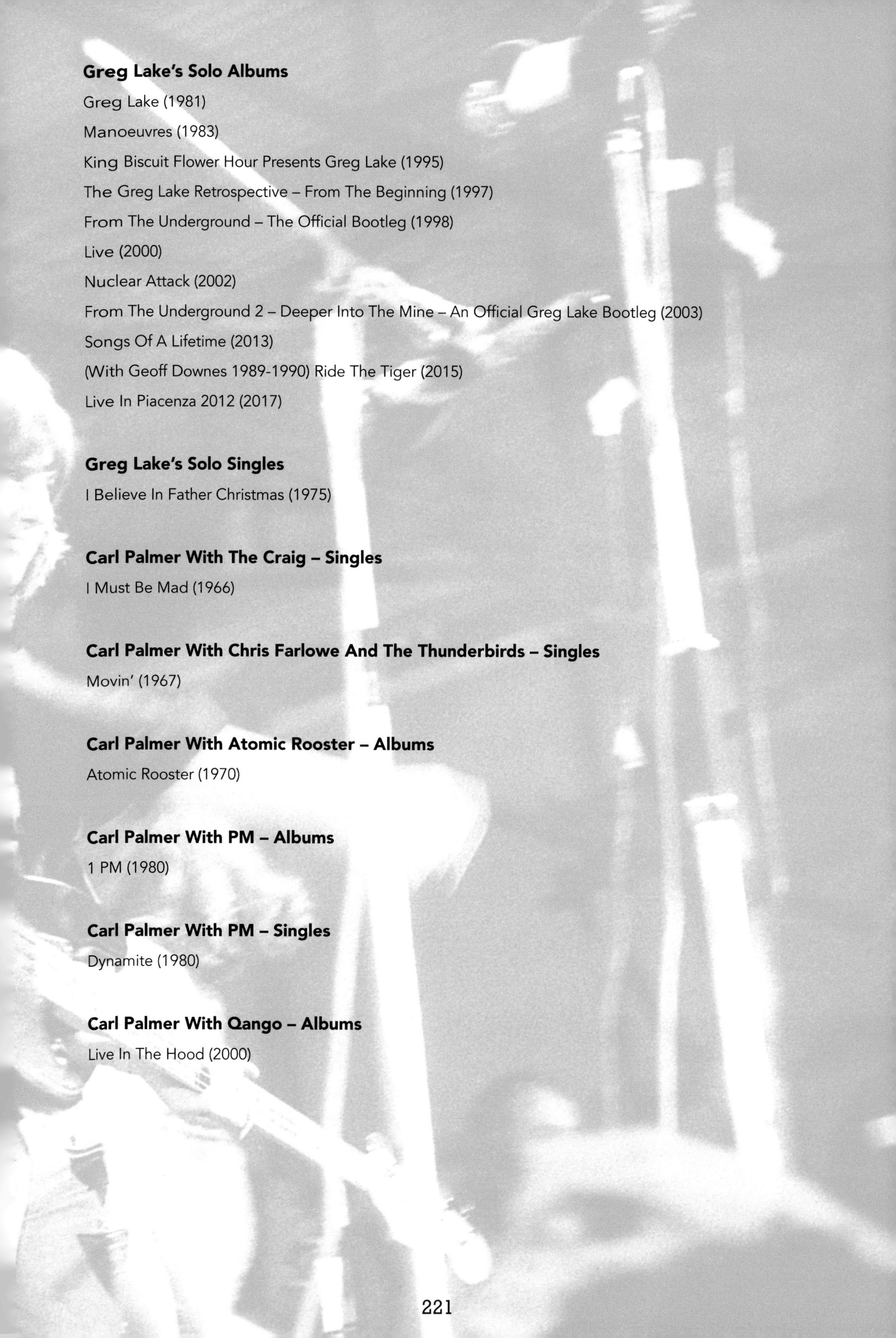

Greg Lake's Solo Albums

Greg Lake (1981)

Manoeuvres (1983)

King Biscuit Flower Hour Presents Greg Lake (1995)

The Greg Lake Retrospective – From The Beginning (1997)

From The Underground – The Official Bootleg (1998)

Live (2000)

Nuclear Attack (2002)

From The Underground 2 – Deeper Into The Mine – An Official Greg Lake Bootleg (2003)

Songs Of A Lifetime (2013)

(With Geoff Downes 1989-1990) Ride The Tiger (2015)

Live In Piacenza 2012 (2017)

Greg Lake's Solo Singles

I Believe In Father Christmas (1975)

Carl Palmer With The Craig – Singles

I Must Be Mad (1966)

Carl Palmer With Chris Farlowe And The Thunderbirds – Singles

Movin' (1967)

Carl Palmer With Atomic Rooster – Albums

Atomic Rooster (1970)

Carl Palmer With PM – Albums

1 PM (1980)

Carl Palmer With PM – Singles

Dynamite (1980)

Carl Palmer With Qango – Albums

Live In The Hood (2000)

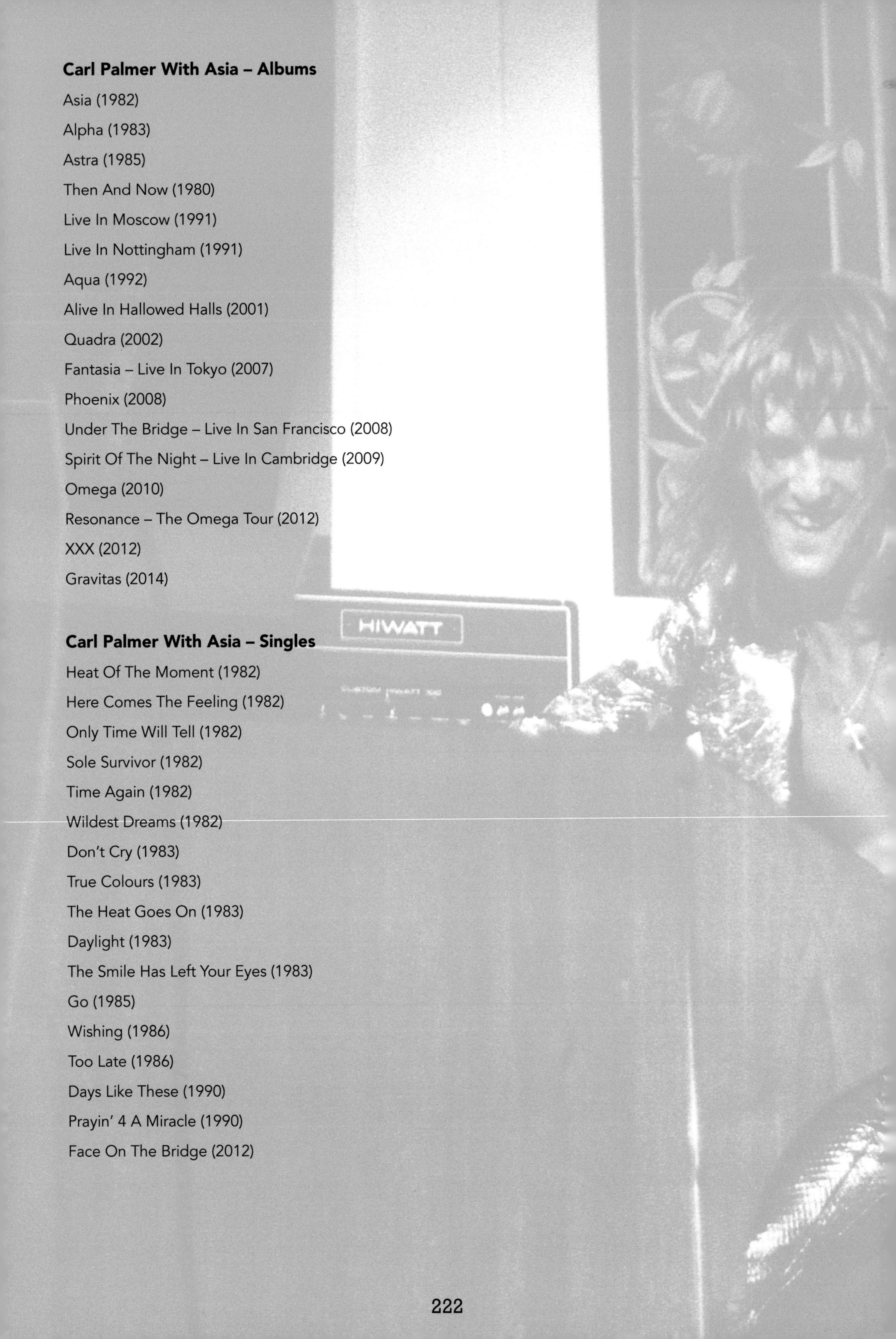

Carl Palmer With Asia – Albums

Asia (1982)

Alpha (1983)

Astra (1985)

Then And Now (1980)

Live In Moscow (1991)

Live In Nottingham (1991)

Aqua (1992)

Alive In Hallowed Halls (2001)

Quadra (2002)

Fantasia – Live In Tokyo (2007)

Phoenix (2008)

Under The Bridge – Live In San Francisco (2008)

Spirit Of The Night – Live In Cambridge (2009)

Omega (2010)

Resonance – The Omega Tour (2012)

XXX (2012)

Gravitas (2014)

Carl Palmer With Asia – Singles

Heat Of The Moment (1982)

Here Comes The Feeling (1982)

Only Time Will Tell (1982)

Sole Survivor (1982)

Time Again (1982)

Wildest Dreams (1982)

Don't Cry (1983)

True Colours (1983)

The Heat Goes On (1983)

Daylight (1983)

The Smile Has Left Your Eyes (1983)

Go (1985)

Wishing (1986)

Too Late (1986)

Days Like These (1990)

Prayin' 4 A Miracle (1990)

Face On The Bridge (2012)

Carl Palmer's Solo Albums

Carl Palmer Band – Working Live Volume 1 (2003)

Carl Palmer Band – Working Live Volume 2 (2004)

Carl Palmer Band – Working Live Volume 3 (2010)

Carl Palmer's ELP Legacy Albums

Live In The USA (2016)

Pictures At An Exhibition – A Tribute To Keith Emerson (2016)

Live (2018)

CREDITS

All photos have been licensed from the respective agencies and individuals for exclusive use in this book and remain the copyright of the said photographers and / or agencies. A few could not be credited and the copyright holders are invited to contact us.

Photo research by Jerry Bloom.

Special thanks to Laura Shenton, Lee Millward, Alan Perry and Mark Scalise at ELPArchive.com

Editorial Control: This book requires total independent editorial control. It has not been authorised or approved by ELP or their respective managements, or the estates of Keith Emerson and Greg Lake.

Robert E. Howard's

CONAN

ADVENTURES IN AN AGE UNDREAMED OF

System Design
Benn Graybeaton, Nathan Dowdell
& Jay Little

Line Development
Jason Durall & Chris Lites

Writing
Chris Lites

Approvals
Patrice Louinet & Jeffrey Shanks

Editing & Proofreading
Sally Christenson, Jason Durall,
Joshua Klug & Richard August

Cover Artwork
Liam Sharpe

Interior Artwork
Gio Baroni, Jorge Barrero, Shen Fei, Michele Frigo,
Nick Greenwood, Robert Jenkins, Diana Martinez,
Andrë Meister, Christian Quinot, Martin Sobr,
Michael Syrigos & Ricardo German Ponce Torres

Cartography
Tobias Tranell

Art Direction
Mischa Thomas

Lead Graphic Design
Michal E. Cross

Layout
Thomas Shook

Additional Graphic Design
Dan Algstrand & Malcolm Wolter

Produced by
Chris Birch

Operations Manager
Garry Harper

Community Support
Lloyd Gyan

Publishing Assistant
Sam Webb

With Thanks to
The Robert E. Howard Foundation,
Professor John Kirowan, H.P. Lovecraft,
Fred & Jay at Cabinet Entertainment

Published by
Modiphius Entertainment Ltd.
2nd Floor, 39 Harwood Road,
Fulham, London, SW6 4QP
United Kingdom

2nd Printing. Printed by Livonia Print, Ventspils iela 50, Riga, LV-1002, Latvia.

TABLE OF CONTENTS

CONAN THE MERCENARY

Conan laughed and lifted the jug. "When you allow the elevation of a man, one can be sure that you'll profit by his advancement. I've earned everything I've won, with my blood and sweat."

— "A Witch Shall Be Born"

Sell-swords, dog-brothers, mercenaries — these are but a few of the names given to those who are paid in coin to shed blood. From the time first development of the sword and a form of trade, a sword-arm could be bought. Nemedian scholars say it is the *second* oldest profession. Indeed, the profession of arms is as necessary a part of society as the farmer, the blacksmith, and even the king — after all, what king rules without men to fight for him?

In the Hyborian Age, standing armies are not the standard affair we know today. While some few kingdoms such as Aquilonia employ full-time militaries, many more kingdoms use conscription to raise armies when the cry of war is heard. Filling out these pressed ranks, composed of boys shaking with fear, farmers thinking of their harvest, and old men waiting for the end one way or another, are mercenaries. Professional soldiers, whose loyalty is to no crown or ideology but to the glint of coin and the bloodlust in their hearts. It is to these men and women this book directs itself — to their way of life, and into their resulting adventures, that we now delve.

THE SELL-SWORD'S WAY

The life of the mercenary is heaped in gore and glory. In your ears ring the stories of dog-brothers and sword-sisters who live and die by the sword... in return for coin. The bodies are heaped all around you, your sword is slippery in your hands, but its blade doesn't stop swinging and the coin doesn't stop piling up.

Conan the Mercenary offers new character options; details on places like Koth, Shem, Ophir, and Khoraja; a host of mercenary companies; a mass combat system for handling company-sized skirmishes; non-player encounters; and more.

Chapter 1: Mercenary Characters

This section offers new castes, stories, archetypes, educations, and war stories to create mercenary player characters. It also covers new equipment, armor, and weaponry.

Chapter 2: Gazetteer

While mercenaries fight all over the known world, this book focuses on the fractious and ambitious kingdom of Koth, the opulent and rich Ophir, the loose city-states

AUTHOR'S NOTE

Following a series of articles which I have submitted for peer review among our singular group of academics, the following describes by foray into the role of paid combatants in the Hyborian Age. These accounts come mostly from post-Hyborian Ages sources, though a few primary texts remain.

For once, the subject is rather straightforward and relatable not only to our own agreed-upon antiquity, but our modern world, as well. Who has not read accounts of foreign nationals fighting for pay in the now-unfolding Spanish Civil War?

The Hyborian Age, it seems, suffered from yet another iteration of the needs imposed on countries in times of war, and was perhaps one of the first to experience such societal tensions.

-J.K., October 22, 1936.

JOURNAL OF THE WANDERERS CLUB

MERCENARIES IN THE HYBORIAN AGE

By Prof. John Kirowan (PhD, FRS, FRAI, FRGS)
Guest Lecturer, Department of Anthropology
Miskatonic University
Arkham, Massachusetts

All Americans know something of the lone gunslinger, working for hire wherever needed. While this figure is no doubt largely a fiction from dime novels of the prior century and the pulp magazines of these times, it comes from the very real world of the professional soldier-for-hire. From Macedonia to Renaissance Italy, we know the work of mercenaries in the larger affairs of empires.

This gives us a familiar rock on which to gain purchase in the Hyborian Age. You see, their mercenary companies — with names such as "the Nemedian Adventurers" — are not dissimilar from our own. Of surviving translated documents, the letters and diaries of one Amalric, a mercenary captain of this age, feature prominently. Even the legendary figure of Conan crosses with the life of what the age terms "dog-brothers".

In our current times, we confront the rise of nationalism in Europe and elsewhere. These men fought for no cause, but instead only for money. The loyalty they give was bought — from the great Aquilonia to mysterious Khitai, such forces turned the tide of battles and on their pikes hung the fate of empires.

We look, then, through the hourglass of time at men who fought and died in an era many consider mythic. It is my purpose herein to lend both humanity and veracity to their existence. Where the tidal waves of jingoistic fervor may consume the nations of men, there are always stalwarts who fight merely to feed themselves and for the lust of gold. I am reminded of letters written from the trenches of the Great War and wonder, would we all not be better off with wars fought by such able veterans, rather than the youth herded like cattle into those horrific meat-grinders of Verdun, the Somme, and Galipoli not two decades ago?

that comprise Shem, and Khoraja — a kingdom founded by mercenary armies ages ago!

Chapter 3: Mercenary Events

Few things move the world like war, and mercenaries can be counted to be in the thick of it. But what sparks these endless wars and rebellions? Plague, religious upheaval, and sorcerous acts which breach the boundaries of the Outer Dark are all covered here, as inspiration for your adventures.

Chapter 4: Encounters

Found here are mercenaries, soldiers, gilded knights, as well as those who hire them. Find out who holds the real power behind the jeweled thrones of the Earth, who leads the most feared Free Companies, and what sorcerous foes harry mere soldiers. Also presented here are horrors to rob sanity, from the realm of dream and nightmare!

Chapter 5: Hither Came Conan...

In this phase of Conan's career, we see progress as he grows in power, skill, and fame... if not fortune. A seasoned warrior and leader of soldiers, Conan the Mercenary is presented here in all his deadly glory.

Chapter 6: The Mercenary's Way

The life of a mercenary in the Hyborian Age is one of danger, thrills, and bloody war. What sort of companies are best known in this epoch? How does one gain ranks, and more importantly, what loot is to be had when the carrion clear the field of the dead?

Chapter 7: Battles

Without a sense of order, any combat involving more than a handful becomes chaos. These rules allow the gamemaster and players to orchestrate conflicts at a company-wide scale, to determine the outcome of battles between sell-sword and soldier alike!

Chapter 8: Mercenaries of the Age

Lastly, presented here are two formidable mercenaries — a sword-sister and a dog-brother — who might be encountered on the battlefields of the Hyborian world. Will they be allies, or deadly opponents?

MERCENARY CHARACTERS

"They'll follow me. I'll promise them a camel-train of gold from the palace. Khauran will be willing to pay that as a guerdon for getting rid of Constantius. After that, I'll lead them against the Turanians as you have planned. They want loot, and they'd as soon fight Constantius for it as anybody."

— Conan, "A Witch Shall Be Born"

While a dog-brother may tell a young cur that mercenaries are born and not made, this isn't the case. This savage world is an anvil upon which one's mettle is beaten, pounded, and all too often broken.

Yet the mercenary is no tavern keeper, farmer, or winemaker. This is the profession of arms, and only those of real strength come out of the forge. The rest remain behind on the field of their first or second battle — their stories untold; their names forgotten.

A mercenary's work is a job, and one may have many jobs in one's time. But to a soldier for hire, there is nothing else that matters. The mercenary marches and sleeps and whiles away time until the true test comes. The life of a mercenary is one of boredom punctuated by sheer terror and thrills to which nothing else in this life compares. Mercenaries are a fraternity, united by both money and a rude code of honor. They come from all kingdoms and places, emerging from any location in which men and women grow dissatisfied with the tedium of civilized life.

Your character creation follows the steps outlined in the *Conan* corebook, but each step has new options. Use these new choices — or rolls — to create soldiers of fortune and blood. Then, have them pray to whatever god they believe in that they last more than a handful of battles. A mercenary's work is hard, often deadly, and leads only to fortune as one rises in the ranks.

The following additions serve to expand the options available to players selecting mercenary characters. Any step not presented below is found in the *Conan* corebook. As always, the player can choose or roll, as desired.

MERCENARY HOMELANDS

Mercenaries are well traveled and visit many lands. They are likely to have a birthplace and a home country that are quite independent of each other. If a player wishes, they can choose or roll for their Homeland twice, or pick two results. One is their birthplace, and the other is the country they were primarily raised in. Pick only one to derive benefits from, not both. This confers no additional benefit, but may serve to inspire the player in depicting a well-traveled veteran of the often petty, always bloody wars of the Hyborian Age.

ANCIENT BLOODLINES

A player character with this talent can use the basic description from the CONAN corebook, unmodified. However, said player character may choose one of the bloodlines below for flavor.

- **BLOOD OF BORI:** While not as ancient as the lineage of sunken Atlantis, or the mysterious Zhemri of Zamora, those descended from Bori give name to this age. It is the Hyborians who rule in the West, having risen from barbarism to form the civilized world. When a character with this talent fails a Personality test, they are filled with pride and disdain for anyone who would question the blood which made the world (as they see it).

- **FELL BLOOD OF ACHERON:** The remnants of dark Acheron remain not only in ruins and memory but also in blood. After the Cataclysm, Acheron rose to a power of which Turan and Aquilonia can yet only dream. The Sons of Bori are nothing compared to this more ancient, pure blood. That barbarous people may have pulled down the towers of Python, but they will see the whips of Acheron at their backs again. A character with this talent that fails a Personality test is filled with anger and entitlement, perhaps even with a surge of that sorcery-tainted blood that burns in their veins.

MERCENARY CASTES

All mercenaries are warriors of some stripe, but few of them come from the warrior caste of the cultures into which they are born. Most mercenaries are the cast-offs of society who find an income one sword stroke at a time. Those from a caste that breeds knights are likely to be fallen members of their given unit. At the gamemaster's choosing, mercenaries with the warrior caste can choose the traits Gloryhound or Greedy to reflect how their fellow dog-brothers perceive them. Once one is lauded for status at home, it is hard to give up the desire to have tales of daring heaped upon them.

Players characters originating in one of the countries described in this sourcebook may roll or pick from the castes presented in the corebook. They are largely identical, with some slight changes, described below.

- **Escaped Serf/Slave:** Koth traffics heavily in slaves, and it is not unlikely such a player character had a Kothic master.

- **Outcast:** A great many mercenaries become soldiers of fortune precisely because they have burned all their bridges behind them.

- **Petty Nobility:** Such a character has fallen. Perhaps they seek to regain their title by rising among the ranks of dog-brothers and sword-sisters?

- **Priesthood:** Mitra is the prevailing god in the Hyborian nations, but one need not choose to follow his light. Like the Petty Noble, a priest in a mercenary company may have fallen out of the light.

CASTE DESCRIPTIONS

Two new castes are offered for mercenary player characters: Born Soldier and Child of Camp Followers.

Born Soldier

Caste Talents: *Sentry, Vagabond*
Skill Gained: Discipline
Story: See *Mercenary Stories*, page 7
Social Standing: 1

You were born to war. Whether pressed into the service of your homeland at an early age, or raised by the captain of a mercenary company, you have little memory of anything except battle. To you, war is a profession and a calling. Many men and women take up arms in times of trouble, but few live by that same sword and seek out trouble of their own volition. The born soldier yearns for battle. The born soldier thrives... nay... *needs* the rousing fury stoked in one's veins by the clashing of arms!

Child of Camp Followers

Caste Talents: *Survivor, Scrounger* (see page 7)
Skill Gained: Survival
Story: See *Mercenary Stories*, page 8
Social Standing: 0

You were born to a camp follower, one of those motley folks that travel behind mercenary companies like carrion following battle. Your innocence was brief with all the adult pleasures and horrors of the world surrounding you. In time, you decided you wanted to take up a blade with those whose gold and crumbs your people scrambled for.

Other mercenaries are ill at ease with you until you prove your worth. They do not look well upon those who take their scraps, though they find them useful. In time, you will distinguish yourself and write your name in blood amongst the dog-brothers you now call family.

CASTE TALENT

The following talent is provided for the Child of Camp Followers, and can (at the gamemaster's discretion) be used for other player characters who could reasonably acquire this talent in their youth.

Scrounger

Having spent your life in the ranks of camp followers taught you how to survive. Yet, it is not the sort of survival that involves living off nature's bounty, but rather the scrap that civilization leaves behind as the mercenary cavalry's hooves stamp them flat as autumn leaves. You can find things to eat, use as tools, and trade where others see only junk. Treat this as the *Living Off the Land* talent, but only in places where the civilized exist or existed. This includes the mercenary company and the camp followers, or *tross*, as the mercenaries disdainfully call them.

MERCENARY STORIES

Based on your player character's caste, roll on the following tables or pick the result that most appeals to you. As in the **Conan** corebook, these suggest background options, and inform the person your player character became as an adult. In all our years on this Earth, our early ones prove the most formative. For the mercenaries, this involves harsh lessons in death, honor, glory, and the cheapness of life.

Additionally, each story has an associated Trait, evoked during play to regain spent Fortune points.

BORN SOLDIER STORIES

Roll	Event	Trait
1–3	Count the Dead	Witness to Brutality
4–6	The Early Deaths	Vengeful
7–10	The Promotion of the Fool	Realist
11–14	We Few...	Bond
15–17	The Killing Blow	No Mercy
18–20	In These Bodies, I Hide	Survival

Count the Dead

The dead were heaped upon the horizon like a hill of flesh. You were but a child as you watched the mercenaries strip them of valuables, pry out gold teeth from still living men, and joke about the brutality of war. Death walks beside you, a constant companion. The world is an anvil, and character is either forged or broken on its iron. Yours was never broken.

The Early Deaths

Your father, your mother, or both were killed in battle. Perhaps you watched them die. Perhaps you merely saw their corpses borne back to the camp on their shields. Either way, you remember well the army which slew them. In time, you will take tenfold violence upon them in recompense.

The Promotion of the Fool

The ranks of an army have fools and men of honor. Often, it is the fool who is promoted or, more likely, given command by circumstances of noble birth. Few such men or women are fit to lead, yet they are an ever-present threat on every field of battle. The enemy is oft not half as dangerous as the idiot who leads you. In knowing this, you've become a realist. That alone saved your life on more than one occasion.

We Few...

Women and men become dog-brothers and sword-sisters when blood is spilled together. This bond becomes particularly strong with those who war for a living. You cannot count the times another soldier saved your life, or you theirs. These are bonds and, if honored, reward the soul who keeps them... in this world or the next.

The Killing Blow

You may have hesitated that first time, but now it is second nature to you. An enemy which gives no quarter shall receive none either. A wounded enemy is nothing but a burden, lest they have intelligence. Thus, even a reparable wound is not treated in the field. Men are killed where they lie, their brains pierced by the merciful, their agonies drawn out by the cruel. Kill them and be done with it, you say. Sparing an enemy's life puts no coins in your pouch.

In These Bodies, I Hide

Your company was decimated. You alone survived, but you had to do so through the most gruesome of means. You pretended to be dead, laying among your brothers and sisters while their bodies were rudely stripped of any valuables. The enemy stayed that night in your camp, and you spent more than a day laying in the festering pile of corpses as the flies gathered and the carrion birds feasted. When the enemy left, the birds that fed on your friends fed you. You walked out of that hellish site, the last and only survivor.

CHILD OF CAMP FOLLOWERS STORIES

Roll	Event	Trait
1–3	The Open Road	Well-traveled
4–6	Children Are Seen and Not Heard	Spy
7–10	Deprivations of the Poor	Survivor
11–14	The Law of Possession	Selfish
15–17	Harsh Punishment	Disciplined
18–20	The Cat	Merciful

The Open Road

The road is home. You do not remember ever having a permanent residence, but simply the next camp. The revelry of the drunken mercenaries and harlots sung you to sleep. A boot in the ribs knocked you awake. When lucky, you rode on a wagon. When not, you trod along with the others. Yet, for all that, you have seen much of the world and would not trade it for a stable life. You have seen the Scarlet Citadel jutting over the moody Khorshemish nightscape, and slept in the deserts of the zuagir beneath the canopy of fiery jeweled stars.

Children Are Seen and Not Heard

Camp followers and mercenaries alike find children get in the way. If you were quiet, you learned something. In fact, the company commander once caught you listening in on his plans for the morning's battle. At first, his lieutenants raised their hand to you, but he bade them to stay punishment. Instead, the captain had you infiltrate the camp followers of the rival mercenary company. No one noticed you, but you got wind of the enemy's plans and, on the morning of the battle, they were slaughtered. Keeping your mouth shut and eyes open has its advantages.

Deprivations of the Poor

By pulling up your tunic, you could easily count your ribs after those long months with hardly a bite to eat. The mercenaries had not warred in some while, and the camp followers subsisted on meager food stores, then the horses. Some died, but not you. You stole a scrap of bread here, a rotten apple there, and made friends with a mercenary, tending his armor for him, in return for the remnant meat left behind on the hambones they cooked in the great fires. This deprivation happened more than once, but it did not wreck you. Instead, it made you stronger.

The Law of Possession

If they cannot prove you stole it, then it is yours. You learned that the hard way when another child in the camp took your luck-stone, a rude marble you found on a dead gambler who was knifed in the night for cheating. You got it back. Then, you realized that there were things others had which you, too, could take. The law of the camps says whoever holds it owns it... more or less. The mercenaries who steal from each other get hung. In the camps, punishment for theft isn't nearly as merciful, but it's much harder to get caught. Being generous never did anyone any good, did it?

Harsh Punishment

"This is somewhere between civilization and barbarism, child," your master said as he whipped you. It was for your own good. If you cannot learn the trade, you shouldn't be apprenticed. Kind words do not hold in the mind as long as the scars on the back from the lash. You've grown to the level of master, and understand discipline is the foundation on which craft is built.

The Cat

A white cat, hidden in the pouch of a dead man along the road. The mercenary that found it cast it aside. A dog can hunt, suss out game, but a cat has no practical purpose. The others trudged by it as it eyed them pleadingly from the mud. You picked it up, rescued it. You cannot say why. You fed the cat from your meager food and, one night, when a scout from an enemy army slipped into the ranks of the camp followers, he started slitting throats and looting. Your throat would have been next, if it hadn't been for your cat who yelped, scratched the man in the eye, and woke you. Your dagger found his heart as if guided by unseen hands. Sometimes, it pays to be merciful.

MERCENARY NATURES

The free companies and their ilk attract all manner of people — those devious, bright, dull-witted, larcenous — any type of person may find circumstance causes them to hire out their sword arm. The natures in the **Conan** corebook are suitable for mercenary characters, but two new natures are provided below.

Professional

You are a professional to your core. Dereliction of duty to the company is worse than disloyalty to a monarch or forsaking one's god. There are ways of doing things, and they are not meaningless. In fact, they save lives. The company is a machine and, if a single part fails, the whole ceases to operate. You drill formations and maneuvers. You spar at times. Your blade is always sharp. You never go into battle unprepared. Your dog-brothers and sword-sisters can count on you. The lazy break against the enemy's shields. The professionals hack through them.

Attribute Bonus: +1 to Willpower
Mandatory Skills: +1 Expertise and +1 Focus to Discipline, Observation, and Resistance
Elective Skills: +1 Expertise and +1 Focus to two of the following skills: Command, Melee, or Warfare
Talent: One talent associated with any of the above skills

Blood-crazed

You need to kill. Drawing blood is not enough. Enemy or stranger… it matters not.

Attribute Bonus: +1 to Brawn
Mandatory Skills: +1 Expertise and +1 Focus to Melee, Observation, and Resistance
Elective Skills: +1 Expertise and +1 Focus to two of the following skills: Craft, Melee, or Survival
Talent: One talent associated with any of the above skills

> *The only sounds were the quick scuff of feet on the sward, the panting of the pirate, the ring and clash of steel. The swords flashed like white fire in the early sun, wheeling and circling. They seemed to recoil from each other's contact, then leap together again instantly. Sergius was giving back; only his superlative skill had saved him thus far from the blinding speed of the Cimmerian's onslaught. A louder clash of steel, a sliding rasp, a choking cry — from the pirate horde a fierce yell split the morning as Conan's sword plunged through their captain's massive body.*
>
> — "Iron Shadows in the Moon"

MERCENARY ARCHETYPES

In addition to those archetypes found in the **Conan** corebook, the following choices are allowed for player characters wanting to add something more specifically mercenary to their characters. Each new archetype represents the sort of dog-brothers and sword-sisters found in almost any company of sell-swords.

ARCHETYPE	
Roll	Archetype
1–3	Asshuri
4–5	Captain
6–7	Champion
8–13	Mercenary*
14–16	Messenger
17–18	Unseasoned Youth
19–20	Veteran

*See **Conan** corebook, page 31.

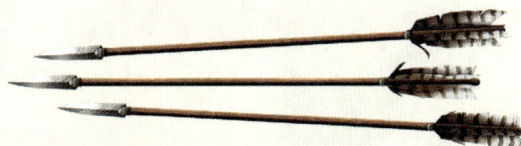

ASSHURI

These proud warriors are usually Shemitish: rarely are outsiders inducted into their ranks. Trained from birth, they are fiercely devoted to their companies. Life in the *asshuri* instills camaraderie and discipline. Those who leave find work as mercenaries. Outside of Shem, many *asshuri* refuse to fight against other *asshuri*, though inside *Shem* they are all-too-willing to do so.

CAREER SKILL: +2 Expertise and +2 Focus in Ranged Weapons
CAREER TALENT: *Accurate* (CONAN corebook, page 77)
MANDATORY SKILLS: +1 Expertise and +1 Focus to Animal Handling, Melee, Parry, and Survival
ELECTIVE SKILLS: +1 Expertise and +1 Focus to two of the following: Command, Observation, or Warfare
EQUIPMENT:

- Scale hauberk with helm (Armor 3: Torso, Head)

- Shortsword, dagger, and medium shield

- Shemitish bow with 3 loads of arrows

- Riding horse

- Desert robes

NOTE: *Asshuri* are commanded in Shemitish. Those with another Homeland must choose Shemitish as their free additional language (CONAN corebook, page 44, *Language*), or take Skill Focus in Linguistics and chose Shemitish.

CAPTAIN

Ruthless, intelligent, and committed to the job — so long as it pays — the captain leads a company of mercenaries, negotiating for contracts and ensuring they are carried out. A captain must balance loyalties: to gold, to their troops, and to their mission. While gold comes in, the captain is beloved. If fortunes change, a captain may end up murdered by their own company. Captains are found in taverns, barracks, prisons, and even royal courts — their skill at arms matched by their ability to negotiate a deal and to recruiting those to earn it for them. Between jobs or even armies, a captain is always alert, aware, and ready for opportunity.

CAREER SKILL: +2 Expertise and +2 Focus in Warfare
CAREER TALENT: *Strategist* (CONAN corebook, page 91)
MANDATORY SKILLS: +1 Expertise and +1 Focus to Parry, Melee, Persuasion, and Command
ELECTIVE SKILLS: +1 Expertise and +1 Focus to two of the following: Acrobatics, Stealth, or Counsel
EQUIPMENT:

- Mail coat and helmet (Armor 3: Arms/Torso/Legs/Head; Heavy)

- Two weapons of choice

- Riding horse

- Clothing

- Maps of the current region

CHAMPION

The champion is not merely accustomed to combat, but is seemingly born to it. Every mercenary company has their "best", and others waiting in their shadow to claim that title. Thus, every champion knows that their days are numbered. Only in legends are warriors immortalized, and those who fight for coin must be very great to merit any such fame.

Standing armies also have champions, but they serve their ruler, not themselves.

CAREER SKILL: +2 Expertise and +2 Focus in Melee
CAREER TALENT: *No Mercy* (CONAN corebook, page 73)
MANDATORY SKILLS: +1 Expertise and +1 Focus to Acrobatics, Discipline, Parry, and Resistance
ELECTIVE SKILLS: +1 Expertise and +1 Focus to two of the following: Command, Persuade, or Warfare
EQUIPMENT:

- Mail hauberk with coif (Armor 3: Head/Arms/Torso; Heavy)

- Battleaxe, broadsword, or greatsword

- Dagger, shield

- Riding horse

- Fine clothing

MESSENGER

Battle is frenzy; a chaos in which commanders attempt to impose order. During a fray, flags, horns, drums, and screams are signals of command, but are limited in range and usefulness. The messenger can carry complex orders and news. They are adept riders, bold enough to cross battlefields, directly through the enemy ranks if need be. Some are tricky, larcenous sorts, others hardened at survival, while others are experienced soldiers, fleeter of foot than with a blade.

CAREER SKILL: +2 Expertise and +2 Focus in Animal Handling
CAREER TALENT: *Born in the Saddle* (CONAN corebook, page 59)
MANDATORY SKILLS: +1 Expertise and +1 Focus to Athletics, Languages, Ranged Weapons, and Survival
ELECTIVE SKILLS: +1 Expertise and +1 Focus to two of the following: Acrobatics, Healing, or Melee
EQUIPMENT:

- Brigandine vest (Armor 2: Torso) and helmet (Armor 3: Head; Heavy)

- A spear, lance, or bow and 1 load of arrows

- Melee weapon of choice

- Fast horse

- Survival kit

UNSEASONED YOUTH

Every soldier begins somewhere. Every scarred veteran once had the smooth, unsullied face of youth. Camp boys in the *tross* dream of becoming real mercenaries or soldiers. They lack the wisdom born of experience, or the rightful fear of death, but what they do have is vitality and enthusiasm. Most are barely out of childhood, though they are all-too-willing to fight, and to prove themselves to the old grognards and veterans in the company. Those who survive become dog-brothers or sword-sisters, and those who do not are forgotten.

CAREER SKILL: +2 Expertise and +2 Focus in Acrobatics
CAREER TALENT: *Agile* (CONAN corebook, page 56)
MANDATORY SKILLS: +1 Expertise and +1 Focus to Athletics, Persuade, Melee, and Society
ELECTIVE SKILLS: +1 Expertise and +1 Focus to two of the following: Animal Handling, Parry, or Stealth
EQUIPMENT:

- Sword and other melee weapon of choice

- Cheap riding horse

- Heavy clothing and set of spare clothing

VETERAN

A soldier who has seen more wars than winters garners respect. Those who have seen many of each are approached with caution. Their best days are behind them, but the veteran can still split a foe's skull to the teeth with the broadsword at their side. With wisdom born of bitter experience, the veteran is less inclined to charge headlong into certain death, and for this, they are respected by others in their company.

CAREER SKILL: +2 Expertise and +2 Focus in Society
CAREER TALENT: *A Modicum of Comfort* (CONAN corebook, page 82). At the gamemaster's discretion, this can be swapped out for the *Veteran* talent.
MANDATORY SKILLS: +1 Expertise and +1 Focus to Insight, Thievery, Parry, and Persuade
ELECTIVE SKILLS: +1 Expertise and +1 Focus to two of the following: Counsel, Observation, or Stealth
EQUIPMENT:

- Brigandine Jacket (Armor 2: Arms/Torso)

- Mace or club

- Melee weapon of choice

- Cheap riding horse

- Cheap clothes with military insignias of dubious origin

MERCENARY EDUCATIONS

Mercenaries come from many background and educations. There aren't any that are banned for mercenaries nor which need be added. From the lowest illiterate stripling, to the tutor-educated prince, all and anyone might find themselves in the ranks of such bloodthirsty sell-swords as outlined here.

WAR STORIES

Mercenaries are as much about the tales they tell as the deeds they have done. A mercenary character will often embellish their tales. After you have rolled your real War Story, roll two additional War Stories and treat them as "Tall Tales", rumors that have been told about you and are occasionally known to your fellow mercenaries. Some may even have a grain of truth. It is up to the player whether they have shared these tales or not. You do not gain the skill bonuses to these Tall Tales, however. The player may choose to make these stories "true" by later spending experience or customization points on these skills as the player character progresses.

Every soldier is wont to roll up their sleeves and show the scars they earned on a given field, but that same soldier must have the *gravitas* of one who has seen death to convince other brothers of the blade. While mere peasants may not tell a lie from truth, a fellow mercenary can tell if a man has truly spilled blood. If they have, they are as likely as not to forgive embellishment, as they may very well do the same.

There are also those about whom nearly every story is true. These are warriors of legend, reavers, slayers, mercenaries who may one day tread the jeweled thrones of the earth beneath their sandaled feet.

	WAR STORY	
Roll	Select War Story	Skill Improvements
1	Defeated a Company Champion	+1 Expertise and Focus to Persuasion and Melee
2	Nearly Slain by a Horde of Foes	+1 Expertise and Focus to Survival and Parry
3	Last Survivor of Slaughtered Unit	+1 Expertise and Focus to Resistance and Survival
4	Punished for a War Crime	+1 Expertise and Focus to Discipline and Resistance
5	Gained (and Lost) a Dog-brother	+1 Expertise and Focus to Observation and Discipline
6	Gained (and Lost) a Position of Rank	+1 Expertise and Focus to Discipline and Society
7	Served as a Spy in an Enemy Town or City	+1 Expertise and Focus to Persuasion and Society
8	Gained the Favor of a Sorcerer	+1 Expertise and Focus to Observation and Sorcery
9	Saved A Town or Village	+1 Expertise and Focus to Craft and Survival
10	Endured a Plague or Disease	+1 Expertise and Focus to Resistance and Survival
11	Shipwrecked as a Marine	+1 Expertise and Focus to Athletics and Sailing
12	Stranded in the Wastelands	+1 Expertise and Focus to Athletics and Resistance
13	Survived a Duel	+1 Expertise and Focus to Parry and Resistance
14	Lifted a Siege	+1 Expertise and Focus to Discipline and Warfare
15	Survived a Massacre	+1 Expertise and Focus to Stealth and Survival
16	Sacked a City	+1 Expertise and Focus to Melee and Thievery
17	Charged in the First Wave	+1 Expertise and Focus to Melee and Survival
18	Engaged in Banditry	+1 Expertise and Focus to Stealth and Thievery
19	Survived A Sorcerous Foe	+1 Expertise and Focus to Discipline and Sorcery
20	Acted as a Captain's Bodyguard	+1 Expertise and Focus to Insight and Warfare

PERSONAL BELONGINGS AND GARMENTS

Roll	Personal Belongings	Garments
1–2	A jade ring taken from an Eastern foe	A pair of silken slippers looted from the dead
3–4	A small pouch of yellow lotus, saved for a special occasion	A fur-lined, hooded cloak
5–6	A small wooden carving of a home with small figures of your parents and siblings inside	A pair of snake-skinned gloves stitched with gold thread
7–8	A fine set of cutlery, silver with obsidian inlay	A long, wide scarf in an ornate pattern, now since faded, useful as a sash or turban
9–10	The manacles you wore for a brief time	A slouch-brimmed hat
11–12	A short rune stave, carved with a blessing	Thick woolen garments and high-strapped sandals
13–14	An arm-ring like a coiled serpent, made of pure silver	A thick shagreen belt with a golden boss for a buckle
15–16	A small totem staff with the gods of your village carved upon it	A thick woolen kilt, a rough tunic, and sandals
17–18	A coin of ancient Valusia, stamped with the face of a savage king	A long leather tunic, that once had scales riveted onto it
19–20	A small icon of a god from a far-away land, made from jade or ivory	Tattered and stained garments, stolen from a dead man

WEAPON AND PROVENANCE

Roll	Weapon	Provenance
1–2	Dagger	Your friend's. They died in battle. Better you take it than some stranger!
3–4	Shortsword	Bronze handle inlaid with silver.
5–6	Broadsword	Acheronian. If only you could read the sigils...
7–8	Bow	...made in Hyrkanian fashion. They may be born in the saddle, but they just as readily die in it.
9–10	Battleaxe	... this was your first killing, fighting against the people of the North. Its owner died well.
11–12	Tulwar	... you still bear the scar its owner gave you.
13–14	Bearded Axe	... given by a friend you saved in battle.
15–16	Spear	A madman claimed a Pictish legend once wielded it. It has yet to fail you!
17–18	Broken Shield	... emblazoned with a coiled serpent eating its own tail.
19–20	A katar	Vendhyan formations are strange, their weapons equally so.

MERCENARY NAMES

Homeland	Male	Female
Khoraja	Bacchus, Cyril, Khor, Khossus, Shupras, Taurus, Thespides, Tribunas	Anastasia, Domnola, Eudocia, Nicasia, Vateesa, Yasmela
Koth	Amalric, Agnellus, Basil, Bonifatius, Constantius, Gregorius, Maximin, Priscian, Prudentius, Sergius, Strabonus	Aetheria, Firmina, Honorata, Iren, Leocadia, Meloda, Placidia, Silvia, Sophia, Vesta
Ophir	Alceu, Almarus, Aureliu, Caiu, Custantinu, Fantino, Manfredi, Marcu, Massimianu, Pertinax, Quintu, Savaturi, Tibberiu, Veru	Accursia, Àita, Calcedonia, Calògira, Candelora, Fara, Gerlanda, Ignazia, Itria, Nedda, Orazia, Rocca, Vatessa
Shem	Ahikibani, Enlil-Ennam, Ibbi-Adad, Kalibum, Kalumum, Mar-Iltum, Naram-Sin, Ninazu, Sin-Gamil, Sin-Lidish	Belît, Bittatum, Delondra, Nammu, Ninil, Ninki, Ninshuel, Radjni, Taram-Uram, Urbau

OTHER CHARACTER ASPECTS

The following tables allow players to roll for, or to select, items that are more singular to mercenaries and the lands covered in *Chapter 2: Gazetteer*. These can be substituted for those in the **Conan** corebook, if desired.

NAMES IN THE CENTRAL KINGDOMS

The *Mercenary Names* table (page 14) are appropriate to each nation of depicted herein, and are presented for use and as inspiration by players and gamemasters.

APPEARANCE

Player character appearance — including hair, skin, and eye color, body type, facial features, and other physical characteristics — is entirely up to the player to choose. Should the players and gamemaster wish to know what natives of these kingdoms look like, consult the suggestions below. Remember, the Hyborian Age is one of traveling and mixing of blood. While the following are traits shared commonly among such races, they are by no means the only variety.

- Khorajans are essentially Kothian in descent, their country having been part of Koth until relatively recently. However in recent decades, their stock has become infused with more Hyborian blood and thus they are lighter-skinned. Some few have blonde hair and blue eyes.

- Kothians are tan folk of some height. Men often wear ringleted beards, and women braid their hair. Kothic people are known for their sharp, hawkish noses.

- Ophireans are slightly darker skinned than their Hyborian cousins, often with dark hair and brown eyes. Of medium height, they bear some similarity to Argosseans, though the former often dress with more flash.

- Shemites are of dark complexion from the suns of their lands and almost always dark-haired. Men wear blue-black beards, while women often braid their hair or interlace it with beads. Shorter than the average Hyborian, Shemites tend to be compactly built, though this is not always the case. In the meadow lands, Shemite complexion turns fair, even pale, and frames are lither and less generally powerful.

MERCENARY TALENTS

Mercenaries face a variety of fluid conditions both on and off the field. Work comes as it will, borne by winds blown from fickle gods. One week you are rich in coin, the next you're hiring your sword-arm to a local tough in the bad end of Tarantia.

Along the way, mercenaries learn to pick up a variety of useful talents with which to kill, enrich, and defend. These talents are included in this volume, but need not be restricted to mercenaries. The gamemaster is encouraged to allow other player characters to learn the talents below.

VETERAN

Mercenaries do not reach old age without learning how to fight and how to avoid a fight. The tongue is sometimes as useful as the sword, though the veteran knows to trust their blade first. Convincing others that there are options other than killing is a rare talent, and one largely reserved for those quite capable of doing the killing.

Prerequisite: The character must have fought in an army or mercenary company.
Experience Point Cost: 200

When persuading a group of mercenaries or soldiers not to take a particular action, the veteran can spend 1 Doom to reduce the Difficulty of the test by 1 so long as the soldiers are not in combat.

Veteran Talents

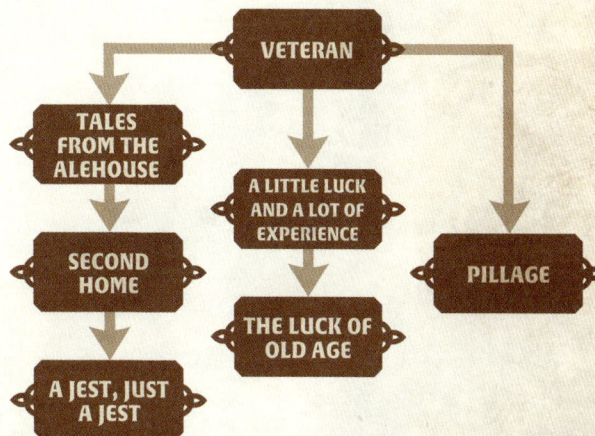

A Jest, Just a Jest

Prerequisite: *Second Home*
Experience Point Cost: 600

You are well practiced in preventing violence amongst peers. If a brawl or argument breaks out between characters who share a Homeland with you, you can spend 2 Doom to make a joke or buy suitable entertainments. The division is momentarily forgotten, and the fractious parties calm.

A Little Luck and a Lot of Experience

Prerequisite: *Veteran*
Experience Point Cost: 200

The first time you are Wounded in a combat encounter, you can spend 3 Doom to be knocked down instead of Wounded.

The Luck of Old Age

Prerequisite: *A Little Luck and a Lot of Experience*
Experience Point Cost: 400

Before entering combat, you can make a Daunting (D3) Warfare test. Any Momentum scored from this test grants you 1 Fortune point, which can only be used to avoid Harms.

Pillage

Prerequisite: *Veteran*
Maximum Ranks: 2
Experience Point Cost: 200

Once per combat, so long as you have a hand free, as a Free Action you can either use the *Ransack* talent or engage in opportunistic thievery (see page 136 of the **Conan** corebook).

Second Home

Prerequisite: *Tales from the Alehouse*
Maximum Ranks: 3
Experience Point Cost: 400

You have many places you call home, and can benefit from all of them. Every time *Second Home* is purchased, you gain a new Homeland and all the benefits of that Homeland, including language.

Tales from the Alehouse

Prerequisite: *Veteran*
Experience Point Cost: 200

You have heard many strange tales from the years spent fighting for pay. When making a Lore test, you can substitute your Command skill.

OTHER TALENTS

The following talents are common among mercenaries, but may be taken by any player characters if they meet the prerequisites.

A Single Honest Blade (Parry)

Prerequisite: *Deflection*, Parry Expertise 3
Experience Point Cost: 200

When carrying a single weapon, and using the Parry skill on a Reaction, the character gains cover soak against all Melee attacks equal to their Parry focus −2. If the character is using a shield, they can use either the benefit of this talent or the benefit of the shield, but not both.

Brutal Reaction (Melee)
Prerequisite: *Deflection*, *No Mercy*
Maximum Ranks: 2
Experience Point Cost: 400

When you suffer damage from a Melee attack, you can spend 2 Doom to make an immediate improvised Melee attack. This attack is a Daunting (D3) Melee test dealing your usual damage for an unarmed strike. As this attack doesn't cost an Action, no Momentum can be carried forward. The attack either hits or misses. If you have 2 ranks of *Brutal Reaction* and the *Riposte* talent, *Brutal Reaction* is triggered on any Melee attack that hits, even if it doesn't do damage.

Hazardous Disarm (Parry)
Prerequisite: *Flamboyant Disarm*
Experience Point Cost: 600

When making a *Flamboyant Disarm* against a foe in a Mob or Squad, you can pay 1 Doom and inflict 3 ⚔ damage to a Mob or Squad member of the gamemaster's choice. The damage inflicted has all the Qualities of the disarmed weapon.

Ferocious Wounds (Parry)
Prerequisite: *Stage Fighting*, Persuade Expertise 1
Experience Point Cost: 400

When you wound a foe, your penchant for the dramatic allows you to panic the weak-willed. Once you have inflicted a wound, your weapon gains the Fearsome 1 Quality for the rest of the combat. This doesn't add to any weapon already having the Ferocious Quality.

Flamboyant Disarm (Parry)
Prerequisite: *Riposte*, Parry Expertise 2
Experience Point Cost: 400

When you perform a *Riposte* you can instead perform a *Flamboyant Disarm*. A *Flamboyant Disarm* costs 2 Doom, but automatically triggers a Disarm of any one-handed weapon, and allows you to make an instant Threaten Action against the foe you have disarmed.

Hostage Taker (Melee)
Prerequisite: *Grappler*, Melee Expertise 2, Persuade Expertise 2
Experience Point Cost: 400

When wounding a foe, rather than delivering a blow that would kill the foe, you can knockout, bind, or otherwise restrain that foe so that they might be later be interrogated or ransomed back to their families.

If It Bleeds... (Discipline)
Prerequisite: *Iron Will*, Discipline Focus 3
Experience Point Cost: 400

When facing a foe that has suffered a Wound, you gain 4 🦅 Morale Soak against that foe and all its abilities.

...It Can Be Killed (Discipline)
Prerequisite: *If it Bleeds...*
Experience Point Cost: 600

When facing a foe that has suffered a Wound, you automatically restore Resolve up to your Discipline Focus. If this means that all your Resolve is restored, you can count 1 Trauma as automatically treated.

Shieldwall
Prerequisite: *Skirmisher*
Experience Point Cost: 200

You treat all shields as large shields so long as you are in a Squad with at least one other character with a shield.

Skirmisher
Prerequisite: Warfare Focus 1
Experience Point Cost: 200

You can fight in a Squad with one other character and not lose your Reaction.

> *As if in answer to that desperate cry, there was a rolling thunder as of celestial chariot-wheels, and a figure stood before the slayers, as if materialized out of empty air.*
>
> — "Iron Shadows in the Moon"

THE TOOLS OF WAR

ENGINES OF DESTRUCTION

Soldiers see many battlefields, if they survive long enough, and many kinds of weapons of war. Among these are huge, devastating devices collectively known as siege engines. These mechanical terrors are the height or technological development in the Hyborian Age. They can crush city walls, devastate clustered ranks of armored men, and bring the battle directly to the enemy while protecting the attacker.

Ballista/Scorpio

The ballista is vaguely analogous to the crossbow, but on a far larger scale. It fires a huge missile which, ostensibly, looks like it would lack accuracy. This is not the case at all. A trained soldier can pick off individual targets with this weapon. If enemy troops are wary of archers, who fire small arrows, the ballista scares them outright. Being hit by one of these missiles tears off limbs, severs heads, and can even split a foe in twain.

A ballista is made mostly of wood bolted together with iron plates. They are wheeled but heavy. The crew of a ballista can move it at the rate of one zone per round. When not in combat, ballistae are pulled by animals.

Like the ballista, the scorpio is a one-person torsion spring "catapult" that looks like a large crossbow, but fires powerful bolts. It is easier to build, maintain, and operate than the ballista, and is often issued in larger numbers. The scorpio still requires a fixed position to fire, though it can be moved by a single person. A scorpio cannot, however, be carried, and they are sometimes fixed to chariots so that they can be relocated at speed.

Battering Ram

A battering ram is one of the primary means of breaching a gate. Be it a castle or city wall, the gate is weaker than the solid rock around it. The most primitive of these tools are simply logs cut to be held by many soldiers who, of their own brawn, bash the end of it into the gate. Often, the end is tipped with iron or steel for better effect.

More advanced versions of the battering ram are suspended from a roof which also serves to protect those underneath. The pendulous motion of the battering ram so hung gains greater force than men alone can muster. The roof is made of wood, but coated with fire retardant sap. Even so, most such shields eventually give way to a sufficient barrage of rocks, flame, or boiling oil. The soldiers operating the ram must be quick about breaking down the gate if they are to survive.

Boiling Oil

The simplest weapons are often the most effective. Who can say what person first looked at a pot of boiling oil — probably in preparation for a meal — and thought "Imagine what this would do when poured upon besiegers?" Doubtlessly, that person existed long, long ago. Humans have found clever ways to kill each other for as long as they have walked the earth.

Boiling oil, though, is a cruel means of killing your foe. First, anyone hit screams in pain. Second, the oil eats right through the flesh, burns muscle to smoke, and finally settles on the bone. The skin of a soldier can literally fall off like an ill-fitting tunic. The horrific sight of such a death is demoralizing in the extreme.

CREW

Siege weapons have a new Size characteristic, called crew. This means the weapon requires more than one person to operate. If the table lists Crew X, X is the number of crew required to use the siege engine effectively. If the crew of any weapon falls below the minimum listed, the difficulty of using the weapon increases by one step for every absent crew-member.

The term "Crewed" also appears in place of Encumbrance. While some of these engines can be pushed by an individual, none can be carried by one person only.

Were this not enough, the oil is an area of effect weapon. Poured down from walls or through murder holes from vast, iron pots. Dozens of men can die in an instant. Since the weapon need not be aimed, those using it do not overly expose themselves to missile fire. Boiling oil is a horrible weapon. It is likewise very popular with defenders.

Mangonel

Like a trebuchet, the mangonel fires a variety of objects at a low trajectory but incredible speed. It lacks the accuracy of the larger, more advanced trebuchets, but makes up for this by being less complex. Soldiers can learn to use a mangonel more quickly than other siege engines of its type.

Rocks are the most common ammunition spit forth by these weapons. Directed at either defensive walls or troops, these rocks hit with tremendous impact.

Rocks are not the only objects flung by these sling-like weapons. Pots of flammable liquid are hurled with tremendous velocity and explode like grenades. But there are stranger loads for the mangonel still. The carcasses of dead animals, festering with disease, may be flung over a city's walls, hoping to infect those inside. Severed heads are also sent to the enemy, causing terror and failing morale. If it can fit it into the mangonel's bucket, it can be fired.

Siege Tower

Besieging a fortress, city, or town is a dangerous affair, even more so for those who first attack the walls. Ladders and ropes leave soldiers exposed to a host of deadly attacks from the defenders. A siege tower is a massive wooden tower designed to provide cover for those fools who must make the first assaults.

Generally rectangular, a siege tower is as tall as the walls it attacks or taller. If taller, archers rain down arrows on the defenders, as do others inside the wooden walls of the engine. Huge wheels allow men to push the tower into position. Of course, the sheer size of the tower attracts missile fire. A successful hit from a trebuchet can wreck these towers.

If the tower gets close enough, and hasn't yet been set aflame, a gangplank falls from the front, allowing the troops inside to charge over the wall and into their target. Being the first soldier to so charge is not a position for which most mercenaries volunteer. Those who are designated as the first wave of attackers are often paid better (if they survive) or are possessed of unusual bravery or sheer madness.

Trebuchet

A trebuchet marks a civilization at its technological height. The siege engine is comprised of smaller, less complex machines which together make a terrible weapon. A counterweight system flings projectiles weighing more than three hundred pounds at the enemy, with unparalleled force.

By necessity, these machines are large and require a well-trained and disciplined crew. They are not easy to move, but, in a siege, can mean the difference between victory and defeat. The massive size of the stones (or other objects) shot from these siege engines can break through defensive walls in a single hit, or reduce an incoming siege tower to splinters. When flung over the walls, they easily destroy houses and reduce human targets to a fine, red paste.

EXOTIC MELEE WEAPONS

It suffices that most soldiers have a sturdy weapon at hand. The more complex a weapon becomes, the harder it is to train with and maintain. Yet humans are ever inventing new ways to kill one another, and some of these are quite effective. None of these weapons are common, but a veteran in a mercenary company is bound to have come across one

SIEGE ENGINES							
Weapon	Reach	Damage*	Size	Qualities	Availability	Cost	Encumbrance
Ballista	L	5🔱	Crew 2	Vicious 2, Intense (Bolt); Area, Knockdown, Stun (Stones)	3	5	Crewed
Battering Ram (Crude)	1	6🔱	Crew 6	None	1	1	Crewed
Battering Ram (Covered)	1	8🔱	Crew 12	Piercing 1	3	5	Crewed
Boiling Oil	1	3🔱	Crew 2	Incendiary 2, Spread 1, Area, Volley	2	2	Crewed
Mangonel	L	4🔱	Crew 1	Area, Vicious 2	3	5	Crewed
Scorpio	L	5🔱	Crew 1	Vicious 2	2	6	Crewed
Siege Tower	2	—	Crew 20+	None	6	12	Crewed
Trebuchet	L	5🔱	Crew 4	Area, Vicious 3	4	8	Crewed

*Damage from a siege engine assumes a near miss. A direct hit from any of the above will likely slay even the mightiest hero. The gamemaster is encouraged to use Doom to increase this damage as they require on a case by case basis.

or more during their service. Chances are, a soldier can tell you much about these weapons, if they survived being on the receiving end.

Mancatcher

A strange kind of pole-arm, the mancatcher features two steel prongs on the end which form a kind of pincer. Springs at the tips of these prongs allow a man-sized object to enter the pincers but not escape from them.

In a way, the mancatcher is a directed snare. While infantry can be trapped by this weapon, its main purpose is to pull cavalry from their mounts. This may cause injury to the rider, but the goal is to get the enemy on the ground, keep him briefly trapped, and deliver the killing blow with a more traditional weapon while the formerly invulnerable rider lies helpless.

Repeating Crossbow

The simple action of a lever strings, pulls, and reloads bolts automatically. The bolts are fed from a wooden box atop the crossbow. A soldier need not expend time and effort reloading this weapon as with a normal crossbow.

From Khitai, the weapon is simpler than it first appears, and is ingenious in design. Khitan armies often replace traditional archers with these weapons. The high rate of fire and ease of use makes these missile weapons very popular and deadly. May the gods forbid humankind ever creating a more effective way of automating slaughter.

Sword-breaker

This is something of a misnomer, as the "sword-breaker" does not break a sturdy blade. Instead, it has two grooved slots on either side of the upper hilt which catch other swords. The effectiveness of the weapon lies not in its ability to break another sword, but to trap an enemy's blade and follow up with a counter-maneuver which may disarm them.

The downside to this weapon is the added weight of the prongs that catch another sword unbalance the sword overall, and it takes no small amount of training to properly use one. Unlike Swift Strikes made with other weapons with an off-hand, the sword-breaker does not grant a reduction

in the Momentum cost; but a Swift Strike or parry from a sword-breaker reduces the Momentum cost of a Disarm by 1.

AKBITANAN STEEL

Famous across the world as a symbol of quality and excellence, Akbitanan steel is legendary both for its rippling patterns, reminiscent of ocean waves, and the keen edge that it can be sharpened to. Stories abound of such razor-sharp edges severing a human hair that falls across it, even as the blade lies still in its mount. Likewise, they are nigh impossible to break.

> *Thrusting his dagger point into the crack, Conan exerted leverage with a corded forearm. The blade bent, but it was of unbreakable Akbitanan steel.*
>
> — "Servants of Bit-Yakin"

Akbitanan steel is a thing of beauty and the superstitious hang many powers on its strange patterns and sheer quality. It is said that one destined to die at the point of such a blade can see their fate in the patterns of the steel, and the many terrible whispers about the metal have granted it a reputation that can affect even the most seasoned warriors.

Akbitanan steel is almost never encountered in any other state than that of a completed weapon, and the swordsmiths that specialize in the secrets and mysteries of steel are happy to allow ill-informed speculation to shroud their techniques with stories of volcanic heat, winter snows, meteoric iron, and the quenching power of human blood. In addition to those who know how to prepare authentic Akbitanan steel, there are those who know how to make convincing forgeries of the legendary material. These blades are often softer and weaker than regular steel, as more care has been made to make the blade look correct, than to make a blade that is serviceable in battle.

EXOTIC MELEE WEAPONS							
Weapon	Reach	Damage	Size	Qualities	Availability	Cost	Encumbrance
Mancatcher	3	4🔱*	2H	Grappling, Knockdown, Non-lethal	4	6	1
Repeating Crossbow	M	3🔱	2H	Volley, Vicious 1	5	10	1
Sword-breaker	2	4🔱	1H	Parrying	3	5	1

*No direct damage. Harm from falling applies.

AKBITANAN STEEL QUALITIES		
⚜	Quality	Effects
0	Poor-quality Forgery	Fearsome 1 and Fragile
1 or 2	Battle-worthy Forgery	Fearsome 1
Effect	Akbitanan Steel	Fearsome 1, and roll from *Akbitanan Steel Effects* table below

Purchasing Akbitanan Steel

Akbitanan steel is very difficult to find. The basic test to find a blade made of this wondrous material is a Daunting (D3) Society test. The price of Akbitanan steel is ten times that of a regular weapon. If twenty times the normal cost is paid, the basic test to acquire the blade is reduced to a Challenging (D2) test.

The Powers of the Metal

Once it has been found, there is a high likelihood that it will be a forgery of poor or middling quality. Even these forgeries have power over the minds of their enemies. All unbroken, Akbitanan steel weapons used in Displays, even the basest of forgeries, increase the damage of that Display by their Fearsome rating. Beyond this, the actual capabilities of the weapon are determined by rolling 1⚜ and consulting the table below.

AKBITANAN STEEL EFFECTS	
⚜	Effects
0	Increase Fearsome to 2
1	Increase damage by +1⚜
2	Increase damage by +1⚜ and Fearsome to 2
Effect	Gains extra Quality

When an Effect is rolled, the gamemaster gets the option as to what ability the weapon possesses. This does not improve an existing quality. However, the gamemaster has the ultimate decisive authority. Should the weapon gain Intense or Vicious, the weapon should also gain Fragile. If this leads to the weapon having Fragile twice, the weapon will reduce its damage by 2⚜ for every effect rolled.

Spotting a Forgery.

Only a master smith will be able to determine whether a blade is a forgery. If the smith has never handled Akbitanan steel, this will be a Dire (D4) Craft test. Smiths that have handled actual Akbitanan steel will find the test to be a Daunting (D3) test. Warriors who have handled Akbitanan steel may attempt to substitute Melee or Parry as a means of deducing a blade's authenticity, but this will increase the test to an Epic (D5) Craft test.

If the seller knows the blade to be a forgery (and most do not), an opposed thievery struggle can be attempted to spot the forgery (see page 98 of the **Conan** corebook). Attempts of this nature against an opponent who believes the blades to be Akbitanan steel will automatically fail.

Crafting Akbitanan Steel

Akbitanan steel is a petty enchantment and follows all the rules for such things. It takes a minimum of three ingredients to make, and the work cannot be completed without a dedicated workshop. Both a Daunting (D3) Alchemy and a Daunting (D3) Craft test are needed to complete the process. Failure of either test, or a Complication, creates a poor-quality forgery (see table above). Failure of both tests leads to a complete failure where nothing is produced. Success produces a battle-worthy forgery (see table above). Spending 2 Momentum will transform the blade into actual Akbitanan steel, with a random table result of 0. This number can be increased by 1 for every additional point of Momentum spent.

GAZETTEER

That day Conan, king of Aquilonia, had seen the pick of his chivalry cut to pieces, smashed and hammered to bits, and swept into eternity. With five thousand knights he had crossed the south-eastern border of Aquilonia and ridden into the grassy meadowlands of Ophir, to find his former ally, King Amalrus of Ophir, drawn up against him with the hosts of Strabonus, king of Koth. Too late he had seen the trap.

— "The Scarlet Citadel"

Though mercenaries may find work in any kingdom, for war is a constant among rulers and kings, four nations in the center of the West are particularly notable for fielding mercenary armies. In Ophir, diamonds are plucked from the ground like daises, so say those jealous of that kingdom's immense wealth. Koth, while not a Hyborian kingdom, rivals the powers of those sons of Bori north of her. Kothic people are a mix of that Hyborian stock and the southern Shemites who command the vast meadowlands and deserts of that ancient land. Finally, there is Khoraja,

a kingdom itself founded by mercenary adventures who long ago sliced a nation from Koth as a butcher flenses a piece of meat from a great flank.

Ophir's scheming Hyborian king and queen will, in their time, conspire with Koth and the dread wizard Tsotha-lanti to capture King Conan of Aquilonia. But that is another tale, and one which the young Cimmerian mercenary can scarcely dream of. We see these kingdoms as they were in his days, with the dog-brothers and sword-sisters of these lands — fighting for coin, bloodlust, and glory.

KHORAJA

Khoraja was once part of Koth itself before gaining its independence many hundreds of years ago. That might have been a historical footnote had fate and geography not conspired in Khoraja's favor. Shamla Pass, one of the only ways through the great mountains, rising as wave of stone, it is a bulwark against the southern kingdoms, and the chokepoint of a major trade route.

Such an important trade route would not have been lightly let go by those ancient kings of Koth, and thus any learned scholar must ask — how did this upstart

state maintain its independence against such a powerful kingdom?

A SLICE OF KOTH CLEAVED BY BRAVE ADVENTURERS

What trickles down from legend is the oft-repeated phrase "... *Khoraja, carved out of the Shemite lands by Kothic adventurers...*" Such are the storied beginnings of Khoraja, but these must be separated from genuine fact as ascertained by historians.

From whence does the wellspring of Khoraja's ruling family flow? Mercenaries, purely and simply.

Khoraja is quite literally a mercenary kingdom. Though, the ruling aristocracy would likely cut one's tongue out for saying so. After all, who would kneel in fealty to a king who ruled not by something other than divine right and blood? One may now, of course, ask the same of that barbaric king who holds the greatest throne of the earth, but these were simpler times. How then might a rabble such as mercenary dog-brothers make a kingdom from the pastoral lands of Shem?

In those dimly remembered days, the establishment of a firm, Mitran theology had not yet solidified. The barbaric founders of the Koth had cast aside their worship of the savage god Bori in exchange for the seemingly more civilized Mitra. Yet with belief came power, and those who controlled the tenets of this belief were likely to control the kingdom of Koth. Little wonder, then, that schisms occurred and Koth fell into an internecine holy war. Of course, the points of faith and devotion over which the young kingdom warred were *pabulum* for the *hoi polloi* — the rulers themselves craved power, not religious purity. While some among the warring factions cleaved closely to their faith, the greater hordes warred for territory and, as in any war,

money. It was among these gold-inspired mercenaries that the first Khorajans sprang.

> *Sounds of revelry had died away in the gardens and on the roofs of the city. Khoraja slumbered beneath the stars, which seemed to be reflected in the cressets that twinkled among the gardens and along the streets and on the flat roofs of houses where folk slept.*
>
> — "Black Colossus"

As the wars saw zeniths and nadirs over the course of a century, it did not escape a single mercenary company's attention that a major, wealthy Shemite city lay for the taking. No doubt, Koth itself would have claimed this land were it not bogged down in civil war. What a perfect time to lay siege to the city and loot its riches... and so they did.

A City Plundered and a Kingdom Forged

The company's name has been scrubbed from the palimpsest of history — overwritten with a more dignified story of

royal origin — but dusty scrolls and aged minds still hold the truth. The Shemite city, which some scholars maintain was called Khoraja even then, fell to the mercenaries during a short siege. When the smoke of battle cleared, and the blood dried on the streets, the sell-swords realized they had no pressing reason to leave the city they'd just taken.

With Koth still mired in war, the dog-brothers set up permanent residence in Khoraja. In the mind of a mercenary there are few things better than the looting of rich cities; among those few things, however, is permanent possession of that wealth. Why risk returning to the bloody fields of Koth when this city was already theirs? They did not return.

In time — no one now knows quite how long — the city state of Khoraja became a kingdom, securing the fertile lands north of the Shemitish deserts, as well as the strategic Shamla Pass. Dog-brothers and sword-sisters, those filthy curs of blood and coin, became kings and queens. By the time Koth was united under the bloodline which would lead to King Strabonus, the onetime sell-swords had a firmly entrenched kingdom. These newly minted rulers rewrote history through the eyes of faith and destiny. The kings of Khoraja rule by blood, but it is blood spilled, not divine in origin

The mercenaries became adventurers, a more palatable term, and they wrote a narrative in which Mitra himself came to them in dreams with a mandate to save this land from the wars around it. So much time has since passed that it little matters what story one now believes so long as one does not speak of the royal family as having curs for ancestry.

PROUD INDEPENDENCE AND MILITANT DEFENSE

Koth looms large on the borders of Khoraja, and many speculate that the kingdom, while nominally independent, in truth pays fealty and treasure to Koth. King Strabonus does not openly decree the actions of Khoraja but, behind the scenes, he has great sway. Still, it is no small achievement that a kingdom with such a rough and tumble origin would, hundreds of years after, maintain any sort of independence at all. Truly, if Koth wished direct and total control over this independent state, they would have to make war. To date, they have not.

As it stands, Khoraja maintains control of Shamla Pass, and serves as a buffer between Koth and the ambitions of southern enemies. Perhaps no better example of this can be found than the story of Natohk the Veiled One, who rose from millennia of slumber and attempted to conquer Koth and her other Hyborian cousins. This story is well known to learned men and commoners alike, and there is no reason to recount it here, for the barbarian king sitting upon the throne of Aquilonia needs no further adulation.

Politics

It is as if Khoraja inherited the fractious nature of its birth mother, Koth, and thus political instability is far from infrequent. The small royal family occasionally produces a would-be upstart, and the throne comes into play. Other kingdoms, too, interfere in Khorajan affairs. The culprit here is most often Koth, though the king of Khoraja was once kidnapped by Ophir. While the machinations of political enemies are not on the scale of Koth, they are just as intricate and unforgiving.

THE CITY OF KHORAJA

In its time, the city of Khoraja has gone by many names, but the current name is the only one people remember. Previously a Shemite trading town, it rapidly grew due to its proximity to the famed Shamla Pass. By the time Kothic mercenaries conquered her, Khoraja was well established and wealthy. That holds true to this day.

A populous city, Khoraja is, like Khorshemish, a mix of northern and southern cultures. Domed towers sit next to the square turrets of northern defenses. Though not as large as other well-known cities, Khoraja is equally cosmopolitan. Trade flows through the city like water torrents when winter ice breaks for spring. Stygians, Shemites, Turanians, and even Kushites move north looking to trade and work, while Kothians, Aquilonians, Corinthians, and the like move south in search of the same. The utility and ease provided by Khoraja for all these peoples and economies is one reason why it has not been sacked for so long. Surely, its riches are tempting.

Broad streets dominate the walled town, giving an open feeling seldom seen in other such busy cities. As in any city, though, the night gives shade to business which shies from the light of day. Khoraja's black market economy equals the entire wealth of smaller sized cities. Weapons, lotus, slaves, and secrets pass through one gate and out another. Still, Khoraja is not equal in illicit dealings to the likes of Shadizar and Zamora the Accursed. All things considered, it is a relatively safe place for travelers.

The royal palace stands at the approximate center of the city, with splendid gardens and cressets which shine under the wine-dark mantle of night. The gardens are bright, boasting plants from the far reaches of the Earth, but they are also well guarded by both man and beast. There is more than one assassin who found themselves prey to Puntian leopards when political discourse turned to daggers.

A permanent garrison of Khorajan knights barracks near the palace, though most rotate between the forts and citadels along the Kothic border.

Outside the city are the bones of thousands of soldiers, victims of long forgotten wars, their remains buried under the clean swards of green earth. The city of Khoraja is a

SHAMLA PASS

Long before the age of men, great mountains rose against the sky between what is now called Shem and Koth. Passage through these mountains has always been slow and treacherous, save for a few natural passes such as Shamla.

Control of the pass has historically given power to whomever occupies the location and can defend it. Shamla Pass has seen the sandals of Stygian, Kothic, and Shemitish soldiers in history still readable in scroll and stone. Prior to that, fallen Acheron, too, trod over this ground in her bloody conquests, and whispers suggest races that were not men fought and died for this pass long before even Acheron.

Today, Khoraja holds this doorway between the kingdoms founded by the Bori and those more ancient countries to the south. While Shem is more a collection of city-states than a nation proper, the venerable Stygians lock the eye of Set upon Shamla Pass and have, in the past, made attempts to wrest it from the control of their northern opponents.

Barring any conflict which might arise, the pass remains open — a stable route for travel. However, such valuable real estate is, of course, always coveted.

renowned stop for mercenary troops seeking wars in Koth, or looking to sign on with the Turanian military.

Religion in the City

A fane to Mitra, sheathed in white marble, lies inside the palace, though few but those in residence ever see it. Its vaulted chamber is vast but not domed, distinguishing it from the temples of Ishtar who likewise finds supplicants in Khoraja.

Whatever wars of religion afflicted the city in times past are gone, and there is little rivalry between the Mitra and Ishtarian faiths in Khoraja. Further away from the capitol, such rivalries become more pronounced, though not recently violent.

Even still, there is a wide road which once divided the faithful of Mitra and Ishtar, and still serves as a line of demarcation between those who carry more Shemitish blood and those who carry the bloodlines of Koth.

MERCENARIES IN KHORAJA

In a kingdom founded by mercenaries, it is little surprise to still find them there today. To say the border between the northlands and the south is tense is to vastly understate the situation. While Shem serves as a buffer to Stygia, it would

A DARKER FANE

History accumulates as it is written and, like pages in a book, the keen eye can discern the strata of eras marking the passing of the city's ages. Most of Khoraja was rebuilt after the Kothic invasion and, prior to that, little evidence remains of the human dwelling.

However, at least once a year, some scholar or fool adventurer comes in search of a supposed pre-human religious site located deep under the current city. There, inside a basalt temple of impossible geometry supposedly stands a statue of a profane god-thing. The creatures said to have worshiped this affront to sanity are described as equally horrific.

Some few stones, broken and worn by time, are found during excavations every now and then, bearing glyphs no man has yet been able to decipher.

HISTORY'S IRONY

The story of civilizations is not without a sense of poetic justice. As Khoraja was founded by mercenaries — howsoever they try to forget — it was perhaps fate or the will of Mitra that salvation came to Khoraja in the form of a mercenary called Conan. The canonical stories of the mighty reaver include a tale wherein he was given charge of the kingdom's army and met a terror which had slumbered since the days of Acheron.

As this sorcerer, Thugra Khotan, pushed north with his unholy horde, it was Conan who prevented his ambition from turning into reality. Indeed, were it not for a mercenary of savage birth, Khoraja, and perhaps all the nations founded by the Hybori, would have fallen under the fell influence of the Outer Dark.

often, mercenary companies come to Khoraja on their way somewhere else, and the king sees fit to keep them on retainer whilst in country. The open-armed attitude of Khoraja toward those who others call curs is a protection all its own. Mercenary companies are generally fond of Khoraja, and would not idly see it invaded. After all, there are rumors it was founded by freelancers such as themselves.

Of course, like any kingdom, Khoraja is not immune to coup attempts. Where the knights of Khoraja are loyal to the king, any would-be usurper would hire those loyal to the coin. The royal family may be small, but it is not entirely friendly. Further, several more powerful kingdoms would have interest in seeing power shift on the throne. Currently, Khoraja gives general fealty to Koth, but a change in ruler could easily change that and thus change the balance of power in this strategic location.

A MIXTURE OF KOTH, ADVENTURER'S BLOOD, AND OLD GODS

Khoraja is quite literally carved from parts of Koth and Shem, and it is no surprise its culture reflects this strange origin. The spirit of the mercenaries — indomitable, wild, war-like — still runs through the blood of Khorajans. While the nation is small, and oft subject to the threats of larger kingdoms, it does not freely bend its knee.

Khorajan Art

Koth and Shem share some aspects of aesthetics, but Khoraja integrates these admixtures more thoroughly than either kingdom could on their own. Pottery leans toward Shemitish style while architecture broadly cleaves to that of southern Koth. Minarets look over walls of crenelated battlements of Hyborian design, while markets might be mistaken for a *suk* in Askalon. There, in the open-air stalls, beads of semi-precious stones festoon the tan wrists of merchants trading in the idols of gods from one end of the world to the other, engraved swords dragged by caravan from Vendhya, and mosaics in the tradition of Argos and Aquilonia. The militant undercurrent runs through most art and, while Khorajans are proud of their public works, most outsiders feel they are rather crude and overly prideful for such a young, small nation.

pose little enough hindrance should the servants of Set wish to invade. Likewise, the growing might of Aquilonia, too, might choose to push south. All would likely pass through Khoraja.

Khoraja boasts some five hundred knights and various other soldiers, but the greater number of her defenders are sell-swords. Along the border forts, mercenaries keep watch for the flaring ambitions of the great kingdoms. Still, for all the tension, it has been some while since war broke out, and thus the pay is relatively low, and the bloodlust of many a dog-brother shall not be satisfied here. More

Khorajan Culture

Society's stratification throughout the region finds less purchase here. While nobles and commoners are not mistaken for one another, Khoraja lacks the deeper bloodlines of Koth and Shem. She lacks also the same sense of permanence, at least at street level.

Now, one must not mistake this for a slack nobility nor an egalitarian one. The noble family invests itself fully in the lie that they come from the blood of kings, not dog-brothers. But, in the *suks* and taverns, the alleys and squares, men and women have a sense that they might rise to greater heights than those they were born to.

One day, perhaps, that spirit shall well up and turn into rebellion. Today, however, is not that day.

Khorajan Religion

The kingdom officially cast off the worship of Mitra in favor of Ishtar, though Mitra's temples yet exist. They are not often visited by most, but rumors hold the king's sister consults such a site for oracular visions. While this may not be true, Mitra is not looked upon askance so much as part of another time. Ishtar is today and tomorrow, while Mitra is a story left far behind.

A number of household deities were also borrowed from Koth, Shem, and elsewhere, and each Khorajan family carefully selects their deity to help identify their role in society. These minor gods all serve Ishtar and, perhaps more than actual icons, might be seen as a hybrid of holy idol and family crest.

RUINS OF KHORAJA

At the intersection between two worlds, Khoraja is rich in the ruins of vanished civilizations reduced to broken column and buried road by time and war. Two such ruins are described below.

The Ivory Tower

Somewhere, just as the meadows recede into the Shemite desert to the east, a tower stands; a single, white finger against the sun. No one who has described the bone white stone tower has ever been able to find it again. Their stories, though, are remarkably similar — while traveling through the desert, they espied a white tower which at first was mistaken for a mirage. Yet, upon getting closer, they realized it was real.

The tower stands at least one hundred feet high, alone on a flat salt plain surrounded by dunes. Atop the tower is a piece of immense glass or crystal in the shape of a shield. When the light hits the crystal from a certain angle it reflects like the mirror in a lighthouse. However, instead of merely redirecting the light, the tower produces a polychromatic display. At this point in the tale, a doorway (some even say a mouth) opens in the tower. As the sun moves and the rainbow effect fades, so does the door. One man claimed his companion ventured inside, but the tower vanished before the witness' very eyes. That same witness allegedly saw his companion again, decades later, in a market. The companion had not aged and quickly fled when his former friend approached.

The tower is actually one of the rare physical gateways to the realm of dream, in this case Kuth of the Star-Girdle (see *The Book of Skelos*, page 20). The tower is only sometimes there — on the winter and summer solstice when the sun reaches its zenith. The rest of the time, the tower exists in Kuth. It is an intrusion of that other reality into the waking world. How those who enter get back, or if they ever truly do, is unknown.

The Statue of Khor

Outside the city of Khoraja, perhaps half a mile, stands a large hill atop which is a damaged statue. The hill looks man-made. The statue is known as the Statue of Khor. Supposedly, Khor was the mercenary captain who first sacked the city which now bears his name. The story holds that the suffix "aja" means city in an old form of Shemitish. Serious scholars do not agree, but the statue of a tall, warrior-like figure gains attention now and again.

Twice in the last two decades, the upstart rabble has used the statue as a meeting place for popular revolt, believing the spirit of Khor will ensure their overthrow. None have been remotely effective. A few groups have dug into the hill, hoping it's some type of barrow. The rulers of the city invariably send knights to disrupt these attempts, thus fueling speculation that the statue is indeed tied to the real story of Khoraja's founding. The statue itself was defaced in antiquity. Those who believe the story also believe the royal family defaced the monument to help hide their humble origins.

KOTH

It has been said that Koth might rival Aquilonia, if it could keep itself unified. Plagued by internecine warfare, the king must constantly put down rebellions from varying city-states. Even then, Koth is a power to be reckoned with, and the king strives to acquire and sustain control so that he might indeed challenge Aquilonia's position as the most powerful of the Hyborian Nations.

For now, that is not to be, and thus Koth is a constant source of employment for varying mercenary companies. Whether one fights for the king or an upstart, ambition and coin are plentiful for a reputable sell-sword.

THE LAST OF THE SONS OF BORI

The Sons of Bori, in their rise from barbarism, founded Koth further to the south than other nations. Here, the Hyborian peoples ceased expansion into the pastoral lands of Shem. Yet Shemitish and Stygian blood both run through the Kothians, making them distinct from their northern cousins. Koth is as far south as the Hybori conquered, though they continued with raids into what is now Shem. Hitting the mountains separating the two lands, the Bori halted and settled.

> A week's ride northward the desert ran into a tangle of barren hills, beyond which lay the fertile uplands of Koth, the southernmost realm of the Hyborian races.
>
> — "Black Colossus"

They did not settle comfortably.

Almost as soon as Koth gained its independence from the Acheronian Empire, the Kothians began to war among themselves. Many centuries passed before a now forgotten warlord hammered and welded Koth into the kingdom known today. Some even say it was a woman, though King Strabonus holds hard punishments for any who speak such lies.

Whoever did beat the Kothic people into a proper culture, upon their death the fighting continued, albeit much more tentatively. Koth found itself a powerful nation of warrior-folk, and the various lords of the demesnes were loath to simply throw that away. In part, that same sentiment keeps Koth united today — it is better to rule as a nation than fall as squabbling factions.

AMBITION AND PENURY

Of course, Koth is renowned throughout the Hyborian Nations as the most irascible of kingdoms. King Strabonus' hold on the throne is perpetually threatened by the ambitions of his rivals. The Kothian spirit suffers not the yoke idly and, coupled with the penurious ways of Strabonus and his tax collectors, rebellion is not uncommon. None have yet succeeded in toppling the king from his throne in Khorshemish, but that is little promise they won't continue to try.

While Strabonus continues to put down the rebellions of various city-states and provinces, Tsotha-lanti the sorcerer works behind the scenes. Some claim he is the real power behind the throne, though this carries no water with the common people. They would rather imagine themselves led by a power-hungry tyrant than one who dances with the Outer Dark.

Whatever the truth, King Strabonus is the face of Koth, and his name is never spoken of without fear or derision in the courts of the Hyborian Kingdoms. The king's designs on other nations are well known, and all rulers near his borders eye him warily. Only mighty Aquilonia stands fully ready to take on Koth should it come to war in the north. Corinthia, Nemedia, Ophir, and others tread carefully around Strabonus, though they would never admit such a thing.

Rumor holds that at least some of the attempts to overthrow Strabonus, or break free of his grip, are funded by rival kingdoms. What better way to keep his covetous eye off their lands than to keep it focused on his own?

Kothic Intrigue and Mercenaries

Upstart leaders, would-be tyrants, and scheming nobles constantly maneuver and conspire for better position, eyes locked on the throne as the ultimate prize. The more cautious among them work behind the scenes, while the bold foment open rebellion. For the mercenary, work in Koth rarely dries up. Whether it be Strabonus trying to quell revolt, or the king of a city-state attempting to launch one, mercenaries fill out the ranks of local armies.

It can be hard to trust one's own troops at times — whose side might they really be on? More than once in Koth's bloody history, troops seemingly committed to one side turned to the other. Better to buy loyalty then, for the mercenary at least stays bought (or so the theory goes, at least). A sack full of Kothic silver is often a better guarantor than the word of a "high born" man.

So, too, does Koth's intrigue demand smaller groups of intrepid adventures who are willing to assassinate, spy, serve as agent provocateurs, kidnappers, and more. While the armies must, of necessity, take large groups, the cloak-and-dagger work demands fewer soldiers with sharper skills. Many years before Strabonus' birth, the princess of Khorshemish, his sister, was spirited away by mercenaries. As selfish and greedy as his son would one day become, Strabonus' father denied the ransom and put the bounty instead on the heads of the mercenaries. The girl was never seen again.

One of the most famed, feared, and sought-after companies, the Free Companions, oft times settle in Koth when winter sets in, the wars grind to a slow, icy halt, and they choose not to pursue other campaigns in the warmer climes of the South. They are not the only company to do so, for all Kothic rulers of any worth see the wisdom in keeping such men well-fed and ready for battle.

Hyrkanian Mercenaries

A curious situation arises in Koth: the appearance of the Hyrkanian mercenaries in the west. Traditionally, the horse clans are bound to no central purpose, yet some choose to serve their cousins in Turan in return for coin. However, the steppe calls again, and they return to the nomadic life to which they were born.

TSOTHA-LANTI

Eyes the color of oil, black and reflective, gaze from a face more akin to that of a predatory bird than a man. This thin, angry brushstroke of a man hides his bones under silken fineries, and his true intent behind the walls of his Scarlet Citadel.

Mothers tell tales of Tsotha-lanti to cow their children into obeisance, while slave traders threaten to sell their stock to elicit the same. His name is a curse. His attention is worse. It's Tsotha-lanti who men say is the real power behind the throne. His machinations are long ranging and, ultimately, seek goals beyond this world.

His work takes him to the border of the Outer Dark and beyond. The horrors there, of gaping, slavering mouths and eyeless menaces, wait for Tsotha-lanti to feed them the supple flesh of young girls or the hard muscles of strapping young men. His taste for both is in no way carnal. To Tsotha-lanti all are but ingredients for his spells and schemes.

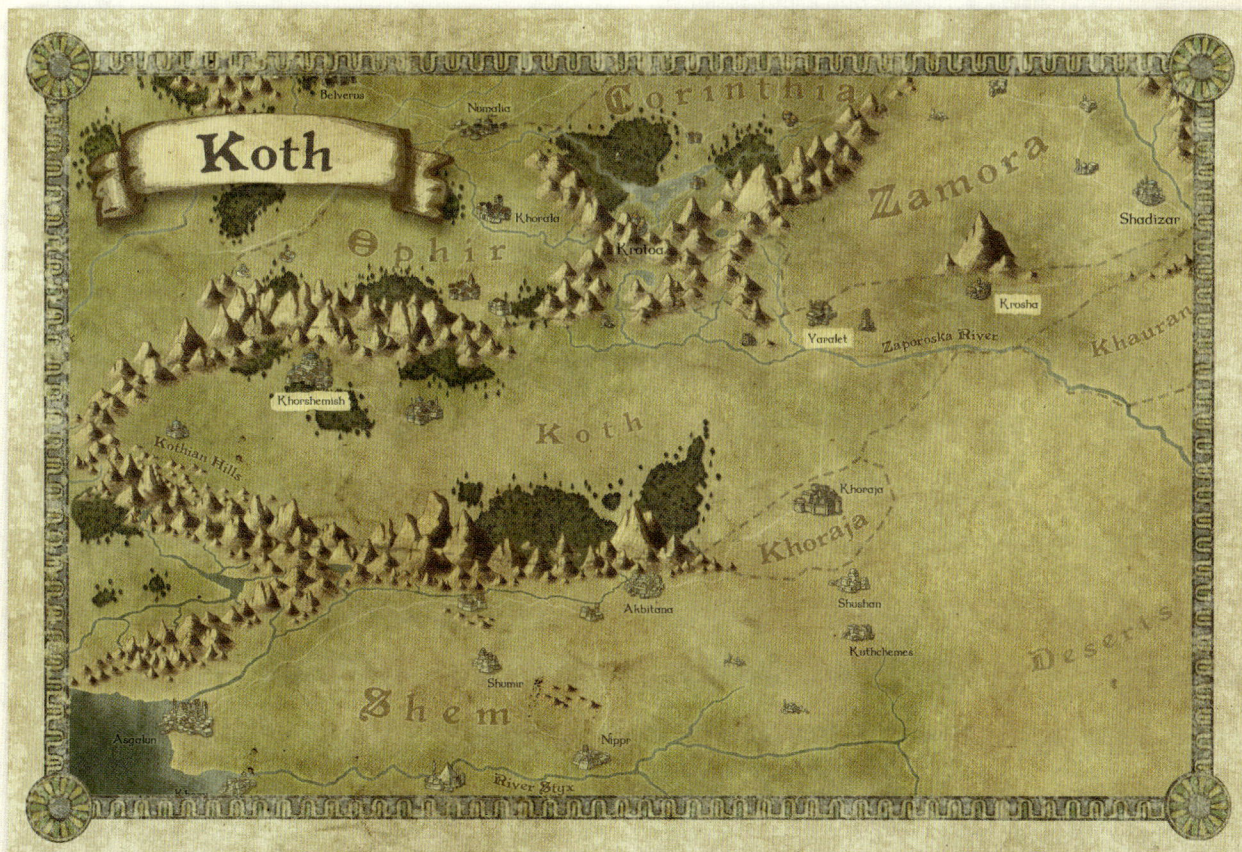

A small contingent, perhaps 15,000 men, has settled on the eastern fringe of Koth. They still live in the yurts of their home and forsake the soft ways of civilized city folk, but they do not return to the steppe. They do not go home.

Why? No one can say for sure. They hire themselves out to any in Koth, or elsewhere, that pays. They are all cavalry and much feared in the area — for who has not heard of the ferocity of the mounted Hyrkanian hurling arrows with pinpoint accuracy from his curved bow?

Strabonus has employed these nomads in the past, but he is not fool enough to take them as a gift. Every summer, more join their ranks, and the king begins to suspect that they are spying for either Turan or themselves. He has also begun to suspect they are a slowly forming horde.

Slavery in Koth

There are no kingdoms under the sun in which slaves do not toil, for the price of empire is ever on the backs of the lowly and the lowest. Koth, however, turns slavery into an economic engine unparalleled in the west. Long before Strabonus, Koth's rapid development depended on slave labor, mostly in the form of conquered foes. But the rise of civilization brings also the rise of slavery as a lucrative trade, and the coffers of Khorshemish spill with the gold from that cruelest form of human commodification.

Ironically, while the Kothic people do not suffer under whips readily, they are more than willing to enslave their fellow men. Sometimes, this includes fellow Kothians, though there are laws governing when and how a Kothian can be entered into slavery. Thievery, murder, conspiracy, treason, and debt are all valid reasons and conform to law. However, proving one is Kothic is not always so simple.

In practice, Koth's slave traders pay the king's overseers to look the other way from time to time. One cannot press this largess too far, though, for the crown comes down hard on any man who holds too many of its charges in shackles.

Foreign slaves have neither rights nor laws to protect them. Anyone of blood borne beyond the borders of Koth is bought and sold at will. Laws govern disputes between slave traders and customers, but the slave is never considered in any of these.

Koth's reputation for its slave trade is somewhat unfair. While it is true they have the busiest slave markets in the western lands, all other nations likewise have stables full of sweaty, human flesh ready to be sold upon the block. In those rare moments when a person feels guilt over their own role in such business, they point to Koth as the worse example, thus expiating some measure of responsibility, if only in their own minds.

One should note that the Hyborian Age suffers little in the way of such sentiment. Slavery is an accepted practice from the Western Ocean to the Vilayet and beyond. Such savagery found in civilization is oft times more barbaric than anything the so-called primitive kingdoms of the frozen far-north and the sweltering south would ever condone.

A MIX OF PEOPLES AND TRADITIONS

Though Koth is a thoroughly Hyborian state with a Hyborian populace, its proximity to both Shem and Turan have influenced the culture of the land. In the east, Turanian architecture often dominates cities and towns, while in Koth it stands side-by-side work more evidently northern. Shemitish craftsman wandered into Koth long ago and stayed, injecting the art with a quality and style uniquely their own.

Kothic Art

Frescoes and mosaics of unparalleled creativity adorn the squares, public buildings, and wealthy homes of Kothians. The typical subject matter involves the gods, most particularly Mitra and Ishtar (see below). Second to the gods are the Kings of Koth, as well as the princesses, who are immortalized in chalcedony, lapis-lazuli, and other semi-precious stones.

Pottery is a blend of Shem, Turan, and the Hyborian lands, being decorative even in the most modest homes. Beautiful urns oft times sit in altars to household gods in peoples' homes. One can, at a glance, see the entire lineage of a family upon such altars.

Koth would like to match the ostentatious displays of gold which Ophir is famous for, but there simply is not as much of the precious metal to be found in the mountains of Koth. Instead, the wealthy buy up heaps of gold from the traders moving between the south and the north. To display gold, in Koth, is also a sign of divinity. Gold, after all, is the metal of the gods.

Kothic Culture

As previously noted, Kothians are a rebellious lot. It is little wonder they fall only under the sway of a strong man like Strabonus, or a sorcerer like Tsotha-lanti. Even so, they are malcontent and proud, quick to anger, and slow to forgive. Kothic identity is based on a principle of supremacy by blood. They claim to be the direct heirs to Old Acheron and their rightful place in this age. It is, they assert, their destiny to rule the lessers.

Koth's calendar is a riot of festivals and holidays drawn from varying cultures. They celebrate the birth of the world on the Day of Anu, but also reserve a week each for Mitra and Ishtar. Koth has more holidays where the lower classes do not work than any other kingdom, largely because the slaves never cease working on those days-.

Where Ophir has slipped into decadence, and Aquilonia is at the apex of its power, Koth believes its time is ripe. Only Turan, the fastest growing empire in the world, gives Koth a run when it comes to raw ambition. Perhaps, in time, Kothians will wield such power as Turan or Aquilonia, but they will need to learn how to temper that with caution.

Kothic Religion

Like most of Kothic civilization, theology and religion are a mix of Shemitish, Turanian, and Hyborian influence. Certain theologians scoff that Koth "is the home of all gods under the sun, for the Kothians hedge their bets". It's more accurate to say that Koth's geographical position make it a unique blend of competing religions which have syncretized over time.

Mitra dominates in Northern Koth, though Ishtar has gained favor in the south. Anu and Bel are both worshiped along with other household gods. Altars to these household deities are found in nearly every home, though larger altars to Mitra or Ishtar often shadow them.

Clerics wield some influence over local populations, but the very profusion of different gods keeps that influence in check. Indeed, the kings of Koth may well have encouraged the worship of multiple deities, lest one temple become too powerful.

Tsotha-lanti forges pacts with demons, but he is not alone in revering them. In cities and large towns, in backwoods and burgs, some still worship the gods who ruled the Earth before humanity. They worship Yig and Tsathoggua. They give fealty to Azathoth and Great Cthulhu, names which drive mortal minds to madness. These folk are a minority. Do not all plagues start that way?

CITIES OF KOTH

The cities of Koth are known for their fractious nature. There is not a lord or baron who does not think of occasional rebellion. It is only through the ruthlessness of King Strabonus, and the sorcerous power of Tsotha-lanti, that this kingdom remains united.

That is a blessing for the purer Hyborians to the North, for while Koth puts down internecine threats, her might must look inward. One day, this will cease to be the case.

Khorshemish

Mighty Koth boasts one of the greatest cities of the west in the form of its capital, Khorshemish. The city was built atop the ruins of an Acheronian city, not long after the Hyborians brought down that dark, sorcerous empire. Though few citizens are now aware, their city has its foundations on the bones of a city three millennia older. Beneath the flagstones and squares of Khorshemish lurks a host of treasures both valuable and deadly.

Accessing these ruins is not easy, for the current sewers hardly connect with the ancient city below. Indeed, even the Scarlet Citadel, which sits in the city center like a malevolent finger, has few passages as old as Acheron, and of those that were, many were sealed ages ago by Khossus V who saw his diggers go mad while excavating parts of the former city. What might be found under Khorshemish is left to the ramblings of mendicants and drunks.

The current city is magnificent. While Strabonus is a miser with his gold in nearly all affairs, he spends it for the benefit of Khorshemish — or at least on projecting power and opulence. The actual populace of the city enjoys only a small fraction of the coin spent to make the city a wonder. Her minarets sparkle like jewels in the night, made of highly polished bronze and even crystal.

A great wall surrounds Khorshemish. The city is built on an escarpment and rises ever upward as one ventures toward the center. There, the royal palace is situated behind yet another wall, and Kothic knights are barracked within the compound.

Khorshemish's grand bazaar resembles the *suks* of Shem, but is also an admixture of Hyborian influence. A dozen languages catch the ear, while spices from as far away as Khitai scent the air. On one end of the bazaar is the "Great Block" where slaves are sold. Skins of every hue sweat under the sun as they are put on the block and auctioned to fat merchants whose skins are of just as many hues, but who fortune has treated considerably better. More slaves are bought and sold in Khorshemish than anywhere else in the west. So plentiful are the slaves, even lesser merchants and craftsman can afford to own one or two. The city's economy runs on the backs of those in bondage.

Khorshemish's thieves' quarter is a den of iniquity, but Strabonus keeps it sectioned off from the city proper. Behind a wall as old as Acheron, the poor, the treacherous, and the squalid lurk and do their unpleasant business. This is tolerated by the town guard so long as such degenerates do not pass through the gates, without proper papers, into Khorshemish itself.

Yaralet

A broad river feeds Yaralet, whose eastern influence is apparent in its minarets and temples. Located just as Koth's temperate climate breaks into the wide desert, the city has seen its share of battle and conquest. It has been said that Yaralet is "the thrice built city", having been sacked and burned to the ground at least that many times. It is a city of hardy people and brave souls... or, at least, it was.

In recent decades, a pall fell over Yaralet in the form of what denizens call a curse. Doors slam shut at night, bolted more than once from inside. Neither guardsmen, torch-bearer, nor even skulking thief walks the streets once the sun falls, for something stalks the city — something not of this world.

Its very visage is said to drive men mad, and caravans now rarely spend the night. Yet the populace largely remains, keeping their secret to themselves. "Perhaps Prince Than can save us?" mewls a frightened voice into its wine jack — yet the prince has not saved anyone. The more pragmatic folk say instead, "Perhaps no one can save us."

City of Khorshemish

1   Royal Palace
2   Knights Barracks
3   Scarlet Citadel
4   Grand Bazaar
5   Great Block
6   Khossus V Square
7   Temple of Anu
8   Thieves' Quarter
9   Statue to Strabonus
10 Slave Pens
11 District of Wealth
12 Merchant's District
13 Residental
14 South Gate
15 East Gate

Despite the darkness fallen on the city like tainted snow, Yaralet persists, as they did against invaders so many times. But for how long? One day, the caravans may not come at all. The merchants may forsake this stop on the river. The people may leave *en masse*. For where darkness plays the better game, mortal man cannot hope to win the final hand.

RUINS OF KOTH

Acheron once extended over much of what is now called civilization, a mighty empire ruled by cruel sorcery and lost rites. Remnants of that vanished world, as well as ruins of those who came after — still thousands of years ago — dot the land. Seen against a starry night, these vestiges of the past evoke history and wonder. Seen up close, they invite danger and edge against the Outer Dark.

The Bones of Acheron

There is a saying in Koth when a person is put to a challenge, "Our blood washed clean the bones of Acheron!" That may or may not be technically true, but the rise of the Hyborians did occur alongside the fall of Acheron, and those barbarians did swarm the decaying empire in places. Proper scholars feel it goes too far to ascribe the ultimate end of Acheron to the barbarians. History may write a different story.

This saying, though, has some spark of truth in these ruins located atop an unnamed hill in western Koth. There,

something which is not quite a ruin, and not quite a skeleton, is fused in times no living man can now remember. Whatever the creature was, if indeed it was a living being and not a wondrous monstrosity of engineering and craftsmanship, it was enormous. The "bones" form spires taller than those in most contemporary cities. Rib-like curvatures of petrified calcium rise over the city itself like a stone stockade ready to repel invaders, but who in any age would have been brave enough to assault such a place?

Oral history maintains that the city's name was not forgotten but purposely erased from history — to utter it was to invite the Outer Dark down from the void. Scholars, too, have recorded appearances of this city in ancient documents, but in every case the name has been scrubbed out as if the beginning of a palimpsest.

There is another legend which locals also know and speak of when warmed by hearth and wine — the city and its environs are the remains of a dead god. What sort of god would have a hulking, misshapen skull some twenty feet high and bat-like wings spread out like ancient roads? They do not say, or they do not know. Perhaps there was a time when gods walked the earth. Perhaps they still do. Perhaps this was not anything man could, or should, try to comprehend... even in death.

Ishtar's Dial

In the rocky badlands that abut the deserts of the east, a large, flat plane suddenly appears. Upon it rises a series of what appear to be stairs at haphazard, apparently randomly placed angles. In the center of these is a wheel carved from the bare rock. In fact, upon close inspection, the plane itself is the top of an enormous, underground rock.

Where the wheel's spokes radiate to their maximum extension, glyphs appear. They are old; older than humanity. The stairways also have glyphs on the top and side of each step, only they are too narrow to easily climb. Instead, the entire affair is an apparatus not unlike an astrolabe, though it's locally known as a sundial.

During the day, the sun casts shadows which march along the wheel. Over the course of a year, these shadows stretch to each of the "stairs" in turn. So, too, do the shadows "climb" these stairs on certain days, like a serpent's body skittering through the sand.

The wheel itself is broken, cracked by a one-foot wide chasm in the center. Foul, acrid fumes are evident from the crevasse at night. It is the night for which this monument exists. Built by serpent people in a time when Atlantis was young, this device marks when the stars are right to summon an aspect of Yig from the Outer Dark. Perhaps the giant crack is the result of such a summoning. Perhaps men will come who can read the language of the serpent-men and attempt to draw down Yig once again.

OPHIR

Once vassal to Acheron, who coveted the kingdom's wealth, it was only after collapse pulled down the great cities of that ancient empire that Ophir regained independence. While their history predates that of other Hyborian nations, they are still thoroughly the Sons of Bori.

Blessed with fertile land and an embarrassment of gold and precious gems, Ophir is the wealthiest of the western nations. That wealth, though, has caused a desultory condition in the population who have begun to decay, being too used to their ways, jaded by wealth and decadence and able to buy off any potential invaders. They have not had to struggle in far too long.

> *Its young king was captive to the treacherous king of Ophir, who hesitated between restoring him for a huge ransom, or handing him over to his enemy, the penurious king of Koth, who offered no gold, but an advantageous treaty.*
>
> — "Black Colossus"

OPHIR THROWS OFF THE YOKE OF ACHERON

Ophir was part of the Acheronian Empire, a vassal like Koth and, while the nation always had its own king, the true ruler always resided in the purple-towered city of Python. The Ophireans toiled under that yoke, though their wealth allowed them more freedom than other, more unfortunate subjects of the Purple Throne. Yet with the collapse of Acheron did not come joyful independence. Instead, the west entered a dark age. Old roads fell into disrepair, magnificent monuments to civilization were pulled down and replaced by smaller towns and narrower visions. Ophir, along with the remaining civilized peoples, suffered. They were easy prey for the Hyborian barbarians who soon swept through and conquered their lands.

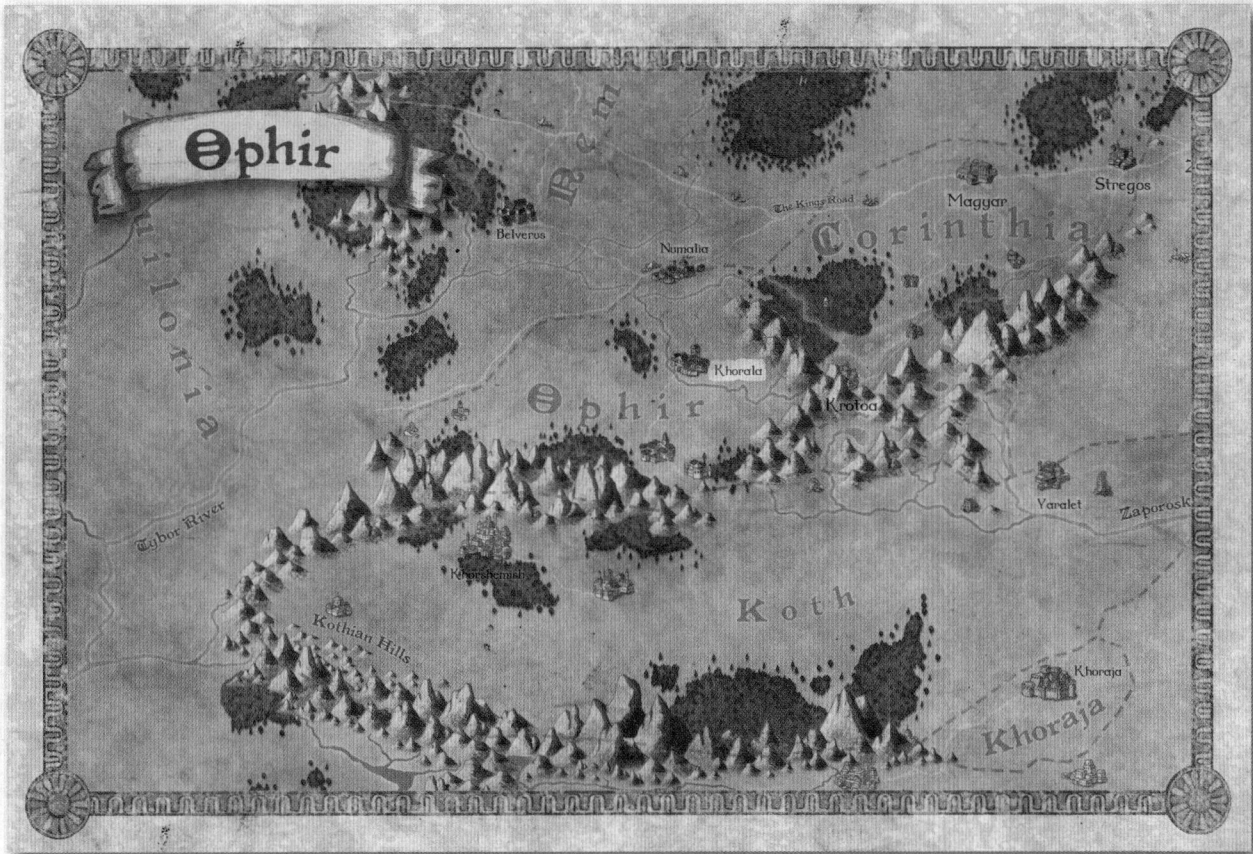

Ophir still retained its wealth, however, and with it preserved some of the older age of civilization. Much of Hyborian culture, art, and custom owe a debt to those in Ophir — philosophers, scholars, and even kings — who carried the torch of civilization through the vast gulf of dark which fell upon the west like a pestilential cloud.

The remnants of before, this detritus of Acheron's height, allowed Ophir an advantaged position in the new world. They quickly became the height of the new kingdoms, though the people here lacked the ambition of their younger counterparts. Ophir may have had the gold, but it would be Aquilonia which would have the raw will to shape an empire. Even that mighty kingdom, though, would never rival Acheron. What was lost would not be regained.

A KINGDOM OF UNIMAGINABLE WEALTH

With older roots comes a more measured national counte-nance. Ophir has not the fiery hate for the outland religions found elsewhere. They tolerate a vast mix of people, and foreigners are not looked on as a lesser species as they are in some of the grander markets of the world. The heights of classical construction — partly in the Acheronian style — still grace the cities of Ophir. Nowhere else does one find eastern philosophy so easily mixed with the more pragmatic notions of the west.

The kingdom is the richest in the west, possibly the world. The gold and precious gems pulled from the mines in the eastern mountains fuel an army who wears gilded armor. Even the merchant class is festooned with gold and diamonds. Only the poor lack these symbols of Ophir's opulence. Ophir has grown fat, though, in the centuries of relative ease and pleasure the bulk of its population enjoyed. People both within and without say the culture is decadent, mimicking the same mistakes which eventually led to Acheron's fall.

The wealthy live lives of leisure, and even lower classes can afford slaves. While the stout and stalwart Hyborian blood fills their veins, as a people, the Ophireans have lost some essential spark. They lack the *elan vital* of their neighbors. While its rulers debate how best to reverse this trend, the rest of the world eyes the gold which is said to litter the ground like pebbles in this meadow-rich land. If the civilization is sliding into degeneracy, it does so slowly. Ophir is still a potent military power and an economic rock.

Politics in Ophir

Ophir's comfortable economy keeps rebellion to a minimum, unlike in Koth. This is not to say that the nobles get along

ACHERONIAN BLOODLINES

Throughout the territory once part of the Empire of Acheron, that ancient blood comingles with the Hyborian lineage which pulled her great cities down. In Ophir, however, some Acheronians took refuge from the fall of the empire. Over millennia, they lost much of the cultural knowledge and heritage to which they were heir. Yet in the hills and mountains, pure bloodlines remain. These hillfolk are solitary and secretive, often killing outsiders. They breed only with one another so as not to pollute their heritage.

It is even rumored that towns and cities, deep in the blank spots on a traveler's map, yet exist, holding the culture of Acheron aloft like a stubborn candle amid history's vast darkness.

readily, but the scheming is far subtler than the open war some kingdoms experience internally.

In the capital of Khorala, the king rules with minor resistance. Edicts issued to lesser nobles are generally obeyed, if not with any great urgency or pleasure. Yet the city-states all keep their avaricious attentions on the gold and gem mines, for to control these is to control the nation. The continuing threat of foreign armies seizing those selfsame mines tends to keep such civil ambitions in check. No city-state, of its own, has a large enough army to take and hold

the wealth to leverage for independence. However, there are such cities which do possess the gold to hire enough mercenaries to establish their own kingdom.

Yet mercenaries are not, by and large, a subtle lot. To see companies plodding over muddy roads by the score would invite suspicion if not direct action from the crown. Issues between feuding gentry and royals is more often handled by bribery. In extreme cases, assassins are employed. In either case, it is common practice to hire outlanders to facilitate either the payment or the more permanent disposal.

Khorala itself is an interesting court. As the king is rather weak, it is really the queen who pulls the strings (see sidebar).

MERCENARIES IN OPHIR

Ophir is awash in gold. So much so that their knights wear gilded armor — something normally only seen in ceremonial plate. They fight with fervor and loyalty. The standing army, too, is well paid and thus motivated. Ophir does not have one of the larger Hyborian armies, however. Their economy is such that fewer men than elsewhere turn to the sword to make their living, and conscription is only called for during emergencies. Otherwise, their standing army is built of professional soldiers, though small in number given the economic power the kingdom wields.

Mercenaries make up the deficit. Where there is gold and glittering gems, mercenaries naturally flock. Khorala City, where the king resides, employs the bulk of these

THE POWER BEHIND THE THRONE

Amalrus is the king of Ophir, but he lacks the ruthlessness and thirst for power great leaders need in this savage age. His wife, Yrrane, possesses both qualities in quantities which would put men to shame. She is the one who spurs her husband to act boldly or duplicitously as circumstances demand.

Queen Yrrane is Brythunian by birth, married into the family of Ophirean kings as part of a treaty solidification when she was only thirteen. Even then, she knew power was what she craved, and that her husband, ten years her senior, lacked the mettle to deliver it. But, were she to be the beating heart inside him, well, what couldn't she accomplish?

Perhaps it was her Brythunian childhood which so starkly drew the difference between a kingdom on the rise and one in decline. Upon arriving in Ophir, she found the people to be a decadent lot, fat with easy gold and the wealth of ages. This had the advantage of making them pliable to her will, but the disadvantage of lethargy.

It was Queen Yrrane who saw that mercenaries were the answer. Among the leaders of various companies, Yrrane has made more "private" arrangements. She once possessed a ring which aided her in these ulterior liaisons but has since lost it. Nevertheless, a goodly measure of the mercenaries who pledge fealty to the crown personally love, or at least ally with, Yrrane. One day, she will use them to seize power. In the meanwhile, she whispers in her husband's ear, influencing him as she does all men, and most other women — with raw beauty and an extremely agile mind.

Of late, her mind has turned to kidnapping. There are kings in the west who are overconfident and expose themselves too readily. Were she to ransom one, she could further her machinations — power may be gained by many means and who knows what she may be able to persuade a captive monarch to countenance, when her wit and beauty are matched with the threat of death.

mercenaries and stations them along the border of Nemedia, where no natural barriers exist. Elsewhere, Ophir is bounded by mountains which make incursions rare. Every city also employs mercenaries, unless their own troops are numerous. In Ophir, a mercenary can easily find work.

That's a double-sided coin, however, for Ophir only hires the best companies. A single defeat, if carried on the gossiping wind, can cause a company to fall out of favor with Ophir for years, if not decades. Their money allows them to pick and choose as they will. The duties of Ophirean service are taxing, but not as dangerous as other soldiering for hire. Ophir sees its share of war, but has not launched an expansionist campaign in some while. Overall, a mercenary could do far worse than a stint in the Ophirean army.

As noted, Queen Yrrane has arrangements with several prominent mercenary captains. Some few of these, after a night's drinking, have spilled this secret to their men. Such information may well be worth more gold than a year's wages to nobles throughout the kingdom.

Besides soldiering, various Ophirean personages employ mercenaries to deal with more private matters — kidnapping, murder, and the intimidation of rivals. Mercenaries are easily deniable, and cautious plotters pay them in raw gold or foreign coin.

A CULTURE REMAINING IN A VANISHED SHADOW

One cannot speak of Ophir without also, perhaps unwittingly, invoking Acheron. As one of the oldest Hyborian nations, and one with few ancestral enemies, Ophir mixes not only the classical influences of Acheron, but absorbed Nemedian, Kothic, and even Hyrkanian influences.

Ophirean Art

Acheron lives in the art of Ophir. Its winding columns and impossibly tall towers are well known throughout the western world. Serpentine motifs are recurrent, though they have eroded over the years to more symbolic, rather than representational, depictions. Pottery flows with intersecting squiggles, and porticos are held aloft by marble carved like coiled rope.

Frescoes and mosaics are also common, though they rarely depict the modern Sons of Ophir, but instead Ophir as artists imagine it in its golden age. There is, pervasively, a sense of loss represented in the craftsmanship of Ophir. The kingdom is old enough to remember independence before Acheron and the dark days which followed its fall. Such psychic undercurrents emerge from the unconscious of the people like icebergs from a Nordheimer sea.

Ophirean Culture

Though falling into decadence, there is no higher culture than that of Ophir among the Hyborian people. Nemedia has its scholars, Aquilonia its grand works and military, but Ophir is steeped in the old ways. Etiquette is a matter of routine and even the lowliest town dweller considers themselves a paragon of civilization. This is not to say that the rude and rough do not exist in Ophir, only that they are looked upon with derision. One must remember, Ophir shepherded an advanced civilization long before Hyborian blood came to dominate the continent. They remember these days in both written and oral history. All in all, other Hyborian kingdoms consider the Ophireans to be full of themselves... but no one says no to their gold.

Extended families tend to live in the same dwellings for multiple generations, and even peasants recount their lineage going back many decades, if not centuries. Pervading the culture is the idea that memory, blood, and objects of art connect Ophir to its glorious past. They even pride themselves, though less openly, on having been a part of the extended Acheronian Empire. Few Ophireans believe that Acheron was a fell kingdom. That, they say, is mere propaganda.

They are wrong.

THE STAR OF KHORALA

The gem known as the Star of Khorala was passed from Ophirean ruler to offspring for countless generations before it was stolen from the current queen. Historically, the gem was set in a fine ring made of an unknown metal. It was the symbol of betrothal for the ruler of Ophir. The gem itself is a rare, black diamond. That alone makes it priceless.

However, the gem and ring have a history that predates Ophir, Acheron, and even Valusia. The gem was first used in a time so far in the past that even the serpent-men wrote of it as ancient history. The "diamond" is not in fact anything of this earth. It is a gem only in human terms. Most likely it came from the Outer Dark, though, curiously, it does not possess the corrupting influence such objects normally radiate. Instead, the single known power of the Star of Khorala is to make anyone fall in love with the person bearing the gem.

In books written in tongues old before the cataclysm, other powers are ascribed. In *The Book of Eibon*, a gem that could well be the Star is referred to as a dream stone. In Acheronian texts, it is a called a summoning rock. Those who have possessed it have ever been fortunate, and Astreas the Scholar recounts a legend in which the Star is a luck stone. None or all of these may be true. Who can say?

The gem is missing, spirited away from Khorala. Queen Yrrane offers a roomful of gold for its return, but neither thief nor adventurer has yet to claim this reward. Perhaps, if anyone does recover the Star of Khorala, the full extent of its nature will become known. The one constant in the gem's existence is this — those lacking royal blood have never possessed it for long.

Ophirean Religion

Mitra is the chief deity of Ophir, and his temples in this kingdom are among the most splendid. Indeed, Ophireans take some pride in the very opulence of their temples to the god, with cities often competing to make the next, greatest monument to mighty Mitra.

In nearly every household, an altar to Mitra is central to the main living area, and folks give thanks before meals. However, there is a hollow quality to this seeming devotion, as if the Ophireans think associating with Mitra is more a matter of prestige than faith. The Ophirean church is, as one might expect, heaped with riches. The clergy speaks in a dead form of the Ophirean tongue, and writes in an even older one.

There are still many devout worshipers throughout the land. While the temples and priests are ringed in finery, there is a movement toward a more common, accessible form of Mitraism gaining popularity outside the cities and royal courts. This movement remains small but passionate. In time, they could cause the priests who live off the faith and gold of others genuine problems.

While some few other gods have temples in many cities and towns, the other notable religion of Ophir is one people do not talk about — supplication to the beings of the Outer Dark. Acheron was built upon the ferocious horror of the Great Old Ones and, though most of their temples and icons were smashed long ago by the Sons of Bori, that eldritch flame is not so easily put out.

Pockets of Acheronian refugees hung on in Ophir and rode out the great dark age with their religion intact. Inside the church of Mitra, a secret cult grows. They worship gods with names like Azathoth and Cthulhu while hiding behind the symbols of respectable religion.

In Shamar, where the Mitra priesthood is strongest, high bishops have begun to investigate this internal corruption. A force of loyal priests has pledged to root out all those who would make pacts with the Outer Dark. Because pure Acheronian blood still runs through the veins of secretive hill folk, the rural peasants, too, are not unfamiliar with these dark gods. Children may go missing in the night. Cattle and other livestock are found with their organs removed, and strange astronomical alignments bring tragedy. Most dismiss this as the superstition of simple villagers and farmers, but they are foolish to do so. In Ophir, the profane gods of the void still hold influence.

CITIES OF OPHIR

Though every city has shadows in which nefarious persons skulk, and has tenements where those without coin bed down like rats, Ophir's magnificent cities have the fewest by far. Gold buys many things, and one of those is keeping the poor and downtrodden out of the eyes of the citizenry. Though small slums find purchase in Khorala itself, they are routinely cleared by hired mercenaries in a continual program of rebuilding and reinvigoration.

Though Ophir slips into decadence, she does not do so without style.

Khorala

Capital of Ophir and home of the Ivory Palace where King Almarus and his family reside, Khorala is called, at least by Ophireans, the "Jewel of the West". While not as populous as Tarantia or Khorshemish, Khorala boasts more public squares, temples, libraries, and monuments than either of those cities. Khorala is the face of Ophir, the face that Almarus and the royal family want the rest of the world to see.

It is also a relatively safe city. Mercenaries serve as guards, and they are plentiful. Torchbearers work on the city's coin to steer travelers in the night where braziers and lamps are infrequent. Those thieves who ply their trade on Khorala find harsh times and harsher punishments. The Square of the Hanged Man is famous for its public executions and gibbets. Thieves do not receive a second chance in Khorala.

The Ivory Palace is a marble marvel made in the days before Ophir was vassal to Acheron. Beneath the palace are a network of old tunnels and sewers pre-dating the current iteration of the city. Who built them is unknown, but the kings of old long since walled off sections leading to any part of the royal compound. A homeless populace calls those tunnels their own and, so long as they mostly stay out of sight, are tolerated.

Khorala boasts the biggest garrison of knights in Ophir, and they serve as the city's primary defense. A large wall likewise offers a bulwark against would-be invaders.

Some of the remaining architecture of Acheron was brought, piece by piece, to Khorala for preservation. The Arch of Time sits in the Square of Mitra, an imposing, black basalt gate covered in bas-reliefs of creatures best not seen in the flesh. It is a curious, anomalous, and jarring monument in a city otherwise given to gold, white marble, and expertly laid roads. Locals have called it a grotesquerie, but no one has ever tried to tear it down.

Khorala sits on edge of the Tybor River. For millennia, the waters served to transport goods throughout the region. The Tybor River is relatively shallow, but thick mud at the bottom stymy cavalry and infantry, increasing the city's apparent impermeability to attack. Nearly all bridges are constantly guarded by either permanent wooden hill forts or mercenary patrols.

Shamar

Shamar rests in the meadows of southern Ophir, a seemingly tranquil, pastoral setting. The area is prone to infrequent, but devastating, earthquakes, however, and Shamar has been leveled at least twice in its history. Originally, the city began as a fortification guarding one of the few passes through the mountains leading to Koth. Over the ages, the fortification became a town, and then a city. It sits along a major trade route in Ophir itself, and sees much traffic because of the pass. Merchants of all sorts travel in caravans, offloading a portion of their goods in Shamar. Shemite traders long ago established a presence in Shamar, and the city holds an entire neighborhood where Ishtar, not Mitra, is revered. Tension between the Shemites and local Ophireans is present, but rarely boils over into violence.

The current ruler of Shamar is the Baroness Helena. She is in league with Queen Yrrane and, when the time comes, is set to control the pass as the Queen sees fit. Such a strategic location could turn the tide of any internecine war, particularly if Baroness Helena were to close off the pass and cut off trade. That would carry some leverage with nobles throughout the land.

There are, perhaps, half a dozen people in the city who know something the rest of the world does not — the earthquakes which have razed the city in the past are anything but natural. Something sleeps, or is perhaps imprisoned, beneath Shamar. One of the squares in the city is strata upon strata of paving covering an ancient, inhuman seal. Before men were a flicker in the eyes of those gods they would later give name to, the Elder Things bound a god of their own under the earth here.

The god's presence is rarely felt, but the citizenry of Shamar is known to have troubled dreams and a melancholic nature unlike most Ophireans. Something perturbs them, though they would never be able to name what it might be. Those people privy to this secret are all irrevocably mad, though only one openly so. The rest are part of a cult whose tendrils reach into dim pre-history. Their goal is simple — to free the Great Old One below. May Mitra, Ishtar, and any other human god man calls on see to it they never succeed.

RUINS OF OPHIR

As a former Acheronian Vassal, it is no wonder that the remains of that land still poke through the earth like infant's teeth. Yet there are cultures before the Cataclysm which, too, have left their mark. Among the gold and diamonds, the silver mines and bountiful land, are things older than time as man can easily reckon. There lay fortunes the king himself might envy, but likewise dangers at which even the stout-hearted shrink.

The Giant-Kings' Redoubt

This strange fortification lies in ruin. Its walls are made with huge, black stones weighing several tons each. They are fit together like a crazy puzzle, but a man could not slip the sharpest dagger between them. The walls that remain are over forty feet in height.

Everything in the Giant-King's Redoubt is built on an awe-inspiring scale. The flagstones which comprise the remnant roads are half as long as a man. Huge cairns, now empty, seem built for men who stood well over ten feet tall. All this evidence caused local oral history to ascribe the site to the Giant-Kings.

However, the Giant-Kings were not giants but merely men, and they did not build this fortress. The people who did are unknown, though some clues give suggestion of their culture. In the center of the compound is a pit. Treasure hunters excavated the bottom of the pit only to find the bones of creatures the world had not seen in eons. Those statues which are still recognizable, as well as reliefs along remaining portions of buildings, suggest the people here worshiped giant lizards of the type still extant in forgotten jungles and lost plateaus. Certainly, the climate in Ophir now is not hospitable to such creatures. Astreas notes:

"It is as if the men of old coexisted with the great lizards and were supplicants before them. One wonders if, perhaps, they made offerings of animals, or even themselves, to such terrible beasts."

The Yellow Dolmen

This collection of capped dolmens appears to have been both an astronomical device and a temple to Bori. Images of the god, as well as several unknown animals, appear on the huge megaliths. The craftsmanship is remarkable given that Bori worshipers were rude savages. Each stone stands between twelve and twenty feet in height and form lopsided circles on the low hill on which they stand.

The stones are not local and must have been hauled a great distance. What's more, the entirety of the site was once purposefully buried. A giant hill hid this megalithic wonder for thousands of years. It was the Acheronians who dug it up for reasons unknown, and the records of this survived the fall of that empire.

Mostly, the site is avoided, for travelers and locals alike report dark, winged forms circling the dolmen in the dusk. At that time, a strange gaseous fog appears which is yellow in color. In hangs over the hill like an obscene crown and dissipates by morning. No one has yet discovered when this phenomenon will occur. Every so often, less knowledgeable (or foolish) travelers stop at the Yellow Dolmen. They return with stories of nausea, hair loss, and sudden weakness. They also claim that freshly-severed human fingers still wet with blood sit upon certain low, altar-like stones. Some wild men or a cult clearly reveres and uses the site today.

The only sounds were the quick scuff of feet on the sward, the panting of the pirate, the ring and clash of steel. The swords flashed like white fire in the early sun, wheeling and circling. They seemed to recoil from each other's contact, then leap together again instantly. Sergius was giving back; only his superlative skill had saved him thus far from the blinding speed of the Cimmerian's onslaught. A louder clash of steel, a sliding rasp, a choking cry from the pirate horde, a fierce yell split the morning as Conan's sword plunged through their captain's massive body. The point quivered an instant from between Sergius's shoulders, a hand's breadth of white fire in the sunlight; then the Cimmerian wrenched back his steel and the pirate chief fell heavily, face down, and lay in a widening pool of blood, his broad hands twitching for an instant.

— "Iron Shadows in the Moon"

SHEM

In the west, the rolling pastoral meadowlands of Shem offer rich bounty for settlers, but these green fields dry up and turn to open desert as one progresses eastward. There, the arid land is dotted by the odd bit of green, as if one has entered a world of only sand and the ceaseless blue sky. Still, the beauty of Shem's deserts rivals those of her meadows, though the former is, of course, far more unforgiving.

Between the ancient empire of Stygia to the south and the mighty Koth to the north, Shem culture is largely unique, and comprises some of the best artisans and craftsman in all the world. The Shemitish religions of Anu and Ishtar resist the dark influence of Father Set whose serpentine eyes rest enviously on all that he wishes were his by conquest. Should Stygia march across the world as once it did, Shem would be the first land lying in its way. There are many whose prayers importune the gods to ensure that Shem's legendary archers and the fearsome *asshuri* be bulwark enough against the spread of that reptilian corruption.

A STORIED HISTORY

Over the course of the centuries following the cataclysm, Shem has been both empire and subject. Once, mighty Stygia called her a vassal state, but Shem broke free of Set's coils and founded its own kingdom in the deserts whose sand drifted from the outskirts of Luxor to the north. There, Ishtar and Derketo, Anu and Bel, became the new gods of those who had gladly abandoned the worship of Set. Yet, as a desert people, with no firm territory, it took time for the Shemites to come into their own. As they moved west into the fertile lands, they settled and built a magnificent culture which survives today.

In antiquity, the Shemitish nomads came out of the desert like a sandstorm and swept all before them; emerging from the stark landscape of the east, they fought their way to the coast of the Western Ocean where they built Askalon over Acheronian ruins. Hyborians, Stygians, far flung Hyrkanians, and even Zingarans were pressed into an empire dominated by Shemite culture, belief, and craftsmanship. At their height, they were unrivaled in their achievements in the fields of steel making, pottery, mathematics, and mobile infantry. Time erodes us all, however, and Shem's glory days are now some half-score centuries behind them.

Yet in the blood of Shemites, *asshuri*, and Pelishtim burns the memory of that faded empire and culture. Perhaps, a leader will one day emerge to lead them back to that golden apex.

The Shemite soul finds a bright drunkenness in riches and material splendor, and the sight of this treasure might have shaken the soul of a sated emperor of Shushan.

— "Queen of the Black Coast"

EAST VS. WEST

While the Shemite peoples first founded their civilization in the deserts of Eastern Shem, the culture changed as it moved west toward the ocean. By the time Askalon became a dominant city on the coast, the people of the east had been conquered by early Turanians. The two bloodlines and cultures mixed, producing a darker skinned Shemitish population whose minarets and temples are unlike those found in the meadowland cities.

There is some rivalry between the paler Shemites of the meadows and the dusky-skinned people of the east. As noted, they come together in common purpose, but it is not unheard of for a city-state from one extreme — fertile or barren — to attack another, especially where the two climates fade into one another.

UNITED MORE BY CULTURE THAN LAW

While Shem is not amongst the dominant empires, nor does she possess the might and ambition of Stygia, her great deserts to the south and mountains to her north provide ample natural defenses. Coupled with the ferocity of her soldiers and the skill of Shemitish archers, it is no surprise that Shem is oft left alone by the ambitious eyes of upstart kings and would-be emperors.

Shem is a collection of city-states spread east to west across the varying topography of a mostly-barren land. The kings of these cities nominally pay fealty to the ruler of Askalon, though the further one strays from the coast, the more a state falls under sway of the desert cities or even foreign powers. Still, for all its lack of consistent laws and edicts, Shem comes together for mutual advantage. There is not any city-state who will not send troops in defense of Shem herself.

SHEMITISH CRAFTSMANSHIP

While the Hybori were pulling down the ruins of Acheron on their way to civilization, the people who would become the Shemites crafted magnificent wares under the aegis of Stygian masters. When they broke from Stygia, the people brought with them all their knowledge of pottery, steel making, textiles, and more.

Throughout the west, and even in remote sections of the east, Shemitish silks, urns, lamps, and weapons are highly prized. Small towns in the deserts of Shem subsist not on hunting and gathering or agriculture, but on their artisanal skill alone.

Ophir, in particular, is enamored with Shemitish goods, and the wealthy nation heaps gold upon wagons headed south and returns with fine clothes, pillows, rugs, pottery, and weapons. Of special note is Akbatanan steel for which the west has no parallel. Weapons crafted in that city-state are superior in quality to nearly all others. For more information on Akbatanan steel, see page 20.

Further, Shem is a nation of merchants and traders. There are no travelers who, as a people, have gone as far as the Shemitish. Their caravans wind their way through Turan to Vendhya and beyond. The only reliable source of goods from the Far East is the Shemitish traders who carry in their minds a secret "road" dotted with oases and cities unpronounceable to western tongues. While others have pulled this secret route forcibly from such traders, almost none have taken the path as Far East as it goes. There is simply too much desert, and too long a delay in profit, for most folk who do not carry Shemitish blood.

Shemite Caravans in the West

To the east, Shem faces relatively little competition in the way of trade, but in the west, this is not the case. Along the great Road of Kings, as well as a hundred less storied routes whose names few bother to commit to paper, Shemitish merchants push through the gleaming kingdoms like rivers who have dug their way over eons. Where other nations depend on trade, none have it in their blood like Shem. They have an extensive network of trade throughout the Hyborian Nations and beyond. In nearly every city, Shemite merchants have established bases of operation and assist one another before they do those of other kingdoms.

When Shem the Empire began to fall from the gods' favor, an economic empire was born instead. Shemitish trade comprises a significant contribution to the economy of the western Thurian continent. This alone is reason why, for now, expanding empires leave Shem alone. To disrupt trade would invite ire from fellow kings.

While they are not the only traders, Shemites have a reputation for quality goods, the swift acquisition of hard-to-find items, and, somewhat miraculously, cutting fair deals. They are shrewd but honest. Any man whose isn't addled would gladly do business with a Shemite over a Zamorian!

THE GLEAMING CITY-STATES OF SHEM

Shemite city-states rule over verdant fields and over desert, but they do not comprise a proper kingdom. The shadows have long fallen on the Empire of Shem. In her place, the city-states glow in the dark like the jeweled mantles of night above. Only, there are far fewer cities than there once were, as if they were snuffed out, each in their time, like the burning stars themselves.

Still, these walled domains carry the torch of Shemitish civilization, and will continue to do so until Shem herself drowns in the sea like her forbears, washed from the land and history in but a moment.

Asgalun

Mighty Asgalun, whose fathers came from the desert's hot sun into the welcome arms of fertile greenery stretching to the Western Ocean. Upon that coast, the early Shemites built Asgalun atop, and sometimes from, the ruins of an Acheronian city. Even today, rounding a twisting alley's bend, one might come upon a wall as ancient as Old Stygia.

Yet upon these foulsome bricks of that fell kingdom is built the civilization of Shem's still-mightiest city. Asgalun — sometimes spelled Askalon — is the chief port of Shem, and the majority of all foreign goods brought by sea enter here. The vast overland trade routes see that Shemite goods make it to many ports besides their own before taking to sea. Such is the variegated nature of trade in the Hyborian Age.

A king sits upon the throne of Asgalun, descended from the Pelishtim Sargonian dynasty, whose lineage stretches back to the first Shemite to conquer the varying tribes and forge them into a people. That unbroken line is, perhaps, more legend than truth, for it is said that the Kings of Asgalun have written over certain lacuna in their bloodlines. In truth, like most cities, Asgalun has seen her share of conquerors and successful sieges.

Built atop the cliffs overlooking the Western Ocean, the city is nigh invulnerable from the sea, and a wall encompasses the entirety of the city where it sits against land. *Asshuri* mercenaries serve in the army alongside other Pelishtim stock.

City of Asgalun

1. Temple of Ishtar
2. Royal Palace
3. Asshuri Barracks
4. Pelishtim Barracks
5. Hall of Records
6. The Great Quays
7. House of Hadad
8. Trading Guild
9. Market
10. First Ziggurat
11. Square of Er
12. Bah'els Tower
13. Hanging Gardens
14. Get of Anu
15. Eastern Gate
16. Southern Gate
17. Southern Quays
18. Gate of Ishtar
19. Bathhouse

As a center of trade, Asgalun is revered, for in her markets it is said all the world arrives. From mysterious objects of the Far East, to totems made by Picts, everything is for sale in Asgalun. Shemite merchants arrive daily, bringing new wares and spices from far-flung places many will never see.

Akbatana

Akbatana, also spelled Akbitana by those from eastern Shem, represents the pinnacle of craftsmanship in all of Shem and beyond. Goods made in the city are prized from Aquilonia to Stygia, such is their quality and beauty. However, it is Akbatanan steel which men of the blade seek. There is no finer steel made in all the world.

The blacksmiths of Akbatana share a story passed down since the first Shemites broke away from Stygia. According to legend, Anu the Bull gave the secret of this steel to men. It allowed the Shemites to forge a kingdom. When they revolted against Stygia, the Shemites had steel blessed by Anu. The Stygians did not and their blades broke like pottery against hard stone. Such is the legend.

Today, every smithy and forge in the city has a shrine to Anu. Every blacksmith in Akbatana belongs to a secret order which swears fealty to Anu and likewise promises, upon painful death, to never reveal the secrets of their steel. Though kings and warlords have tortured Akbatanan smiths, the secrets have never been replicated outside the Order of Anu. Perhaps the god really must bless the steel for it to attain the hardness and sharpness all soldiers lust after.

As noted, all goods from Akbatana are highly prized. While its steel is the most famous, the pottery, leather, silks, and other textiles from the city are the finest in Shem — and that is saying something. The city depends, for its very existence, on the value of its craftsmen and skill of its workers. Situated along an ancient trading route, Akbatana sprung up around an oasis which still exists in the form of a public well in the Square of Ishtar.

While the burly smithies of Akbatana are storied throughout the land, it is Akbatana's women who hold, perhaps, a greater reputation still. Quite simply, they are known for their beauty. Like the stories of steel, the women of Akbatana believe they are descended from, or directly blessed by, Ishtar. They wear veils so that men are not overcome by their full lips and high, curving cheekbones.

The most beautiful girls are inducted into Ishtar's graces at a young age. Some become priestesses of the goddess, but many more become handmaidens of Ishtar, a role which is not well defined outside Akbatanan society. They are not chaste, these handmaidens, but they do not take husbands either. Their status in the city supersedes all others save the ruling elite. They live in three palaces near the city gates, and never walk in public without their veils. The veiled women of Akbatana are spoken of over the flickering tallow of many taverns, but no one outside of the city truly understands their role. They serve as mediators, judges, and symbols of the city. Men may lust after them, but none will ever have them. It is even said by some that they rule Akbatana, and that the royal family are puppets to their beauty and to Ishtar's will.

Eruk

Nestled in the mountains that serve as border between Shem and Koth, Eruk is known by Shemites as "the first city". Legend holds that Sargon, upon forging disparate tribes of the desert into a coherent culture, set his eye to the mountains. He followed the constellation Anu, which was a manifestation of the selfsame god. His people journeyed to the base of the mountains, then some way up until Anu communicated to Sargon that they had arrived at the destination. There, they built a city.

The city is unique in that the most ancient parts are not built but carved from living rock. Such craftsmanship has been forgotten even by the Shemites. Huge columns flank the smooth-tiered steps leading to temples, government buildings, and fine homes. The entirety of the old city is connected by rock handholds, allowing for ease of ascent. These are rarely used today, and the old city remains under watch by the city guard.

At some point in the city's history, the people who carved its wonders lost such skills. Perhaps they were driven off by conquerors, only for their descendants to later return and found the city anew. Today, Eruk proper bears little resemblance to the old structures. Instead, it is a more conventional city which sits on the hills leading to the mountains. The newer city does not ascend the way the old city did.

Pelishtim rule here, and the city lies along a major road and trade route. This seems to be the only reason it continues to flourish as, other than a defensible position, Eruk offers no natural resources save a small stream. It is by no means a desolate location, but Eruk's location seemingly belies common sense.

Why did people scale these cliffs? How did they carve a city from such rock? Where did they go? Anu's will is as much a mystery now as it was so long ago.

Shumir

Shumir is a city run by mercenaries, specifically the dread *asshuri* (see *The Asshuri*, page 47). The family Mok rules over the city from a keep located near the main gate. To say that Shumir is among the more well-defended cities of the age would be an understatement.

The *asshuri* are soldiers for pay and, sometimes, for the sons of Shem. Shumir became theirs some two hundred years ago when the mercenaries rescued the city from Stygian invaders. The Stygians did not progress beyond Shumir, either, for the *asshuri* stopped them in a gore-filled three days and nights on the Plain of Shumir. If Shumir had fallen, the citizens of the city maintain, so would have fallen all of Shem. There are scholars who disagree — they do not live in Shumir.

A prosperous city, the Mok family proved their instinct for commerce was as sharp as their ferocity in battle. Located along a major trade route, the city also boasts a large lake from which water and fish are resourced. This natural bounty is welcome to travelers from the east, as Shumir sits on the border between desert and meadowland. Not a dozen leagues from the city walls, the green meadows wither to yellow stalks and then become mere tufts of grass dotting a landscape blasted by the unforgiving sun.

THE NOMAD CLANS OF SHEM

While her cities draw people from the far corners of the world, the sons of Shem are likewise nomads. In the great deserts, clans wander from oasis to oasis, practicing old forms of Anu and Derketo worship, as well as those of much older religions. Some even continue the practice of demon worshiping which found favor in younger days.

LIFE, DEATH, AND RITUAL IN SHEM

Though once part of Stygia, Shemites are a culture and people all their own. Whilst they toiled under Stygians whips, or served Stygian lords, they never accepted Set as their god. Still, they are not without Stygian influence, but not even the most barbarous fool would mistake one for the other.

THE DESERT CLANS

The clans are each ruled by a chieftain whose word is law. None would go against him unless they were braver than all the hosts of Aquilonia, or more foolish than a man who would kill a snake in the temple of Set. Camels are favored over horses by most clans, but a Shemitish breed of desert horse is renowned for both speed and stamina. Indeed, the clans have a tradition of long-distance races on such steeds, though they do not share the details with outsiders.

This intense privacy continues in most of their affairs. Few men not born to the clans could begin to speak to their ways. Yet the clans answer the call of the defense of Shem the same as the armies of the cities. More than that, the hospitality of the clans is legendary. No man or woman can approach them in peace and be denied shelter, food, and water. The nomad clans do not take that knowledge and heritage which allows them to survive in these barren wastes lightly. Outsiders are not expected to do as well and are thus given aid.

Yet to be among them is never to be of them. The outsider welcomed with smiles is well-treated and honored, but they are just as quickly ushered back to the safety of their towns and roads and cities.

Where the nomad clans are welcoming to those who come in peace, they are equally punitive to those who might bring war. Many an army has tried to push through the eastern desert into Shem, only for the desert night to stretch long shadows under the moon from which the clans seem to appear in an instant. Few survivors have made it out to recount the full measure of these attacks, but each who has claims he was spared precisely to carry a single message — the deserts belong to the clans.

Shemitish Art

Artisans of Shem are among the best in the world. They perfected pottery, chest making, dyes, and forging while in Stygia. These skills they carried into the desert when they left that evil empire behind. With the likes of Anu and Ishtar to guide them, the Shemite people turned their art toward objects of religious significance. There are few objects which do not in some way invoke or evoke some aspect of their gods.

However, few outsiders can read these coded symbols and merely think them decorative. The fine knots of gold filigree around the lip of that cup purchased in Askalon represent the bonds which once tethered Anu and kept him from the world.

The art of steel is another matter. Akbatana makes the finest steel in the Hyborian Age. This is well known. The specifics are not. Some blades are plain, some armor dull in the morning light. Other works are wrought with the finest of designs, prayers, and the names of their owners. Even the most unassuming Shemitish blade swims with the alloys mixed, pounded, folded, and made rigid in the forges of Akbatana.

Shemitish Culture

Friendly but private, Shemitish culture is based on deep tradition, much of it going back to the people's time as subjects — and sometimes slaves — of Stygia. Marriages are arranged by parents and only considered legitimate once a child is produced. One is not truly married under Shemitish law until then. This causes blood feuds for those who, once paired, fall in love but do not have children. The families of both spouses blame the other for the lack of fertility.

While Shemites welcome outsiders, they tend to look down upon most of them. They obviously have no love for the Stygians and consider Hyborian culture backwards, rude, and entirely lacking in subtlety. Nearly every northern oaf manages to insult Shemites in some way, but they are too polite to point this out. Besides, what does one expect from such childish races?

Scented locks, ringleted beards, and silken robes all likely have their origin in Shemitish culture. Other people claim they invented such things, but the Shemites know better.

Shemitish Religion

Shem is a deeply religious nation. In fact, it is sometimes said their religion is as great a bond as their blood. There is likely no village within her borders which lacks a temple, however modest. The sometime uneasy alliance between the nomad clans and the western Shemites is likewise forged in common origins and religion.

While other kingdoms may adopt an official religion, Shem is notable for its belief that their gods are, in fact, the most powerful. Mitra is nothing compared to Ishtar, though Shemite priests rarely attempt to convert those so misled.

Omens come from the stars, some of which burn so brightly that two among them are known as Anu's eyes. This is, in fact, a dual star system, though there are no words for such in this age. The Shemites have a book, whose name is not known to outsiders, which charted the skies for millennia. Their astronomers are nearly unrivaled. Astrologers are highly respected and believed to be able to read the destiny of all in the mantle of night.

RUINS OF SHEM

There is not a land upon the Thurian Continent which has not the dotted ruins, the remaining detritus of other ages. Civilization rises like a wave only to break, again and again, against the stalwart rock of savagery. Among the deserts

especially, travelers report seeing the broken bones of stone poking up from the sand, the last testament of cultures which vanished when the world was new.

Kuthchemes

While located in Shem, Kuthchemes was a Stygian city during the period when that dark empire ruled the Shemites. The specific rituals of these earlier Stygians are lost to time, but it is believed by certain scholars that they were worshipers of creatures and gods from Kuth of the Star-Girdle. That is to say, they followed the business and madness of the Outer Dark rather than Set alone.

The city itself is theorized to have begun as a shrine based on fragments of bas-reliefs and other carvings brought out of the desert. The specific location of the city itself is unknown to the world, though it can no doubt be found in spider-webbed scroll tubes and other books entombed in dust.

The history that is better known is the rise of Thugra Khotan, who set himself to a millennia-long slumber when the barbarians came to destroy the city he ruled. How he came to power is not recorded, though his potent sorcerous talents and connection to the void no doubt assisted his rise. The barbarians who beat down the great bronze gates of Kuthchemes are likewise not recorded, though one presumes they were of Hyborian stock.

In a great tomb at the city's center, a huge white dome pokes up from landscape. Under that dome, whose inside has not been seen a mortal man for three thousand years,

Thugra Khotan waits to wake, for his business with the world is not done. Many brave armies will meet him when he does. May they be led by such barbaric blood as forced his slumber so long ago.

The Demon Stone of Djemballa

A slender finger of rock at a distance, the so-called "Demon Stone" points directly into the dark of night. On certain nights, when the stars are right, it points directly at a planet in the distant void. No naked eye can see that planet, but those old tribes — long dead — could by means unnatural and profane. These unnamed people left rude carvings on the rock which, could one read them, indicate that the stone is the mortal prison of the demon they once worshiped.

Said demon was drawn down from its native planet by means even more unnatural and profane and, for a while, he ruled over and taught the humans below. But some feud on his native planet — to which he was still connected — resulted in his banishment to Earth. That was not the end of his influences in the area.

After the desert savages died off and were forgotten, evidence suggests a town sprung up here. A dry riverbed is bridged by ancient stone, and the remnants of a green stone fountain lie about one hundred yards from the Demon Stone. Oddly, the skeleton of large marine predators can likewise be found in the area. None of these would have lived in a river.

During the days of the nights when the stone points at the lost planet — who men have called Carcosa — the sun draws shadows from the stone which look like the demon itself. Some pass this off as a trick of the eye... others do not.

THE ASSHURI

Not quite a distinct people, and not quite a mercenary company, the *asshuri* likely descended from former nomad clans who settled in the cities. When, exactly, they became mercenaries is not recorded, but they have been in the profession of arms for hundreds of years.

The *asshuri* are perhaps best described as a very extended family, though blood alone does not determine membership. Various branches of the family determine to whom the *asshuri* pledge service, and at what price. They are fierce, well-armed and armored (often in scale mail), and motivated. Among charioteers, they are as respected as the Free Companions.

The extended family breaks down into three smaller groups in Nippr, Eruk, and Shumir. In Shumir, the *asshuri* truly rule — a unique situation. The heads of all three families must agree on the largest contracts before the whole host of the *asshuri* commit. For more information on the *asshuri*, see page 54.

EVENTS

> With a Stygian host on its heels, it had cut its way through the black kingdom of Kush, only to be annihilated on the edge of the southern desert. Conan likened it in his mind to a great torrent, dwindling gradually as it rushed southward, to run dry at last in the sands of the naked desert. The bones of its members — mercenaries, outcasts, broken men, outlaws — lay strewn from the Kothic uplands to the dunes of the wilderness.
>
> — "Xuthal of the Dusk"

The world is fraught with disasters both natural and otherwise. The people count on such events, as they count on the seasons. While the weather is ever unpredictable, and earthquakes give no warning, war boils and festers before it is loosed.

Every village and town can smell war on the wind. The people accept it as a fact of life and call upon whatever gods they worship to spare them from the carnage to come — or to make the carnage as profitable as possible. In those periods where peace reigns, people take what pleasure they can, but are likely ill at ease, for peace is but a respite between unending warfare. For mercenaries, this ensures that they have work so long as they can carry and swing their swords.

KINGDOM EVENTS

Kingdoms from the Western Ocean to distant Khitai have one thing in common — they constantly eye their neighbor's territory for expansion. A kingdom which is not expanding is said to be in decline. That was an old maxim from lost Valusia, but it applies equally today.

Fractious borders are common and truces often not worth the paper on which they are inked. Any truce, any peace, and any alliance is considered temporary by all but the most foolish of rulers. Those who trust too deeply seldom live long enough to truly rue their mistake.

WAR BETWEEN KINGDOMS

There is a tale about two knights in the rain, each waiting for the other to make the first move, knowing that when they do, they have their opponent beaten. Borders are very much like those two lone warriors eying each other, waiting for a first, and terminal, advantage.

A small skirmish between troops on both sides can quickly ignite the fires of war, sending a conflagration blazing across both nations, so tense are relations between many domains. Almost any pretext might lead to war; from the most nugatory of trade disputes, to the suspicious death of a popular religious figure, the tinder of bordering kingdoms is always dry and needs only the smallest spark to set light to it.

As if this were not enough, the lords of provinces and entire kingdoms plot against each other. Maneuvering for advantage is part of a king or queen's duties, and troops massing near a tactical position causes alarm for those who fear losing territory of their own. War is often planned. A clever ruler may well ascribe an invasion to an accident, a lie, or to some insult which was never issued, but he or she probably plotted such an eventuality all along.

Marshaling the national army is a more obvious step, for spies constantly monitor the movements of such troops. One does not know on whose side a mercenary company serves until a contract is signed, and sometimes even that is no guarantee. That makes mercenaries a very effective means of amassing troops without it being as obvious. A company could, for example, simply be marching through a given territory in search of work and then suddenly attack as the spearhead of a guerrilla raid.

For this reason, spies also infiltrate the free companies. Wise mercenaries are always on the lookout for someone who is likely to rat them out. The punishment for such betrayal can be painful and slow, or that spy can betray their own employers, in a dizzying spiral of deceit and counter-conceit.

INTERNECINE WARFARE

The kingdoms of this age are not as stable as those which came before, or so history tells the world. Whatever the truth, peace inside a kingdom is only slightly more common than peace between them. This does not mean that civil war rampages across every nation, but there is almost always a province, a fiefdom, or a city which is ready to rebel. Taxes, conscription, naked ambition, all drive the fringes and fragments of empire to seek independence or control over the direction of the empire itself.

Agent provocateurs from rival nations help foment these putative revolts, and foreign treasuries help fund them. An unstable kingdom is often less a threat than a united one, but sometimes the opposite is also true. Stability is relative, and no peasant or king ever feels as if the way things are at night shall remain the way things are in the morning.

Any time a revolt begins, the ruler of that land seeks to snuff it out with all expediency. The fire caught quickly is more easily put out than the one which grows. The conscripts or professional soldiers of the kingdom — should the kingdom have permanent soldiers — are usually the first to attempt to put down the rebellion, but mercenaries often back them up quickly.

Mercenary companies travel faster and with greater agility than the slow, cumbersome armies of empires. For revolts, speed and flexibility are of the essence.

BARBARIC RAIDS

The long-dead King Arnwald of Brythunia wrote, *"Barbarians are quite like the weather — calm for long periods then suddenly, savagely violent."* Picts, nomads, Cimmerians, and other northrons gather quickly like dark clouds and descend upon civilization with little warning.

Sometimes, these are merely a series of raids or a reminder to the world of soft-men that the savage world must be bought off lest they pull down the founding stones of their great cities. In either case, the conflict is usually short and resolved either by a show of force or a ransom paid by king to chieftain.

There are other times, however, when the clouds gather and the storm rages longer than any thought possible; Acheron was pulled down by rude primitives, and Python sacked by barbarous hordes. There is little to prevent a mass of painted savages from pouring into one's kingdom unless that kingdom secures its borders well. Such borders are largely meaningless to the degenerate people of the hills and forests!

Mercenaries might find themselves patrolling these nebulous buffer zones between civilization and savagery, serving in forts, or quickly hired and brought to the line to stem the tide of angry flesh rising like a tsunami.

In many respects, mercenaries are better matched to uncivilized armies than the more ordered, rigid structure of troops in places such as Nemedia, Zingara, or Zamora. Mercenaries understand the life of the professional soldier in ways conscripts simply do not. Even those kings who keep large standing armies cannot hope to prepare them for the volatile and unpredictable tactics of crazed, barbarous enemies. Aquilonia, though, has made steps in understanding their savage neighbors. Other kingdoms would do well to follow.

RELIGIOUS UPHEAVAL

The polytheistic culture of most nations makes holy war uncommon, but that does not mean religions are not problematic for many rulers. While the king of Ophir wears the crown, even he must bend a knee to Mitra. The church of any major deity wields some measure of influence upon the politics of the kingdom.

When rebellion begins to brew, firebrands often attempt to enlist the aid of various high priests, for when a priest tells the people their god wants them on a certain side, many follow. The churches, too, are home to men and women of equal ambition to kings. Indeed, to rule a nation is a goal for many a megalomaniacal priest more devoted to their own status than the furthering of their god's will.

These machinations are common and relatively predictable. A wise queen knows how to keep the churches of Mitra or Ishtar happy and to keep them from siding with her enemies. But not all religious zealotry comes from traditional, sanctified channels. Growing movements arise among commoners in rural outbacks and crowded cities. Dark gods, far older than humankind, can serve as foci for cults. Supposed messiahs claim to be the true prophets of varying divinity, while some even claim to be the living avatar of such superior beings.

Faith leads to fervor, and fervor can galvanize populations in ways mere fear cannot. Deities are at best aloof, and many believe they care little for the affairs of humanity. Yet many more believe the gods map out the lifeline of every man in the stars long before his birth. What then can a king say to sway such people?

Few mercenaries have direct ties to the throne, though their leaders are well-at-home in many courts. It would not do for the king's knights to slaughter a group of devout believers roaming Ophir, but a company of mercenaries can pose as brigands and wipe them out without proof that the throne was involved. It's a dirty business, but so is war. Killing for coin does not always mean killing those who can properly defend themselves.

NATURAL EVENTS

The eastern philosopher Zei once observed, *"However much man is the root of his own troubles, we must always remind ourselves that nature holds dominion over all. An army may raze a city, but a tsunami may raze an empire. No man can stand against the wilderness."*

This aptly describes the dilemma rulers have faced since humanity first rose to dominion over the earth. No king can control earthquakes, flood, hurricanes, and other disasters. Each is a disruptive factor and, the larger the event, the greater the chaos that follows.

Many towns are not safe from brigands and marauders at the best of times. Should they experience a flood or earthquake, looters flock to the area like flies to fresh corpses. The natural world causes strife through famine and plague, which destabilize the rule of law as surely as insurrection or defeat by one's enemy.

PLAGUE

Like the cyclical turn of the constellations above, so does plague flare and burn out. A single village infected by disease becomes a threat to an entire province, while an infected city can lead to the deaths of countless more across the continent. Records of devastating plagues abound in the annals of the age, though the worst are now far beyond living memory. Locally, however, plagues rear their pestilential head with some regularity, and farmers, villagers, and other peasants fear the stranger who comes with buboes and lesions hidden beneath his clothes. Entire neighborhoods are likewise quarantined, turned into ghettos where one either dies, or waits for all those around them to pass on.

Mass graves, where bodies are tossed like dolls, are covered in quicklime and forsaken. Outside some of the great cities of the day — Agraphur, Khorshemish, and Tarantia — sit low hills where, one or more centuries ago, the dead were piled by the thousands.

Any plague that hits a populated area causes hysteria and havoc. Mercenaries might be employed to quarantine a village or burn it to the ground. A town of some wealth might hire mercenaries to prevent their own troops from doing the same. The pay is high because the risk is great. Even the bravest soldier feels their knees wither when invisible death waits in the very air one breathes.

NATURAL DISASTERS

Rockslides, tornadoes, and hurricanes which no god prevents — all visit devastation on communities large and small. Should a small village be erased from the maps, the kingdom goes on. But if a large town, a city, or an entire region is flooded by the rising river, the whole kingdom suffers. Crops might fail, trade routes are blocked, and armies cannot march.

In cities, earthquakes and fires are greatly feared. A simple stable fire can consume a city far faster than most can imagine. Those pressed into the malls and mazes of the world, with homes little more than shacks, are the first casualties of nature's wrath in such events. People in Askalon still speak of the great fire two hundred years past which burned the poor first, but did not forget the rich. Half the city needed rebuilding once the smoke had cleared and the charred corpses were laid to rest.

Towns and cities so ravaged need protection. If the rulers cannot move their troops fast enough, they may rely on mercenaries. Of course, inviting mercenary companies to guard the weak and helpless is not always the wisest of ideas. King Horak of Shumir, remembered as "the Fool", once hired foreign mercenaries to prevent looting of the city. They did the opposite, and, afterwards, the populace hung the king for his folly.

FAMINE

The necessities of life, once denied, turn men and women into the feral creatures from which they sprang. It takes only a few days without water to kill a person. Emaciated masses, their crops failing, migrate in vast numbers, caring not for borders or laws.

A community without food descends from civilization to savagery in a matter of weeks, but it is those who live to flee that present the greater problem. These desperate folk must be corralled or disposed of. Should they cross into another kingdom, they are likely to be met with death. Wandering about the countryside of their own nation, they may turn to banditry. If the king is unwilling or unable to deal with these bone-thin walking corpses, mercenaries are paid to carry out that dirty business instead.

UNNATURAL EVENTS

Most people will never experience those tumultuous events that begin amongst immortal domains, and in this they are fortunate. The world is savage, and life brutish and short, without adding sorcery and corruption to the mix.

EVENTS RELATED TO CONAN

In the course of Howard's adventures, the Cimmerian visited few places which he did not leave irrevocably changed. It is appropriate to consider some of the events in the regions detailed in this book for which Conan was responsible or involved.

Thugra Khotan's Defeat

The wizard Thugra Khotan (see pages 47 and 70) once ruled the mighty city of Kuthchemes in the eastern deserts of what is now Shem. During Conan's life, Thugra awakes and raises an army of desert nomads against the kingdoms of the Sons of Bori.

By the will of fate, the small nation of Khoraja stands in the way of Thugra's dreams of conquest. His host marches upon that nation and Yasmela, whose brother the king was kidnapped by Ophir, now rules in his place. She consults an ancient fane to Mitra, and that god gives her a message which leads to Conan, a solider in her army, who becomes its general.

Conan proves equal to the task, as he usually does, and defeats the desert horde while dispatching the 3,000-year-old sorcerer. That is the end of the events as they played out in Howard's story.

There is nothing to prevent the gamemaster from using this plot with the player characters. Perhaps Conan is elsewhere, wandering the world toward fortune and slaughter. Perhaps Thugra awakens much earlier, and Conan has yet to be born. Whatever reason, the player characters must face the host of nomads pressed into an army by Thugra Khotan. Is Yasmela in control of the throne when this occurs, or is her brother the king still wearing the crown? Does Mitra give anyone in the royal family a message similar to the one in the story?

Perhaps the player characters might fight under Conan's command. Since Khoraja is small, their army is proportional, and it makes sense that they would supplement their ranks with mercenaries. Even if the player characters do not serve in the Khorajan conflict, they surely hear of it through the stories of those who were there. No dog-brother would fail to recount a battle such as this.

Prince Almuric's Rebellion

Howard only hinted at the full measure of Prince Almuric's rebellion in Koth. At the beginning of *Xuthal of the Dusk*, we learn that Almuric's army was destroyed, the prince himself killed, and Conan and the girl called Natala seem to be the only survivors. Beyond that, Howard remains silent as he quickly dives into the action ahead.

It is logical to assume Conan made a good account of himself that day, despite the defeat, but his deeds did not turn the tide of battle. Conan survived, and that is enough for any man after such slaughter. What happened during the rebellion, how it festered and grew, is left to the gamemaster.

Prince Almuric and his motives are detailed on page 73 of this volume. The player characters might get in at the beginning of the insurrection, working as couriers between their company and other mercenaries Almuric wishes to hire. They could spy for either Almuric or Strabonus, or come in nearer the climactic battle in which the army is virtually extirpated.

Such an opening would serve well as the beginning of a campaign. The army is in disarray, survivors are being hunted down, and those who live attempt to cut their way south with the enemy in pursuit. Like Conan, the player characters may find themselves trapped in the desert, or they might flee in a different direction altogether. Conan and Natala found the mysterious, fantastically weird city of Xuthal. What do the player characters find?

The world does not, however, exist by itself. Alongside everything mortals take for the whole of reality is a shadow realm, the Outer Dark, and from that gaping maw of incomprehensible evil comes powers that dwarf the tragedy mere nature can visit upon the world.

RISE OF A SORCERER

Sorcery is power, and a kind of power few mortals understand. While it isn't always an affair of pyrotechnics, thunder, and lightning, its influence is vast. Sorcerers manipulate the world, drawing favors from demons and making pacts with gods. Given enough time, they can reach the power of those heinous entities.

In a kingdom such as Koth, a sorcerer rules behind the throne, but it was not always thus. Tsotha-lanti did not come to power overnight but, when he did, the effects were felt throughout the western world. In time, he may even cause the great nations to go to war.

In your game, a sorcerer might appear from lowly means or be woken from millennia of slumber. The late Thulsa Doom, who fell before Atlantis sank, may not be as dead as annals say. Priests that truck with the Great Old ones may present the ruse of divinity, but their power comes from that same Outer Dark. It corrupts them, in time, just as it corrupts the world around them.

Whether they raise an army, manipulate a king, or seek to bring the gulfs of starry hell upon the earth, the world must react. Wars flare in times such as these, and mercenaries find no shortage of work. Of course, any dog-brother worth the name will think twice before marching against a wizard. They must either be paid very well, or left in the dark about the true nature of their opponent.

RETURN OF A GOD

Bel, Mitra, Asura — these are names known to hundreds of generations. These gods are old, but there are far older, more powerful beings that existed, and still exist, beyond the mortal realm. Mighty Cthulhu slumbers beneath the depths of the same oceans that drank Atlantis. Somewhere in a place which is not a place at all, Shub-Niggurath radiates a malevolent influence over men. Countless, nameless, and unspeakable cults gather round these beings and worship them. But what if one of these cults could bring their god back?

Imagine the world where humanity toils under the will of creatures whose very visage destroys the brain. Imagine if Bel and Anu were replaced with temples to Nyarlathotep and Nodens? What cities and civilizations might spring up in such a world if, indeed, any person survived?

The very intimation that such a thing might occur is repellent to all sane beings. There are few rulers of men who would allow such an attempt at resurrection, at awakening, to go unanswered. Like the fire of battle that becomes the conflagration of all-out war, the return of a god is not something kings passively watch. Of course, the will of man pales next to the naked power of demons, gods, and things which are beyond even the understanding of divinities.

INCURSION FROM THE OUTER DARK

Not all points of intersection between this world and that incomprehensible penumbra are intentional or even new. There are places in the world where the line between the two realms is soft, and terrible things leak through. So, too, may humans pass accidentally into those other fearsome fiefdoms of terror. The Outer Dark aligns with this world from time to time and, when it does, chaos usually follows.

Take a sorcerer whose intent is to summon demons to do his bidding on the field of battle — only he fails to bind them. A tear opens between the two worlds, and more than just those demons the sorcerer called on come through. In *The Book of Eibon*, accounts of an entire city so destroyed are hinted at. Men and women are easily torn apart from within by demonic forces seeking mortal form for some strange purpose or, not uncommonly, merely for sport.

The appearance of a rift causes troops to flee the area, and the locale itself to be abandoned and called cursed. Some of these rifts close of their own accord. Others are closed by the death of those fools who opened them. But the eons of this earth are long and strange and not all doors opened are easily closed.

For a mercenary, such events are best dealt with in one way — expedient retreat. There is no dishonor in fleeing from that which cannot be killed.

ENCOUNTERS

Inside the tent Conan emptied the wine-jug and smacked his lips with relish. Tossing the empty vessel into a corner, he braced his belt and strode out through the front opening, halting for a moment to let his gaze sweep over the lines of camel-hair tents that stretched before him, and the white-robed figures that moved among them, arguing, singing, mending bridles or whetting tulwars.

— "A Witch Shall Be Born"

From Khorshemish, that scheming city where the dread wizard Tsotha-lanti rules, to the deserts of Shem where nomads dwell and tribal custom reigns, a host of adventurers, knaves, allies, and monstrosities await the mercenary. Herein are descriptions of some of those characters, their motives, and terrors lurking in the darker areas of any map where civilization ceases and the wild begins.

DOG-BROTHERS AND SWORD-SISTERS

The mercenaries of the West are many and varied. From highly disciplined Nemedian Adventurers to more rough-and-tumble groups of near-brigands. These are the men and women who die for pay so that the mighty empires might flood their ranks with fresh troops. Their names are often forgotten, unheralded by history... except here.

ASSHURI MERCENARY (TOUGHENED)

Part family and part hired soldiers, every *asshuri* can trace the story of their unit and their blood back for at least five generations. Once, they were nomads, and their tactics

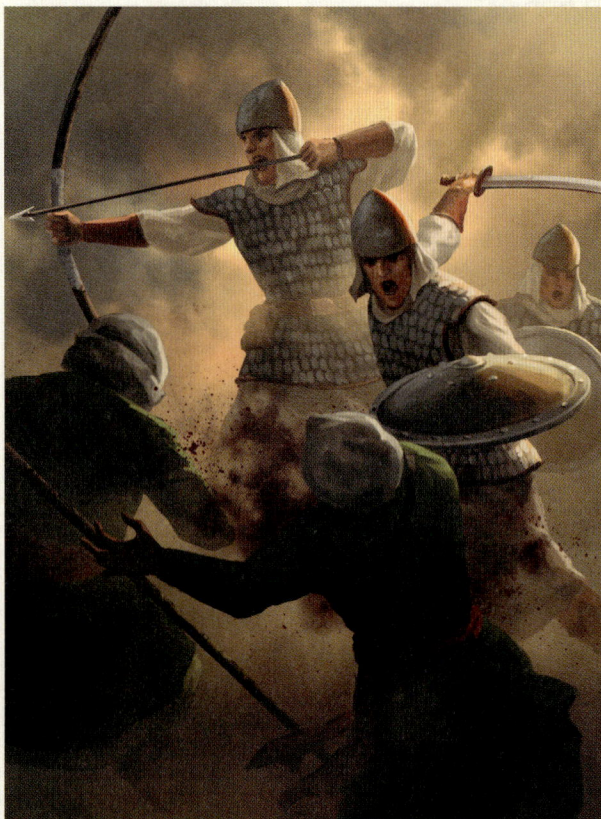

reflect some of that untamed ferocity still. The *asshuri* spent many hundreds of years perfecting the art of war, and they should never be mistaken for undisciplined wild men.

Asshuri go for the sure kill, never consumed by ire or bloodlust. Their pleasure comes from the perfect execution of tactics, form, and willpower. They pride these qualities over more typical mercenary traits like avarice and bloodthirstiness. They are extremely professional in their contracts and their methods of fighting.

Scimitars are their favored blades, and they rarely venture into any campaign without their legendary charioteers. The *asshuri* clans are backed by a great deal of money and history. There are those in Shem who see them as a threat to the Shemitish army itself. Should the *asshuri* ever decide to revolt, the consequences for Shem would be dire.

ATTRIBUTES

Awareness	Intelligence	Personality	Willpower
8	7	7	8

Agility	Brawn	Coordination
9	8	9

FIELDS OF EXPERTISE

Combat	2	Movement	2
Fortitude	2	Senses	—
Knowledge	—	Social	1

STRESS AND SOAK

- **Stress:** Vigor 8, Resolve 8
- **Soak:** Armor 3 (Mail), Courage 2

ATTACKS

- **Scimitar (M):** Reach 2, 3 🗡, 1H, Cavalry 2
- **War-cries of the Asshuri (T):** Range C, 2 🦅 mental, Stun

SPECIAL ABILITIES

- **Cavalry Blades:** *Asshuri* can grant Cavalry 1 to any weapon while mounted. This can increase Cavalry weapons to Cavalry 2.

DOOM SPENDS

- **Practiced Charge:** When mounted and charging a character with greater Reach, an *asshuri* can pay 1 Doom to gain Reach equal to their opponent.

FREE COMPANY MERCENARY (TOUGHENED)

True dog-brothers, Free Companions care about gold, loot, pillaging, and the man who has their back — often in that order. Any man or woman who can cleave their foeman's skull may join. The Free Companions have no past of which they speak, but their company name and standard is well known. Few want to meet them in battle, for they are vicious, ravenous, and skilled.

They have little in the way of a standard kit; each member is responsible for outfitting themselves. Cavalry serve under a select few commanders, but the greater host are footmen, slogging through the mud of sieges like Messantia, Numalia, and Belverus. They have spilled blood in the Pictlands and in the deserts of Turan. They are a group of professional soldiers, murderers, and throat-slitters who, for the most part, are notoriously hard to kill. While other mercenaries call them dog-brothers, standing armies call them roaches, for you cannot stamp them out.

The Free Companions take pride in their roles as rogues, scoundrels, and soldiers of fortune. Their honor, such that it is, applies only to the soldiers beside them. They fulfill their contracts conscientiously, but they quickly turn to banditry and worse if a king severs their employment.

Characterizing an average member is difficult, such are their myriad pasts. Anyone facing them can count on three things — the mercenary will be vicious, look out for their brothers, and protect their own hide. However, once roused to anger or avarice, a Free Companion is as relentless as any starving wolf. General Arbanus of Brythunia once said, *"You have to stab them twice to make sure they're dead,"* after the Battle of the Plains in which his army narrowly escaped from the Free Companions.

ATTRIBUTES

Awareness	Intelligence	Personality	Willpower
7	7	8	9

Agility	Brawn	Coordination
10	10	10

FIELDS OF EXPERTISE

Combat	3	Movement	—
Fortitude	2	Senses	1
Knowledge	1	Social	1

STRESS AND SOAK

- **Stress:** Vigor 10, Resolve 9
- **Soak:** Armor 3 (Mail), Courage 2

ATTACKS

- **Sword (M):** Reach 2, 6 🔥, 1H, Parrying
- **Small Shield (M):** Reach 2, 4 🔥, 1H, Knockdown, Shield 2
- **A Thousand Curses (T):** Range C, 2 🔥 mental, Stun

SPECIAL ABILITIES

- **Cutthroat Mercenary:** Free Company mercenaries are skirmishers second to none. When in Squads of two or three mercenaries, they can roll +1d20 on all Melee attacks
- **Quick Fellowship:** If a Free Company mercenary finds themselves alone, they can form a Squad with any other mercenary within Close range as a Free Action.
- **Shield Brothers:** If a Free Company mercenary is in a Squad with a character holding a shield, they can add +1 🔥 to any Soak test.

DOOM SPENDS

- **Behind You!:** A Free Company mercenary in a Squad or Mob can spend 2 Doom to make a Reaction roll despite being in a Squad. The Squad grants no bonus dice to this roll and damage is dealt to the mercenary first.

KOTHIC KNIGHT (TOUGHENED)

The kings of Koth are constantly ready for their men to turn against them in some petty rebellion or another. It is an untenable position for a standing army and necessitates the use of many, many mercenaries. Yet there exists one unit whose loyalty is unwavering — the knights of Koth.

Training begins as soon as the children arrive in one of the camps or barracks throughout Koth. Martial skill is ingrained along with loyalty. In truth, indoctrination into the knighthood is more about fealty than skill. However, as each child trains for many, many years, few emerge without skill and rigid devotion alike.

The king is the only person to whom they answer. From their first day away from their parents, they are taught that the royal family is their new blood, and the gods care nothing for the affairs of rude humanity. Humankind alone forges kingdoms, carves culture from base savagery, and builds cities where only simple villages once sat. A Kothian knight believes they are the apex of the human race — without equal and beyond defeat.

ATTRIBUTES

Awareness	Intelligence	Personality	Willpower
7	7	8	11

Agility	Brawn	Coordination
9	9	9

FIELDS OF EXPERTISE

Combat	3	Movement	1
Fortitude	3	Senses	—
Knowledge	—	Social	—

STRESS AND SOAK

- **Stress:** Vigor 9, Resolve 11
- **Soak:** Armor 3 (Heavy Hauberk), Courage 4

ATTACKS

- **Lance (M):** Reach 3, 5 🔥, Unbalanced, Cavalry 2, Fragile
- **Sword (M):** Reach 2, 5 🔥, 1H, Parrying
- **Iron Will (T):** Range 1, 3 🔥 mental, Fear

SPECIAL ABILITIES

- **Trained from Birth:** A Kothic knight can re-roll any dice that fails to score a success when making a Melee attack, but must keep the new result.

DOOM SPENDS

- **Fierce Loyalty:** If a Kothic knight would be driven insane by Fear, they can instead spend 1 Doom to keep fighting so long as the opponent is mortal.
- **To the Dying Breath:** Kothic knights hit by Intense weapons can spend 2 Doom to avoid the second Wound inflicted by Intense.
- **To the Last of us:** Kothic knights who have seen two or more of their fellows killed in the current scene can spend 1 Doom to change their type from Toughened to Nemesis, and gain the *Inured to Fear* special ability and add 3 each to Vigor and Resolve.

KHORAJAN SOLDIER (MINION)

The blood of all Khorajans runs with the legacy of the mercenaries who pulled this outremer kingdom from the maw of Koth. While the crown discourages this lineage's veneration, the army does not. It is commonly accepted by the royal family that the soldiery must be allowed to embrace their simple past.

It also makes them spirited, effective fighters. What can one say about the descendants of a mercenary army that took on mighty Koth and won? They must be brave, tenacious, and possessed of rare martial skill. Khoraja's continuing independence, especially under the ambitions of Kothic eyes, is due in no small part to the competence of their troops.

Older formations are the favorite of Khorajan infantry and cavalry. Their commanders study Acheronian scrolls illuminating the art of war and prize simple, effective tactics over complicated siege engines or long baggage trains. Like mercenary companies, the Khorajan army is fast and mobile. However, they are also drilled constantly by their sergeants and assemble themselves into formations as if it were a reflex. Koth's commanders have seen their charges break upon a quickly formed square like waves upon rough cliffs. Each soldier also takes trophies in battle, and a grisly collection of adornments often hang from armor and belt.

ATTRIBUTES

Awareness	Intelligence	Personality	Willpower
8	6	7	8
Agility		Brawn	Coordination
8		9	8

FIELDS OF EXPERTISE

Combat	3	Movement	1
Fortitude	2	Senses	—
Knowledge	1	Social	—

STRESS AND SOAK

- **Stress:** Vigor 5, Resolve 4
- **Soak:** Armor 3 (Mail), Courage 2

ATTACKS

- **Sword (M):** Reach 2, 5 🔥, 1H, Parrying
- **Short Bow (R):** Range C, 3 🔥, 2H, Volley
- **To the Death (T):** Range 2, 3 🔥 mental

SPECIAL ABILITIES

- **Formation Fighting:** When in a Squad or Mob of 3 or more soldiers, the soldiers gain +1d20 to attack

DOOM SPENDS

- **Form Up:** By spending 1 Doom, Khorajan soldiers not in melee can reform into Squads or Mobs as a Free Action. This must occur before any Khorajan soldier makes an attack.
- **Grisly Trophy:** Any Doom spent by a Khorajan soldier when making a Threaten attack grants the Threaten +1 🔥 mental damage in addition to any other effect.

A dully glinting, mail-clad figure moved out of the shadows into the starlight. This was no plumed and burnished palace guardsman. It was a tall man in morion and gray chain mail — one of the Adventurers, a class of warriors peculiar to Nemedia; men who had not attained to the wealth and position of knighthood, or had fallen from that estate; hard-bitten fighters, dedicating their lives to war and adventure. They constituted a class of their own, sometimes commanding troops, but themselves accountable to no man but the king. Conan knew that he could have been discovered by no more dangerous a foeman.

— **The Hour of the Dragon**

NEMEDIAN ADVENTURER (TOUGHENED)

Said to live and die by their swords, the Nemedian Adventurers are a wide-ranging company of mercenaries, knights, soldiers, and others that sell their loyalty for coin. Unlike the Free Companies or the White Company, the Adventurers have no formal organization, no designated leader, and are more a loose fraternity than a military organization.

Adventurers commonly garb themselves in grey mail, and wear no banners or heraldry, signifying their lack of allegiance to any cause. They are famed throughout Nemedia, and generally have little difficulty finding work in military companies anywhere within the western kingdoms.

The Nemedian Adventurers are described in additional detail on page 92 of this book and on page 52 of *Conan the Thief*.

ATTRIBUTES

Awareness	Intelligence	Personality	Willpower
7	8	8	8
Agility	Brawn		Coordination
9	10		9

FIELDS OF EXPERTISE

Combat	3	Movement	1
Fortitude	2	Senses	1
Knowledge	1	Social	1

STRESS AND SOAK

- **Stress:** Vigor 10, Resolve 8
- **Soak:** Armor 3 (Chain Hauberk), Courage 2

ATTACKS

- **Two Handed Sword (M):** Reach 3, 7 ⚜, 2H, Vicious 1
- **Arbalest (R):** Range M, 5 ⚜, 2H, Unforgiving 1, Vicious 1
- **Mocking Laughter (T):** Range C, 2 ⚜ mental, Stun

SPECIAL ABILITIES

- **I Know You:** Due to their extensive knowledge of livery, mercenary companies, and royalty, a Nemedian Adventurer can make an Average (D1) Social test to determine the identity of a knight or noble warrior.
- **Mounted Swordsman:** A Nemedian Adventurer is extensively trained with the two-handed sword and may use it as if it were Unbalanced instead of 2H, wielding it from horseback.
- **Respected:** When dealing with Nemedians, the Difficulty of any social action the Adventurer attempts is reduced by one step.

DOOM SPENDS

- **Band of Brothers:** A Nemedian Adventurer is rarely without allies, and can spend 1 Doom to get word out when in any social center or military camp to reach the nearest Adventurer. The ally will arrive in 3 ⚜ days, with each Effect meaning an additional Adventurer arrives with the first.
- **Opportunity Calls:** A Nemedian Adventurer is always able to find lucrative opportunities for glory, and can spend 1 Doom point to be at the "right time and right place", sometimes seemingly if by coincidence. For more unlikely appearances, this may be increased to 2 Doom.

NOMAD CLAN WARRIOR (MINION)

Like a sandstorm, the nomad clans appear out of the desert bringing chaos and death, only to disappear into the dunes again. Deserts are no easy place to travel, let alone live. The nomad clans of Shem are tough, mysterious, and fearsome. One must possess all these qualities to survive the rigors of the clime in which they thrive.

They favor the curved swords of Turanians over the straight blades of the Meadow Shemites. Archers are few, as the clans rely on speed of action to defeat their foes. They ride camels by day, but may take on horses for combat depending on availability.

They give no quarter to menfolk in combat, but generally spare women and children. Armies who have tried to invade Shem, only to be slaughtered in the open desert, have seen their camp followers safely escorted to the borders of clan territory. At times, certain leaders arise to unite the nomad clans. When this happens, Shem's neighbors shake, for an army of these nomads, possessed of a unified will, can topple the mightiest of kings.

ATTRIBUTES

Awareness	Intelligence	Personality	Willpower
8	7	7	8
Agility	Brawn		Coordination
8	9		8

FIELDS OF EXPERTISE

Combat	1	Movement	2
Fortitude	3	Senses	1
Knowledge	2	Social	1

STRESS AND SOAK

- **Stress:** Vigor 5, Resolve 4
- **Soak:** Armor 1 (Desert Robes), Courage 3

trained. They read, write, and know something of courtly ways, unlike the typical Hyborian knight who is, to be generous, more thug than chivalrous defender. Ophir has its share of such thugs, too, but they are less common.

Ophirean knights have the finest armor, horses, and weapons in the west. Their steel is Akbitanan, their horses Hyrkanian, and their camp followers well paid. As most of these knights carry at least a drop of royal blood, they are rarely accompanied by their families like the units who follow most armies.

Further, each Ophirean knight has a squire who tends to their needs — grooming their horses, sharpening their blades, and learning what it takes to become knights. Like their masters, these squires have royal blood, but will never be heir to anything of import. Squires in Ophir tend to be those boys who rejected a monastic life in service to Mitra. That spirit of adventure and desire for danger distinguish them from the rabble of common troops.

ATTACKS

- **Mounted Scimitar (M):** Reach 2, 4💧, 1H, Cavalry 2
- **Cries of the Desert (T):** Range C, 2💧 mental, Stun

SPECIAL ABILITIES

- **Cavalry Blades:** Nomads can grant Cavalry 1 to any weapon while mounted. This can increase Cavalry weapons to Cavalry 2.
- **My Horse, My Brother:** Nomads never suffer any penalty for having horses in combat, and can ambush with mounts at no difficulty increase.

DOOM SPENDS

- **From Nowhere:** When in the desert, nomads can spend 1 Doom to add 2 Momentum to any ambush.

OPHIREAN KNIGHT (TOUGHENED)

Perhaps more famous for their gilded armor than their victories on the field of battle, Ophirean knights are all too often underestimated by their enemies. The reputation for Ophirean decadence and softness carries over into their military, but the kingdom would not continue to survive against willful enemies if this were true.

Knights are selected from the ranks of nobility, often the so-called "second sons of second sons", and rigorously

ATTRIBUTES

Awareness	Intelligence	Personality	Willpower
7	7	8	8
Agility	**Brawn**		**Coordination**
9	9		9

FIELDS OF EXPERTISE

Combat	1	Movement	1
Fortitude	1	Senses	—
Knowledge	1	Social	1

STRESS AND SOAK

- **Stress:** Vigor 9, Resolve 8
- **Soak:** Armor 4 (Gilded Plate), Courage 2

ATTACKS

- **Sword (M):** Reach 2, 4💧, 1H, Parrying
- **Small Shield (M):** Reach 2, 4💧, 1H, Knockdown, Shield 2
- **Arbalest (R):** Range M, 5💧, Unbalanced, Piercing 1
- **Steely Glare (T):** Range C, 3💧 mental, Stun

SPECIAL ABILITIES

- **Noble-born:** Ophirean knights can roll 1 extra d20 when intimidating fellow Ophireans or other nobles.
- **Martial Valor:** Ophirean knights gain +2💧 Morale Soak when in the presence of fellow Ophireans.
- **Squire:** All Ophirean knights have a squire who they can form Squads with. When they do so, they can still make Reaction tests and gain +1d20 to Melee attacks.

SHEMITE ARCHER (MINION)

The Shemite army relies heavily upon their archers. Flocks of arrows darken the sky like angry, diving ravens before Shemite infantry advances. By the time it does, the enemy is weakened. Only Hyrkanian and Bossonian archers match the Shemites.

All archers are also expected to serve as infantry and are dually trained. While they specialize in harrying the enemy with arrows, they are also highly capable with melee weapons. In this way, they are unlike other armies. A typical archer could not expect to withstand an infantry charge, breaking at the first sign of trouble. Shemite archers drop their bows, pull their blades, and form into squares of disciplined infantry. More than a few, unbloodied commanders have made the mistake of thinking these men easy prey.

Every Shemite archer takes care of their own weapons, both bow and blade. In this they are assisted by younger boys, who train to become members of the unit one day. These boys aren't squires, for the archers are not knights, but they are no mere peasants either. Part of the success of the Shemite archers is ascribable to the way tradition and experience are passed down in the field.

ATTRIBUTES

Awareness	Intelligence	Personality	Willpower
7	6	6	7

Agility	Brawn	Coordination
10	7	10

FIELDS OF EXPERTISE

Combat	1	Movement	1
Fortitude	—	Senses	1
Knowledge	—	Social	—

STRESS AND SOAK

- **Stress:** Vigor 4, Resolve 4
- **Soak:** Armor 2 (Brigandine), Courage 2

ATTACKS

- **Shortsword (M):** Reach 1, 4🗡, 1H, Parrying
- **Small Shield (M):** Reach 2, 4🗡, 1H, Knockdown, Shield 2
- **Shemite Bow (R):** Range L, 4🗡, 2H, Piercing 1, Volley
- **Shield Hammering (T):** Range M, 3🗡 mental, Stun

SPECIAL ABILITIES

- **Massed Fire:** If four or more Shemite archers fire at a target, they gain the Area Quality to their attack.

DOOM SPENDS

- **Fast Volleys:** The Shemite archer can spend 1 Doom to gain the Vicious 1 Quality for their arrows.

SISTER OF THE BLADE (TOUGHENED)

Almost all Sisters of the Blade are women; certainly all the officers. They are an anomaly in the world of mercenaries. As most Sisters do not possess the raw strength of men, their tactics favor speed, agility, and ferocity over charges and brute force. They are excellent skirmishers, and one of the few companies for hire that can wage effective guerrilla warfare.

A Sister carries a blade she crafted herself. Each knows the ways of blacksmithing, hunting, and survival. Their founder, a Vanir woman called Freya (see page 110), grew up in a land that suffers not the weak and helpless. Any member of the Sisters of the Blade can operate on their own for long periods. Stealth is likewise important and ambushes common.

You are more likely to have an arrow in your throat or watch your entrails steaming in the snow before you even realize you've become another victim to these deadly warrior women.

ATTRIBUTES

Awareness	Intelligence	Personality	Willpower
8	8	9	10

Agility	Brawn	Coordination
10	8	10

FIELDS OF EXPERTISE

Combat	2	Movement	2
Fortitude	1	Senses	1
Knowledge	1	Social	—

STRESS AND SOAK

- **Stress:** Vigor 8, Resolve 10
- **Soak:** Armor 3 (Mail), Courage 3

ATTACKS

- **Sword (M):** Reach 2, 4 ⚔, 1H, Parrying
- **Small Shield (M):** Reach 2, 4 ⚔, 1H, Knockdown, Shield 2
- **Throwing Axe (R):** Reach 2, 3 ⚔, 1H, Thrown, Vicious 1
- **Rage of Folkvang! (T):** Range C, 4 ⚔ mental, Stun

SPECIAL ABILITIES

- **Deflection:** A Sister of the Blade pays 1 less Doom to Parry with her own sword.
- **Skirmishers:** A Sister of the Blade can Parry attacks when in a Squad or Mob. They gain no bonus dice for doing so, and must rely on their own abilities.

DOOM SPENDS

- **Deadly Opportunist:** For 1 Doom, any unarmed/improvised attack made by the Sister deals Vicious 1 damage instead of Improvised damage.
- **Riposte:** If the Sister of the Blade makes a successful Parry, they can immediately make an Attack for 1 Doom.
- **Disarm:** If the Sister of the Blade makes a successful Parry, they can choose to spend 2 Doom to disarm any 1-handed weapon.
- **Execute:** If the Sister of the Blade causes a Wound and spends 4 Doom, her attack counts as if it had the Intense Quality.

WHITE COMPANY MERCENARY (TOUGHENED)

You'll find no curs or whelps in this lot of killers. Each man or woman serving in the White Company (see page 93) carries the scars of at least a half-dozen campaigns.

These soldiers' martial prowess is on par with the knights of Poitain or the dread riders of Turan. These are professional soldiers in every sense of the word. Yes, they are still mercenaries, but they are the best of them. Well equipped, highly motivated, and battle-ready, each of this company's members can take on — so it is said — a score of regular troops. While this is perhaps an exaggeration, there are former survivors of a White Company charge that swear it to be true. Naturally, though, a survivor doesn't want to sound like they were easily defeated.

Akbitanan steel and Hyrkanian horses are common among higher-ranking officers. The company prefers hand-to-hand combat and generally eschews archers. Should they need a contingent of archers, they hire Bossonians, Shemites, and Hyrkanians of the steppes.

ATTRIBUTES

Awareness	Intelligence	Personality	Willpower
6	7	6	9

Agility	Brawn	Coordination
9	11	9

FIELDS OF EXPERTISE

Combat	2	Movement	—
Fortitude	1	Senses	—
Knowledge	—	Social	—

STRESS AND SOAK

- **Stress:** Vigor 11, Resolve 9
- **Soak:** Armor 3 (Mail), Courage 2

ATTACKS

- **Two-handed Sword (M):** Reach 3, 7 ♆, 2H, Vicious 1
- **Lance (M):** Reach 3, 6 ♆, Unbalanced, Cavalry 2, Fragile
- **Steely Glare (T):** Range C, 2 ♆ mental, Stun

SPECIAL ABILITIES

- **Professionals Without Peer:** White Company mercenaries roll +1d20 on Melee attacks and all Reactions.

DOOM SPENDS

- **Endure Wound:** So long as a White Company mercenary has Vigor, they can pay 1 Doom instead of taking a Wound.

MONSTROUS FOES AND HORRORS

When one leaves the confines of civilization, a host of horrors may await those bold enough to explore forbidden places. Yet there are monstrosities constructed from cities, from the guilty minds of men. Whether conjured from the mind, or made of flesh and blood, monstrous adversaries await one in the dark corners of the Earth.

IRON STATUE, LIVING (TOUGHENED, HORROR)

Mortal men turned to iron by some ancient sorcery, these statues resemble the tall and powerful warriors they were, but only in form. Iron is stronger and hardier than flesh and blood, and their fists and weapons strike harder than any mortal assault. These statues are inanimate most of the time, but they regain their motion when touched by moonlight.

ATTRIBUTES

Awareness	Intelligence	Personality	Willpower
6	6	3	6
Agility	Brawn		Coordination
6	15 (2)		6

FIELDS OF EXPERTISE

Combat	1	Movement	—
Fortitude	2	Senses	1
Knowledge	—	Social	—

STRESS AND SOAK

- **Stress:** Vigor 17, Resolve 6
- **Soak:** Armor 4 (Made of Iron), Courage 4

ATTACKS

- **Iron Fists (M):** Reach 1, 8 ♆, Grappling, Stun, Knockdown

SPECIAL ABILITIES

- **Braindead**
- **Inhuman Brawn 2**
- **Unliving**
- **War Engine:** Attacks made against inanimate objects gain the Intense Quality.

NIGHTMARE MOUNT (TOUGHENED, HORROR)

These creatures are not steeds in the mortal sense, though they take the form of such when drawn down from the Outer Dark. They may appear as horses, yaks, donkeys, and camels. Thugra Khotan gained such a Nightmare Mount by pact. His appeared in the form of a camel.

These beasts never look quite mortal, and one need only glimpse them to see the eldritch fire burning faintly around them. Their hooves leave glowing tracks for minutes after their passing. As unnatural mounts, nightmares do not slow for any terrain. These creatures have been seen running over corpses heaped like hillocks as though along a smooth, paved road.

While a pact creates a contract between sorcerer and demonic mount, that arrangement is not inviolate. These are demons, not animals to be cowed by the will of men. The mount serves the wizard in a limited capacity only. Parameters must be drawn that, if broken, cause the pact to cease.

The reason for this is very specific, though few know it. These demons are not stupid, mindless minions who caper like broken marionettes in the Outer Dark — each of them is a real and powerful demon. They are bound by other, more puissant, lords as punishment for failed service. Conscripted into the form of an animal is a humiliating, though effective, punitive response for displeasing beings man was not meant to know.

Any of these demons' actual appearance is abhorrent to the human mind. One cannot see their true form and escape with nerves intact. On occasion, the creatures evidence some aspect of their true form on this earthly plane — wings spread, smoky tendrils leaking from nostrils, eyes tripling in size and becoming faceted like those of an insect. Even a slim betrayal of the mortal coil can drive a man to lunacy.

While these demons in question serve as punishment, none are expected to forfeit their lives in the mortal world. Should the danger become too great, they vanish into the interstices between worlds, never to return to their supposed master. How long each demon so punished must suffer this indignity is up to their lord. The worse their transgression, the longer and more odious their servitude.

While the demon holds this form, it cannot speak or otherwise communicate with anyone. It is as if the hideous, malignant mind watches helplessly behind the dumb animal it now inhabits. Such is the torture of those so disciplined.

These creatures may also pull chariots and wagons. When so doing, they convey to the vehicle the same ability to ignore the vagaries of terrain.

ATTRIBUTES

Awareness	Intelligence	Personality	Willpower
10	8	5	9
Agility	**Brawn**		**Coordination**
11	12		11

FIELDS OF EXPERTISE

Combat	3	Movement	4
Fortitude	3	Senses	2
Knowledge	—	Social	—

STRESS AND SOAK

- **Stress:** Vigor 12, Resolve 9
- **Soak:** Armor 3 (Unnatural Flesh), Courage 5

ATTACKS

- **Hooved Maul (M):** Reach 1, 5 🦅, Stun
- **Unnatural Aspect (T):** Range C, 5 🦅 mental, Stun

SPECIAL ABILITIES

- **Familiar**
- **Flight**
- **Mount**
- **Sorcerer:** The nightmare mount may know a variety of spells, but always knows *Form of a Beast* and *Haunt the Mind*.
- **Surefooted:** Nightmare mounts are immune to Hazardous and Dangerous terrain.

DOOM SPENDS

- **Trample:** For 1 Doom each, the nightmare mount may trample man and beast underfoot for 3 🗡. This applies to anyone in the creature's path (assuming they have enough Doom). For mass combat, this applies to an entire unit for every 2 Doom spent. The mount must have a running start of at least 30 yards for this to work.

SATHA THE OLD ONE (NEMESIS)

No mere snake, Satha the Old One is as ancient as Old Stygia, one of the original children of Set. Its piercing, vermilion eyes have seen the ages pass, and its gaze can penetrate beyond any mortal façade to see the very soul. While Tsothalanti refers to Satha as his "pet", there is no taming a creature so old, so blood-bound to father Set himself.

Satha stretches some eighty feet in length. Its wedge-shaped head is larger than a horse. Its jaw, fully extended, could swallow a tall man standing. From that gaping maw extend razor sharp fangs at least a foot in length. Curved like scimitars, they gleam with the deadly venom the creature produces. The creature is frost-white, an albino, having grown in the dark Halls of Horror its entire life.

While Satha currently hunts in the maze of caverns and tunnels beneath the Scarlet Citadel in Khorshemish, this was not always its home. In days long forgotten, Satha was worshiped as an aspect of Set himself. Satha-Lan, an entire city in Old Stygia, served as a necropolis guarded by the great serpent. In the center of that city, long since vanished beneath the unforgiving sands, stood a temple atop which a single spire pointed toward the night. Satha would coil about that spire, and pilgrims would flock to see Satha's priests display their living god.

In Khemi, it is said that the practice of allowing great serpents to prowl the streets at night — consuming who they may — began in Satha-Lan. Surely many a pilgrim gladly sacrificed themselves to the belly of this mighty ophidian horror, consigned to their fate with eyes wide and shining, knowing they went to serve Set's chosen.

What things Satha's sinister eyes have recorded in his millennia on this earth none may ever know. However, it is said that by obtaining Satha's sloughed skin, one can uncover in it, via ritual, all the snake did and knew in the years since the previous molting. Books of such skins are rumored to exist, though no one can confirm having read them. Imagine, the whole of history contained in the scaly castoffs of this magnificent god-thing!

ATTRIBUTES

Awareness	Intelligence	Personality	Willpower
11	3	3	7

Agility	Brawn	Coordination
14	14 (1)	14

FIELDS OF EXPERTISE

Combat	3	Movement	4
Fortitude	5	Senses	2
Knowledge	—	Social	—

STRESS AND SOAK

- **Stress:** Vigor 20, Resolve 12
- **Soak:** Armor 5 (Scaled Hide), Courage 5

ATTACKS

- **Bite (M):** Reach 2, 7 🗡, Persistent 3
- **Envelop (M):** Reach 1, 7 🗡, Grappling
- **Constrict (M):** Reach 1, 7 🗡, Stun, Unforgiving 2, only on grabbed targets
- **Tail Slap (M):** Reach 2, 8 🗡, Knockdown
- **Hissing Display (T):** Range C, 5 🗡 mental, Intense

SPECIAL ABILITIES

- **Fear 2**
- **Inhuman Brawn 1**
- **Inured to Poison**
- **Monstrous Creature**
- **Phobia of Sorcerers:** When Satha first encounters a sorcerer, it must make a Discipline test with a Difficulty equal to the number of spells the sorcerer knows. If successful, Satha gains Doom equal to the Difficulty of the test.
- **Wild Beast:** When attempting a Threaten attack, Satha may attempt a Discipline test using Willpower and its Fortitude Field of Expertise.

DOOM SPENDS

- **Devour:** For 1 Doom, Satha can devour a corpse as a Free Action. Satha immediately gains 3 ⬩ Vigor from this, and anyone witnessing the act must make a Challenging (D2) Discipline test or suffer 1 Despair.
- **Sacrifice to Father Set:** Satha may immediately kill a Minion held in his coils at the cost of 1 Doom. Toughened non-player characters can be killed for 2 Doom. Other characters (including player characters) are immune to this ability; they must be killed using Satha's other considerable abilities.

WAR ELEPHANT (TOUGHENED)

Of all the land animals man has tamed, the war elephant is the most fearsome. Some call this creature a self-propelled siege engine, others "the mount from hell". No soldier wants to be on the opposite side of one in battle.

Elephants are not generally aggressive, but they can be trained to become so. The angriest of such creatures make war elephants. The process to train one goes further than any other mount, and for good reason. In battle, they stampede over the best armored men, break lines through their bellowing cries alone, and even serve to batter down the mighty doors of fortifications — and poor training and indiscipline can lead to this monstrous force being turned against an army's own men, should luck prove against them.

When equipped with a howdah, the war elephant is also a mobile weapons platform. Half a dozen or more archers can rain arrows from atop the beast. The tusks of the creature, coupled with its strength, result in devastating goring attacks which can tear a man in half through sheer force.

Vendhya employs the greatest number of war elephants in their army. When first encountered by western forces, legends say that the men unfamiliar with these creatures simply turned and ran. The fear they inspire is a weapon all its own.

Clever animals, they are also valuable for their ability to use their trunk to pull men from battlements or wreck catapults and ballistae. The trunk of an elephant is far more dexterous than the creature's bulk and weight would imply. Taking such a creature down requires enough arrows to blot out the sun, or enough suicidal troops to get within spear range.

ATTRIBUTES

Awareness	Intelligence	Personality	Willpower
9	6	6	9

Agility	Brawn	Coordination
8	16 (2)	8

FIELDS OF EXPERTISE

Combat	2	Movement	—
Fortitude	2	Senses	2
Knowledge	—	Social	—

STRESS AND SOAK

- **Stress:** Vigor 18, Resolve 9
- **Soak:** Armor 2 or 3 (Tough Hide or Barding), Courage 2 (War-trained)

ATTACKS

- **Stomp (M):** Reach 1, 9 ♦, Unforgiving 1
- **Gore (M):** Reach 2, 10 ♦, Vicious 1
- **Bellowing Trumpet (T):** Range C, 4 ♦ mental, Area, Stun

SPECIAL ABILITIES

- **Fear 1**
- **Inhuman Brawn 2**
- **Keen Senses (Scent)**
- **Keen Senses (Hearing)**
- **Monstrous Creature**
- **Mount 6 (10 with Howdah)**
- **War Engine:** Attacks made against inanimate objects gain the Intense Quality.
- **Wild Beast:** When attempting Threaten attacks, a war elephant may attempt Discipline tests (using Willpower and their Fortitude Field of Expertise) instead of the normal Persuade tests.

DOOM SPENDS

- **Battlefield Behemoth:** A war elephant may spend 3 Doom to ignore a Wound.
- **Inelegant Motion:** A war elephant has a hard time changing course when running. When running, if the elephant wishes to attempt any movement except for a relatively straight line, it must pay 1 Doom and attempt an Athletics test. During this test, it cannot use its *Inhuman Brawn*.
- **Raging Charge:** After taking a Wound, spend 1 Doom and immediately perform *Raging Charge*. The elephant moves to any point within Medium range, threatening anything in its path. This inflicts 9 ♦ with the Area, Knockdown, and Stun Qualities.

KHORAJANS OF RENOWN

In the breakaway kingdom of Khoraja, beautiful princesses mix with arrogant nobles; while some scheme to return Khoraja to Koth, other seek to conqueror her anew. A small nation with many enemies, the royal court is ever aware of their precarious position.

AGHA SHUPRAS (TOUGHENED)

They say Agha Shupras has Hyrkanian blood running though his veins, so natural is he in the saddle and with the bow. This is not true, for Shupras is pure Khorajan, yet he was born to the horse. His family raised horses, among the most prized in the kingdom, and he learned the ways of mounted combat while hunting with his father. Though not of noble blood, his family has found favor with generations of kings, and thus he was able to attain leadership of the Khoraji horse archers after his exploits on the field of battle.

Shupras is quiet but sly. Since he is not a noble, he knows not to speak out of turn, yet he is observant of the varying motivations and machinations of those whose blood does run with royal gold. For his part, Agha has no interest in

rising beyond the station he has achieved. He has been a soldier for most of his life. At age 12, he entered into a local mounted archery tournament and caught the eye of a nobleman whose son he beat. The man quickly offered his family a place in his house, where Shupras became a ward. He trained, drilled, and lived the life of a rider until age 17 when he entered the Khoraji horse archers and quickly made his name.

Within Khoraja, his accuracy is unparalleled, as is his horsemanship. His men respect him, but the noble combat generals do not see him as one of their own. Count Thespides, in particular, dislikes having to consort with someone of lower birth. Yet King Khossus knows there is no man better to lead his horse archers, and thus Shupras' position remains secure.

Tactically minded, he is one of the few cavalry men in the west who have some idea how to counter the Hyrkanians and Turanians, though neither has made forays in Khoraja recently.

ATTRIBUTES

Awareness	Intelligence	Personality	Willpower
10	8	7	10
Agility		Brawn	Coordination
9		9	9

FIELDS OF EXPERTISE

Combat	3	Movement	1
Fortitude	2	Senses	1
Knowledge	—	Social	—

STRESS AND SOAK

- **Stress:** Vigor 9, Resolve 10
- **Soak:** Armor 3 (Heavy Hauberk), Courage 2

ATTACKS

- **Saber (M):** Reach 2, 4 ☠, 1H, Calvary 1, Parrying
- **Hyrkanian Horse Bow (R):** Range C, 5 ☠, 2H, Volley

SPECIAL ABILITIES

- **Expert Archer:** Shupras gains 1 bonus Momentum whenever using a bow from horseback, and can spend 1 Momentum (repeatable) to use the Secondary Target Momentum spend.
- **Horse Lord:** Shupras always attacks first when mounted. This effect cannot be canceled through Momentum spends.
- **Ride Like the Wind:** While riding on horseback, Shupras gains 4 ☠ Cover Soak and is immune to the Piercing Quality.

DOOM SPENDS

- **Animal Bond:** If a mount Shupras is riding is killed, the gamemaster may spend 2 Doom to have him automatically leap to a nearby mount and continue to act, as though he were still mounted on the same creature.

AMALRIC

Amalric is described on page 352 of the **Conan** corebook.

KING KHOSSUS OF KHORAJA (TOUGHENED)

Khossus is a young king with the limitless ambitions of his age and position. His father, the previous king, died on the throne from seeming old age, though Khossus believes the man was poisoned by foreign rivals. His father cleaved closely to ideas of honor and chivalry, which Khossus largely has abandoned. He is not duplicitous by nature, but dons such a mantle as circumstances demand.

He is well liked by the people, for he is neither too harsh nor too aloof. While he believes firmly in the divine right of kings, his father instilled in him the idea that with such power comes responsibility to the people. Khossus frames this duty in expansionist terms. To serve the people, he believes he must secure Khoraja's place as a proper kingdom and not a one-time part of Koth. The king also refuses to acknowledge that this is a land formed by common mercenaries — as did his father and his father before him. Any such talk is punishable by a lifetime in the dungeons of Khoraja City.

While Khossus fancies himself the young blood needed to lead his kingdom, he is not so clever as he imagines. His faithful counsel, Aetarus, tries to temper the king's confidence with prudence, but to little effect. While Khossus is not so rash as to take on mighty Koth or Shem, he would broker alliances and treaties which might allow him to later. His one true fear is that his blood runs with that of common dog-brothers and men of fortune. One day he, and the whole kingdom, may be found out as pretenders and overthrown. Such obsessive thoughts blind him to the plots within his own court as well as the nefarious plans of other kings. Aetarus fears the king leaves himself open to assassination or kidnapping, but cannot convince Khossus to take more precautions when traveling. To fight his own internal fear, Khossus presents himself as invulnerable to the public.

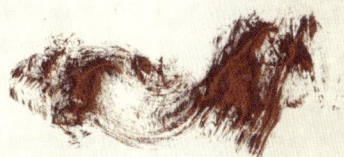

ATTRIBUTES

Awareness	Intelligence	Personality	Willpower
8	8	10	9
Agility		Brawn	Coordination
7		9	7

FIELDS OF EXPERTISE

Combat	1	Movement	—
Fortitude	3	Senses	1
Knowledge	2	Social	4

STRESS AND SOAK

- **Stress:** Vigor 9, Resolve 9
- **Soak:** Armor —, Courage 3

ATTACKS

- **Broadsword (M):** Reach 2, 6🔥, Unbalanced, Parrying
- **A King's Name (T):** Range C, 4🔥 mental, Area, Piercing 2

SPECIAL ABILITIES

- **Bold Leader:** Khossus gains +1d20 to any Social or Combat test.
- **King:** As king of Khoraja, Khossus can command the obedience of any subject and has treaties that offer him extensive reach. Any Social test that scores a success automatically grants the king 3 bonus Momentum. Characters who win any Social struggle against the king automatically trigger a Complication.

DOOM SPENDS

- **Mercenary Blood:** Though long diluted, there still runs the blood of mercenary warriors in Khossus' veins. At the cost of 2 Doom, the gamemaster may have Khossus draw upon this lineage, allowing him to deliver an extra attack. This ability can be used each turn, though it cannot be stacked.

PRINCE KUTAMUN (TOUGHENED)

Kutamun is the second son of the king of a city-state in northern Stygia. He cuts an imposing figure, standing well over six feet in height and broad of shoulder. His formative years were spent in one of the monasteries of Set, where his father sent him since the boy's destiny was not to rule. Until the age of seventeen, he genuflected before Father Set and was initiated into the ways of the priesthood. All that while, though, Kutamun was dissatisfied, feeling he'd been robbed of his rightful place in the world. His blood burned not for cold, serpentine theology but conquest.

As fate would soon engineer, he'd soon have his chance to become the man he always felt Set intended him to be — a leader of men, a warrior. His elder brother was kidnapped by rogues seeking ransom. In the attempt Kutamun's father led to rescue the boy, his brother was killed and the king severely injured. It was then that he recalled his son home where he became heir to the throne.

With his father's injuries so severe that the king could no longer face combat, Kutamun gladly took on the role as the leader of his demesne's host. He quickly made his mark with excursions into Shem, his forces marching across the Styx and dealing swift justice to the nomad clans who dared stray south into mighty Stygia. In time, his victories were not easily counted, and Cstephon himself recognized the man as one of his best. Yet Kutamun wanted more.

In his thirty-first year, Kutamun's father died of the lingering illnesses his wound engendered. At last, the son who had been initially cast aside, assumed the throne. Since that time, Kutamun has sought opportunity to make moves which might ultimately elevate the lands he now rules. Not content to suffer as subject under King Cstephon, Kutamun's court is thick with rumor that their ruler now seeks allies from without Stygia. His people are thus far behind him. Should he lead them to glorious victory, they shall laud him. Should he fail, King Cstephon will have his head — if some other foe does not sheath their blade in Kutamun's royal flesh before.

Kutamun is brave, intelligent, and ferocious. The ambition which burns inside him boils to the fore in the heady din of battle. Sometimes, he is even reckless, though this inspires his men. One day, it may get him killed, but today is not that day.

ATTRIBUTES

Awareness	Intelligence	Personality	Willpower
8	9	9	11
Agility		Brawn	Coordination
8		9	8

FIELDS OF EXPERTISE

Combat	1	Movement	1
Fortitude	1	Senses	2
Knowledge	2	Social	3

STRESS AND SOAK

- **Stress:** Vigor 9, Resolve 11
- **Soak:** Armor —, Courage 4

ATTACKS

- **Exquisite Broadsword (M):** Reach 2, 6🔥, Unbalanced, Parrying
- **Noble Fury (T):** Range C, 3🔥 mental, Fear

SPECIAL ABILITIES

- **Brutal General:** Kutamun knows every ambush spot in his domain. If at any point he can set an ambush, he gains 2 bonus Momentum on the test. The gamemaster is encouraged to use Doom spends to simulate the traps and tricks of this cunning foe (see page 274 of the **Conan** corebook for more information on traps).
- **Immune to Fear**
- **Knowledge of the Snake:** Any player character from Stygia must first pass a Daunting (D3) Discipline test or be unable to attack Kutamun.

DOOM SPENDS

- **Reckless Ambition:** Kutamun's ambition is legendary. At any time where he might gain lands, prestige, or titles he can roll +3d20 for 1 Doom point.
- **Figurehead:** Kutamun's mere presence is enough to inspire devotion. Any Stygian acting in accordance with Kutamun's schemes gains 4 🔥 Morale Soak while Kutamun is present. If Kutamun leaves a scene, any character with this effect can spend 1 Doom to maintain the effect in his absence.

AETARUS (TOUGHENED)

The many seasons of his youth far behind him, Aetarus is now in the winter of his life. It has been a life spent in service to the rulers of Khoraja and, to Aetarus' mind, its people equally. He is of an era that has past and is well aware of his creeping obsolescence. In his day, honor and glory were bedfellows. Today, rival kings resort to kidnapping other rulers and even their children. His day, Aetarus believes, was a more civilized time, and he can, when too much wine finds him, ramble about the encroaching decadence of Khoraja and the cyclized world in general.

In truth, the world has always been one of trickery, extortion, and dubious tactics, but Aetarus first became counsel to the throne under the rule of the current king's father. He was a man of principle, a soldier with a code. Aetarus was, perhaps, spoiled by serving under such a rare individual. Were he to make an honest assessment of those days, Aetarus might admit that his former king was ultimately undone by his ethics, having been killed by plotters to the throne. In the end, though, his son maintained power, and the would-be rebels were put to the sword. Aetarus personally beheaded all the nobles involved. He did so with relish.

Today, the lines of age mix with old scars, for Aetarus was once general to Khossus' father and served as a soldier to his grandfather. Experience tempered the innate brashness of youth, and he is the most trusted adviser to Khossus. Yet the younger king has new ideas and grand

> *In a hurricane of thundering steel, the lines twisted and swayed. It was war-bred noble against professional soldier. Shields crashed against shields, and between them spears drove in and blood spurted.*
>
> *Conan saw the mighty form of prince Kutamun across the sea of swords, but the press held him hard, breast to breast with dark shapes that gasped and slashed. Behind the Stygians the asshuri were surging and yelling.*
>
> — Black Colossus

ambitions — as do all scions to grand thrones. Aetarus worries over expanding the kingdom and reminds the king that mercenaries carved this land long ago, citing that the luck of nations is not an ever-full cup.

He cares for the king, but his ways are not Aetarus' ways. Likewise, he looks kindly upon the king's sister, Yasmela, but remembers the days when even noble women had the mettle to rule. Yasmela, in his estimation, is a fop, caring only for pleasure and the fineries afforded to the elite.

Ever faithful to the family, though, Aetarus shall fill out his days as duty and character demand. As his bones grow old and cold, he wraps himself ever deeper in his ermine cloak. One day, he may disappear entirely — the fate of all men who have lived beyond their time.

ATTRIBUTES

Awareness	Intelligence	Personality	Willpower
9	9	8	8

Agility	Brawn	Coordination
6	8	5

FIELDS OF EXPERTISE

Combat	2	Movement	—
Fortitude	3	Senses	1
Knowledge	3	Social	2

STRESS AND SOAK

- **Stress:** Vigor 8, Resolve 8
- **Soak:** Armor —, Courage 3

ATTACKS

- **Shortsword (M):** Reach 1, 4 🔥, 1H, Parrying
- **Steely Glare:** Range C, 2 🔥 mental, Stun
- **Powerful Reputation:** Range C, 6 🔥 mental, Stun (only against Stygians)

SPECIAL ABILITIES

- **Old General:** Aetarus gains +1d20 to any Command, Persuade, or Warfare test, and can roll up to 3d20 when aiding another in a teamwork test.
- **A Life's Learning:** Aetarus automatically generates 1 Momentum whenever making a Knowledge test.
- **Wise Counsel:** Aetarus offers sound council and can aid another character's Knowledge test with 2d20 and grant the benefit of *A Life's Learning* to that test.
- **Cynic:** When engaging in any opposed Persuade test with Aetarus, a player character must spend 1 Momentum or automatically fail the test.
- **No Treachery Surprises:** Aetarus is immune to ambushes. Any test to ambush Aetarus automatically fails and generates 1 Complication.

COUNT THESPIDES (TOUGHENED)

Black curls of hair scented like the king's garden. A pointed mustache with not a single hair out of place. Silken garb and shoes with pointed, curled toes laced with gold. One need only look, or smell, Count Thespides to know from whence he comes. He wears his affected arrogance like his velvet cape — with pride and haughtiness. Among the nobles who frequent Khossus' court, Thespides is the one who most believes in the divinity of royal blood, his own superiority, and the inferiority of the peasants.

He fancies himself a handsome man and, among civilized folk, he is. Yet under his fine clothes is a strong body, for Thespides is also leader of the storied Khoraji knights. He is, despite his meticulous grooming habits, no stranger to the ways of war.

The current king and Thespides were friends as children, and Khossus values the count's counsel almost as much as he does that of Aetarus. Where Aetarus is cautious, Thespides is bold. Where Aetarus represents the old guard, Thespides sees a new era ahead. The two men do not get along, though both feign to do so in the presence of the king.

As for the king's sister, Yasmela, Thespides is enamored. He would not call it love, but she is beautiful, her dark hair spilling over ivory shoulders like a waterfall of satin locks. His sentiments are fueled by lust, ambition, and the growing feelings Thespides has come to recognize for Yasmela. Any man of noble blood would seek the princess' hand, but Thespides genuinely cares for her. He never admits thus, nor evidences it in her presence. Indeed, he goes to some trouble to appear aloof and uncaring around her, a tactic that has not gained her favors.

While Thespides embodies a paragon of elitism and privilege, he is also a brave warrior, and takes his responsibilities as leader of the Khoraji knights seriously. He is an able commander, though his tactics are circumscribed by his attitude that his knights, being of noble blood, are naturally superior to the rabble they encounter. In time, this could be Count Thespides' undoing. That, or his love for Yasmela, which she is never liable to return.

ATTRIBUTES

Awareness	Intelligence	Personality	Willpower
9	8	8	8

Agility	Brawn	Coordination
8	9	8

FIELDS OF EXPERTISE

Combat	2	Movement	1
Fortitude	2	Senses	1
Knowledge	1	Social	3

STRESS AND SOAK

- **Stress:** Vigor 9, Resolve 8
- **Soak:** Armor 4 (Heavy Plate), Courage 2

ATTACKS

- **Saber (M):** Reach 2, 4 🔥, 1H, Cavalry 1, Parrying
- **Lance (M):** Reach 3, 5 🔥, Unbalanced, Cavalry 2, Fragile
- **Steely Glare (T):** Range C, 2 🔥 mental, Stun

SPECIAL ABILITIES

- **Grandmaster of the Knights:** The Difficulty of all Social and Combat tests is reduced by one step.
- **Unrequited Love:** Any Willpower or Discipline related rolls involving the will of Princess Yasmela have a two step penalty.

DOOM SPENDS

- **Thunderous Charge:** Thespides may spend 2 Doom on a cavalry charge, but only with the Khoraji knights.

THUGRA KHOTAN (NATOHK THE VEILED ONE) (NEMESIS)

When the Hyborians were still pulling themselves up from rude savagery, Thugra Khotan was a powerful sorcerer. In his time, he ruled the ancient city of Kuthchemes, which was older still. Thugra Khotan sought to conquer the world, and made some progress as his armies moved north. They were met by the upstart, degenerate races of the north and stopped. Thugra Khotan and his army were forced to retreat into their city.

His power was legendary, and, it is said, that he ruled Kuthchemes for the lifetimes of four mortal men before those selfsame barbarians swept south and assaulted the city. His sorcery, however potent it was, did not keep the savages from storming the gates and crawling over the walls like vermin.

As his city fell, Thugra Khotan entombed himself under the great dome at the city's center. There, he put himself into a slumber which was neither life nor death, to wait the long ages ahead until he could awaken again. He locked himself inside with an ingenious mechanism on the door. The city fell to ruin and was eventually forgotten. Apart from the fading ink of dusty scrolls, so too was Thugra Khotan.

In life, he was power hungry and lascivious. Where other wizards sought the supple flesh of young, comely women only for their value to the demons of the Outer Dark, Thugra Khotan used them to satiate his libidinous nature. There was no depravity to which Thugra Khotan was immune, and some fifty of Kuthchemes' beautiful daughters were imprisoned in his tomb — buried alive with him, a dark and savage means of prolonging the sorcerer's life for eons.

Having slept for some three thousand years, the black soul of Thugra Khotan now stirs. An inchoate thing, he appears in peripheral glances, a shadowy ink plot in corners and on ceilings. In such a form, he is known as Natohk the Veiled One — none have ever seen his face. This life force finds respite in the city of Akbatana, but reaches out to find willing minds — especially those of a worthy female.

Even for all of this, though, Natohk, and the body of Thugra Khotan in Kuthchemes, is not alive. He still slumbers, on the edge of the Outer Dark perhaps, waiting for someone to at last unlock his tomb and wake him once again. On that day, he will gather an army anew and tread the world under the demonic hooves of the nightmare mount he will summon (see page 63).

ATTRIBUTES

Awareness	Intelligence	Personality	Willpower
11 (1)	14 (1)	10 (1)	12 (1)

Agility	Brawn		Coordination
8	9		8

FIELDS OF EXPERTISE

Combat	2	Movement	1
Fortitude	2	Senses	3
Knowledge	5	Social	1

STRESS AND SOAK

- **Stress:** Vigor 11, Resolve 15
- **Soak:** Armor (Unnatural) 2, Courage 5

ATTACKS

- **Zhaibar Knife (M):** Reach 1, 5 ⚔, 1H, Unforgiving 2
- **Sorcerous Might (T):** Range M, 5 ⚔ mental, Area, Intense

SPECIAL ABILITIES

- **Inhuman Awareness 1**
- **Inhuman Intelligence 1**
- **Inhuman Personality 1**
- **Inhuman Willpower 1 Spells:** Thugra Khotan has access to any and all spells in the Sorcery section of the *Conan* corebook.
- **Inured to Fear**
- **More Powerful Than You Can Possibly Imagine:** Thugra Khotan is a sorcerer of impossible potency and resilience. Any spell cast against him is one step more Difficult than normal.

DOOM SPENDS

- **More than Human:** At the cost of 6 Doom, Thugra Khotan can ignore all damage inflicted upon him for that turn.

PRINCESS YASMELA (TOUGHENED)

Minstrels beyond the borders of Khoraja sing of Yasmela, such a beauty is she. Ivory skin, dark locks of hair, eyes that smolder with seductive intent — there are few men who do not feel a stirring inside when first their eyes set upon her. Yasmela, for her part, is well aware of that, and enjoys such attention. As the most comely of princesses, she can have any man she wants, but none have yet to spark more than a fortnight's interest.

Spoiled, Yasmela enjoys a life largely inside the palace walls with her handmaidens. They loll about in lotus-induced ecstasy, having not a care in the world. It is very easy for persons of purpose and will to dismiss her and, superficially, they are right to do so.

Yet Yasmela has in her something of her royal line — the ability to lead. It has never been tested, and she would not think of herself as any sort of leader. Her quiet moments, though, bring thoughts of dissatisfaction with her empty life. She has not a care in the world. Everything a woman could want is brought before her by supplicants... and yet this is not enough. She watches her brother, inconspicuously, as he makes the decisions which forge history. While she has not the desire to make those same decisions, she does feel there is some greater purpose to her life than pleasure and comfort. Still, when such thoughts leap to mind unbidden, lethargy and lotus smoke quickly consign them to the corners of her mind.

Yasmela is aware that Count Thespides loves her, but she would never return his feelings. He reminds her too much of herself, that part of her which she secretly loathes — the entitlement and lack of genuine purpose. Such is her lot, though. It is only when she speaks to Mitra at his long-forsaken temple that she ever voices any of these nagging thoughts aloud. This worship of Mitra, though idle, is itself a rebellion. The people of Khoraja have long since turned to Ishtar and Shemitish gods. Mitra worship has not been practiced for centuries. What Yasmela thinks she might gain from speaking with a deity her people have abandoned is unclear... even to the princess herself.

ATTRIBUTES

Awareness	Intelligence	Personality	Willpower
8	9	11	8
Agility	**Brawn**		**Coordination**
6	6		6

FIELDS OF EXPERTISE

Combat	—	Movement	—
Fortitude	—	Senses	—
Knowledge	1	Social	4

STRESS AND SOAK

- **Stress:** Vigor 6, Resolve 8
- **Soak:** Armor —, Courage 3

ATTACKS

- **Ceremonial Dagger:** Reach 1, 4 🗡, 1H, Fragile
- **The Power of the Imperial Name (T):** Range C, 4 🗡, Stun, Vicious 1

SPECIAL ABILITIES

- **Rare Beauty:** Yasmela is instantly recognizable as one of the few great beauties of the age. Her beauty invites compliment and entreats others to kneel where obedience to the royal name does not. If Yasmela fails a Social test, she can re-roll any d20 that did not generate a success.
- **Princess of Khoraja:** Yasmela can command the obedience of any subject. Any Social test that scores a success automatically grants Yasmela 3 bonus Momentum.

DOOM SPENDS

- **Distraction:** Yasmela can completely dominate any room she enters. When Yasmela enters a scene, or is first revealed, she can spend 2 Doom to force all characters to make a Simple (D0) Discipline test. Before any character acts they must pay 3 Doom. If the characters score any Momentum, this decreases their Doom cost by 1 Doom for each point of Momentum.
- **Sixth Sense for the Outer Dark:** Yasmela can spend 1 Doom to detect any entity of the Outer Dark within Medium range or 2 Doom to detect any entity within Extreme range.

KOTHIANS OF RENOWN

Koth… a kingdom on the rise with a king who eyes those lands around him as territory that will one day be his. Her wars are fought by both native troops and fearsome mercenary companies, while, in the capital city of Khorshemish, two rival wizards war for the real power behind the throne.

It is a land of soldiers, mystics, and slaves. Some notable examples appear below.

PRINCE ALMURIC OF KOTH (TOUGHENED)

To say Koth is a fractious kingdom is to understate the conditions found there. Penurious Strabonus squeezes the lords of his realm with heavy taxes and demands conscription for his imperial aims. Under such stresses, some men snap while others rebel. Prince Almuric, ruler of an eastern city-state, is of suitable mettle that he does not break.

Raised by a father loyal to the crown, despite the foolishness of those Kothic kings, it may well be that Almuric's father instilled in his son the seeds of rebellion. While he openly raised the boy as an adherent to the divine right of kings, he secretly taught him of the older kings of Koth and the willful sons of Bori who founded their kingdom. There was, his father maintained, a nobility and indomitability running through Kothic veins. While they bent knee to Strabonus, they would only respect and truly follow a strong man.

Such was Almuric's father's belief in the monarchy that he himself could not condone revolt. Many times, young Almuric saw other princes, barons, and counts approach his father asking him to join their cause. His father always refused. Almuric knew one day, when he assumed his father's place, he would not refuse.

Upon his father's death, Almuric began cementing friendships and alliances he intended to later use to usurp the throne in Khorshemish. That, though, would take time. In the meanwhile, Almuric amassed a reputation as a wise ruler and brave leader of men. No shrinking violet, Almuric led from the front, charging into battle as the spear-point of that deadly host he helped forge into the sharpest of spears. This only inspired greater loyalty in his men but, even though they were devoted to him, Almuric knew there was not enough of them.

He has thus spent recent years testing various mercenary companies and making friends with the captains of those grim soldiers. He is nearly ready to assemble an army of dog-brothers and lead them against the crown. Yet, Almuric is indeed as wise as his people say. He understands that Strabonus, a thoroughly ambitious and relentless king, is not the one who makes the decisions for Koth. It is the wizard, Tsotha-lanti who truly rules from the Scarlet Citadel. The red tower dwarfs the palace in height. This is no accident. To take the throne, Almuric must need deal with Strabonus and Tsotha-lanti alike. There is no shortage of peasants in Koth who would wish him success in that endeavor would that they knew his plans.

ATTRIBUTES

Awareness	Intelligence	Personality	Willpower
9	10	12	12
Agility		Brawn	Coordination
10		10	10

FIELDS OF EXPERTISE

Combat	3	Movement	—
Fortitude	3	Senses	1
Knowledge	1	Social	3

STRESS AND SOAK

- **Stress:** Vigor 10, Resolve 12
- **Soak:** Armor 4 (Plate), Courage 4

ATTACKS

- **Broadsword (M):** Reach 2, 7🗡, Unbalanced, Parrying
- **Spear (M):** Range 3, 6🗡, Unbalanced, Piercing 1
- **Leader of the Host (T):** Range C, 6🗡 mental

SPECIAL ABILITIES

- **Rebel Prince:** All Willpower tests are made at +1d20.
- **Enemy of Strabonus:** Any test to thwart Strabonus gains +1d20.

DOOM SPENDS

- **Mercenaries at Hand:** When in his palace, Almuric can spend 2 Doom to summon the aid of two Squads of four Kothic knights (see page 56).

GENERAL ARBANUS (TOUGHENED)

Arbanus is the head of Koth's army, and loyal follower of King Strabonus. He grew up in the Kothian hills on his father's demesne. His father, a minor noble, had three sons, of which Arbanus was the youngest. Military service was drawn for him in the stars long before his birth.

Where his eldest brother would inherit his father's title, Arbanus knew he would only distinguish himself on the field of battle. An ambitious boy, he led charges head on as a mere captain. Again and again, he charged headlong into the fray, his men inspired to frenzy behind him and, mostly, won. Those foes who did beat him, he visited tenfold vengeance upon as soon as he was able to do so.

Often, these enemies were foreign invaders — incursions from the other Hyborian nations being common. However, Kothians are an ill-tempered lot when a strong king sits upon the throne and, with the crowning of Strabonus, strength had indeed returned to the capital of Khorshemish. Before long, rebellions among the city-states became common and Arbanus, never dull of wit, realized he could curry favor with the king by putting down such revolts.

Quickly, he gained a reputation for devastating tactics and savage punishments inflicted upon any who betrayed the king. His cruelty to such treasonous rabble became legendary, earning him the name Arbanus the Impaler. Fields of dying men, wailing in the dusk, became as wine to him. Arbanus would lay down his life for any loyal man, but has no mercy for those who have not an ounce of fidelity inside them.

As his reputation grew, Strabonus took interest in his career, and Arbanus moved from local general, to castellan, to commander of the Royal Army of Koth. He remains the military commander of all Koth's forces today.

His loyalty to Strabonus is unwavering, but Arbanus has no love for the wizard Tsotha-lanti who manipulates the king behind the scenes. As a soldier, he should like to cut the beating heart from the vulture-like wizard. As a man of keen intellect, he knows that Tsotha-lanti commands forces from the Outer Dark and makes pacts with old gods whose very names drive men mad. One day, Arbanus is certain, Strabonus will make his move against the sorcerer. On that day, Arbanus will fight with him back to back.

ATTRIBUTES

Awareness	Intelligence	Personality	Willpower
8	11	13	9
Agility		Brawn	Coordination
9		10	8

FIELDS OF EXPERTISE

Combat	2	Movement	1
Fortitude	3	Senses	1
Knowledge	1	Social	1

STRESS AND SOAK

- **Stress:** Vigor 10, Resolve 9
- **Soak:** Armor 4 (Plate), Courage 4

ATTACKS

- **Spear (M):** Reach 3, 4 🟊, Unbalanced, Piercing 1
- **Sword (M):** Reach 2, 4 🟊, 1H, Parrying
- **You Stand Before Arbanus! (T):** Range C, 7 🟊 mental, Stun

SPECIAL ABILITIES

- **Brutal General:** Arbanus knows every ambush spot in his domain. If at any point he can set an ambush, he gains 2 bonus Momentum on the test. The gamemaster is encouraged to use Doom spends to simulate the traps and tricks of this cunning foe (see **Conan** page 274 for more information on traps).

DOOM SPENDS

- **Horrible Fate:** Any who face Arbanus know a dire fate awaits them. At the start of combat, Arbanus grants one last offer of clemency. At this point he can spend 1–3 Doom to gain Fear 1–3 for that round.
- **Master of Strategy:** In the first turn of combat Arbanus can spend 2 Doom to inflict 3 🟊 casualties on enemy minions. Arbanus can sacrifice X minions in addition to this to roll an additional X 🟊 in casualties. Arbanus can re-roll any 🟊 that fails to roll damage.

ATALIS (TOUGHENED)

With his shaved head and lithe limbs which lack an ounce of fat, Atalis is often taken to be an ascetic or the monk of a local god. He isn't quite either, though the former would be closer to his disposition. As a younger man, Atalis lacked the composure and sobriety which mark him today. He was a thief, and a very good one at that. However, the Corinthian pushed the fates farther than he should have and he was caught stealing not only the gold belonging to a princess of Brythunia, but also her purity.

Atalis was condemned to torture and then a slow death in a gibbet along the port of the city whose king and princess he had disgraced. The torture rendered Atalis cripple, and the gibbet took the last of his will to live. His one good hand

had not the rudimentary tools to pick the lock and, if they had, where does a man who can only walk with effort run to?

No, he was to die and accepted that. Atalis was bright, perhaps too bright for his own good, and he had long come to accept that the gods, should they even exist, care not about the affairs of men — be they king or lowly scoundrel. The days went by. The vultures sat atop his cage, eying the meal to come.

Then the city was sacked by Corinthia. It seems the very princess he defiled was betrothed to the Corinithian heir and, after the incident, one insult led to another until the two kingdoms were at war. The irony was not lost on Atalis, for the very acts which caused him to linger so near death also provided the means for his resurrection. When the Corinthians came, they swept clean the city and looted it. They took the spoils of war... but anyone who was on the bad side of their enemy, such as prisoners, might not be all bad.

Atalis was released. With only one good hand and one good leg, though, he wasn't soon to thieve again. Instead, one of the Corinthians — a scholar — took pity on him and made Atalis his scribe. In but a few short years, Atalis'

knowledge exceeded even that of his master, such was his memory. Philosophy, theology, and the numbers locked in the stars which govern all things became more prized than jewels and gold to Atalis. There was not a book he did not voraciously consume. In time, his master sent Atalis to his superiors in Vendhya, where he studied for years.

He had become a new man — almost. Atalis still had in him the spirit of the rogue, and he found himself in a situation not dissimilar to the one that nearly killed him in Brythunia. This time, though, it was not a simple ascetic that spared him, but the son of a king. Prince Than of Yaralet had come to know Atalis and value his counsel. When the situation in Vendhya began to encroach on Atalis, Prince Than took him from that country to Koth. He has been in Yaralet since, some three years. Something haunts the city and the people within. Atalis' knowledge is vast, and he begins to suspect the truth of the city's situation. When Prince Than is ready, Atalis will be at his side. The philosopher only hopes his knowledge is enough to defend against creatures from the void. His hopes are not very high. Atalis has always been realistic — from the gibbet to the grave.

ATTRIBUTES

Awareness	Intelligence	Personality	Willpower
11	13	11	11

Agility	Brawn	Coordination
6	8	7

FIELDS OF EXPERTISE

Combat	1	Movement	—
Fortitude	3	Senses	3
Knowledge	4	Social	2

STRESS AND SOAK

- **Stress:** Vigor 8, Resolve 11
- **Soak:** Armor —, Courage 3

ATTACKS

- **Ritual Dagger (M):** Reach 1, 3 🔱, Hidden 1, Thrown, Unforgiving 1
- **Knowledge of Beyond (T):** Range 2, 4 🔱 mental, Fearsome 1

SPECIAL ABILITIES

- **Survivor:** Atalis can roll +2d20 on all Fortitude, Survival, and Social tests.
- **Studied Familiar:** When spells are cast outside of combat, he can grant 2d20 to assist the test.

DOOM SPENDS

- **Arcane Knowledge:** Atalis can spend 1 Doom to use *Studied Familiar* in combat.
- **Hunter of Demons:** Atalis can spend 1 Doom to gain Vicious 1 against Horrors.

CAPTAIN KAEL (TOUGHENED)

Few in the Hyborian Age shall ever be remembered. Men and women alike squander their lives, toil for masters they will never know, and in the end, are remembered only in the minds of those who share that fate. Kael took his name from a tale told him as a child, the story of an epic hero of Koth. The tale itself was one minstrels fancied for a time, but had since fallen out of favor.

What his real name is, he tells no one. He is, he claims, a former knight of Koth, granted such title by the king himself after rescuing his cousin. This is almost certainly not true. Many things Kael says may not be true. That's how legends grow, after all.

What is true is the following: the man can fight and has near single-handedly won several battles. Now in his 40s, he made his name early — heaped in gore and knee deep in mud and blood. Other accounts are likely spurious, but

enough mercenaries remember him of old. Today, nearly everyone in the profession of arms knows his name for he is captain of the White Company.

The White Company is a host of mercenaries (see page 93) that changed the tide of history in Argos. For some two decades, they fought for one city-state after another, losing but one battle in 30. Eventually, Kael became a king-maker himself, so powerful were his troops and so dependent the princes upon them.

Retirement was not for him. Seated deep in his heart is the want of glory. Despite the fame of the White Company's banner, Kael carries two reputations before him which need no standard — that of supreme martial prowess and total disregard for death. "The Crazy Kael" his men call him… his enemies likewise.

ATTRIBUTES

Awareness	Intelligence	Personality	Willpower
9	10	12	12

Agility	Brawn	Coordination
11	11	10

FIELDS OF EXPERTISE

Combat	4	Movement	1
Fortitude	3	Senses	2
Knowledge	2	Social	2

STRESS AND SOAK

- **Stress:** Vigor 11, Resolve 12
- **Soak:** Armor 4 (Plate), Courage 3

ATTACKS

- **Two-handed Sword (M):** Reach 3, 7 🔱, 2H, Vicious 1
- **Lance (M):** Reach 3, 6 🔱, Unbalanced, Cavalry 2, Fragile
- **Famed Knight (T):** Range C, 4 🔱 mental, Stun, Intense

SPECIAL ABILITIES

- **Legendary Knight:** Captain Kael eschews joining Squads in favor of self-sufficiency. When facing an opponent, Kael rolls as many dice to Parry as his enemy has rolled to attack him. He adds +1d20 to any attack against Mobs or Squads.

DOOM SPENDS

- **Flee Now!:** When facing Mobs or Squads, Kael can spend X Doom to Intimidate X number of Minions into fleeing rather than face him.

NATALA (TOUGHENED)

Brythunian women are known for their beauty — it is renowned throughout the continent and, wherever lusty men are found, their many charms are eulogized with song and laughter. To say Natala is beautiful, even for a Brythunian, is to say something indeed. Yet her beauty has given her life no advantage for her family, poor peasants indebted to the local lord; they sold her into slavery when she was on the cusp of womanhood.

From one cruel hand to the next, Natala was traded like any commodity until she landed in Shem. There, a petty pimp in Shumir bought her at a bargain from a Shemite slaver, who had lost a small fortune gambling with the pimp. The pimp did not treat her well. Two years she spent with him, enduring the cruelties of his appetite. She became his favored girl in the stable, and he assured her that was why she received the best treatment. At last, tired of his cruelty, Natala snatched a knife from the pimp's belt as he stalked toward her and repaid him for his malice. She ran that night from the small, squalid brothel she had been thrust into, covered in the blood of her former master.

Emotional by nature, Natala is also unaccustomed to watching out for herself. Despite feeling her beauty is the totality of her value, Natala possesses a keen mind and a surprising instinct for survival. She is brave, loyal, and capable of enduring great pain and suffering without complaint. After her flight through the darkness, away from the pimp she had slaughtered, she quickly found herself recaptured — not that, at the time, she cared much. The unexpected guilt which flooded her after she committed the murder left her beset by confusion and panic, and she let herself be taken without much of a fight. Her beauty saved her from too much mistreatment in her new bondage, as did the air she now possessed of self-reliance, of a willingness to do anything to survive. While some around her chafe at the chains around their throats and others submit, brokenly, Natala simply waits, knowing that her opportunity for freedom will come. Her life may be circumscribed by the will of the slaver who owns her, but she is free from the grip of cruel men, and ready to pursue freedom when it presents itself. Fragile, delicate, and graceful Natala may well be, but there is an inner steel within her, which any who test may end up cutting themselves upon.

ATTRIBUTES			
Awareness	Intelligence	Personality	Willpower
6	9	10	9
Agility		Brawn	Coordination
7		7	7

FIELDS OF EXPERTISE			
Combat	—	Movement	—
Fortitude	2	Senses	1
Knowledge	1	Social	2

STRESS AND SOAK

- **Stress:** Vigor 7, Resolve 9
- **Soak:** Armor —, Courage 2

ATTACKS

- **Improvised Bludgeon (M):** Reach 1, 3 ◈, 2H, Stun, Knockdown
- **Eyes of the Vengeful Slave (T):** Range C, 4 ◈ mental, Stun

SPECIAL ABILITIES

- **Seductress:** When attempting a seduction, Natala gains +2d20s to her Personality test.
- **Brythunian Looks:** Natala can add +1d20 to any Social tests where her looks might aid her in influencing another.

DOOM SPENDS

- **Looks Can Be Deceiving:** If the gamemaster has spent Doom to use the *Spare Me* special ability (below), at the cost of 2 Doom, Natala may make a free attack for every failure rolled by her attacker. Even if the attacker passes the test, the attacks may still be made should one or more dice show a failure.
- **Spare Me:** For X Doom, Natala can cause anyone to rethink harming her. A (DX) Discipline test is required for anyone to do her violence. This can be combined with *Looks Can Be Deceiving*, as listed above. Note that this doesn't mean she'll be allowed to avoid combat, just that her opponent will use Non-lethal and Grappling abilities where possible.

PELIAS (NEMESIS)

The smile of a sorcerer is always a mask hiding the absence of humanity beneath. Pelias' mask is practiced and, to those whose senses are not keen, entirely believable. For those able to see beneath this benign surface, though, Pelias' smile is that of an alien creature dressed in a suit of human flesh. Is Pelias actually a demon? No one can say for certain, but he has dealt with demons and gods long enough that perhaps the difference is no longer clear.

Outwardly, he is far more genial than his arch-nemesis Tsotha-lanti. How the two men first came to know each other is the subject of rumor. Some men say they were friends in the days of Acheron. Others claim they are demon brothers set upon the Earth by their father, a god of the Outer Dark. Both men have encouraged such whispers.

In truth, it is far more likely that these two sorcerers are simply free of conscience and beyond mortal reason. Both wield enormous power. To look into their soul causes terror even in the sons of Set. Anything which frightens the scion of an old god should be avoided by any who consider themselves sane.

For at least two generations, Pelias struggled against his rival for control of Khorshemish. While it is popularly believed that both men wanted the throne of Koth, a few learned men believe that they seek something inherent to the city itself. The throne is but a means to something else — raw eldritch power, world conquest, or godhood.

Whatever their mutually exclusive aims, Tsotha-lanti is destined to get the better of Pelias, at least for a time. But any man — or demon — as powerful as Pelias may not be dealt with permanently. Tsotha-lanti's tastes run toward humiliating his enemy rather than killing them quickly. Pelias is not a being one should toy with.

ATTRIBUTES

Awareness	Intelligence	Personality	Willpower
12 (1)	14 (1)	10 (1)	12 (1)
Agility		Brawn	Coordination
10		10	10

FIELDS OF EXPERTISE

Combat	2	Movement	3
Fortitude	4	Senses	5
Knowledge	7	Social	3

STRESS AND SOAK

- **Stress:** Vigor 14, Resolve 17
- **Soak:** Armor 2 (Unnatural), Courage 4

ATTACKS

- **Hidden Talons (M):** Reach 1, 6 💀, Vicious 1
- **Threat of Sorcery (T):** Range C, 5 💀 mental, Stun, Area

SPECIAL ABILITIES

- **Fear 2:** Only against supernatural creatures
- **Inhuman Awareness 1**
- **Inhuman Intelligence 1**
- **Inhuman Personality 1**
- **Inhuman Willpower 1**
- **Patron**
- **Sorcerer:** Pelias has many spells at his disposal, including *Summon a Horror* and *Form of a Beast*. The gamemaster should assume that Pelias has access to any spell he might need.

DOOM SPENDS

- **Supernatural Presence:** For 1 Doom, Pelias can make Threaten Actions against creatures *Inured to Fear*.

KING STRABONUS OF KOTH (TOUGHENED)

Strabonus the Penurious, as his subjects call him, ascended to the throne at age 28 after the sudden death of his father. Strabonus was his only son, though he does have two sisters. The early life of young Strabonus was, like most royals, spent in the company of nannies and tutors. His father made little time for his children, but Strabonus watched him with interest.

Always sharp of mind, Strabonus often out-argued his tutors on points of logic and politics. He consumed the Nemedian Chronicles and other histories voraciously. By the time he was a teenager, Strabonus concluded that his father's rule was weak. Instead of ruling by fear and intimidation, Strabonus' father ruled by treaty, secret deals, and appeasement. The rebellious kingdom, during his father's tenure, was sated by low taxes and public works. It also lacked vision.

Strabonus studiously listened to his father once the elder king brought him into the fold. By that point, however, Strabonus took nearly all his father's teaching as examples of how not to rule a kingdom. His sisters, too, sided with Strabonus and had goals of their own. When the king died suddenly, rumors of poisoning rode on whispering winds throughout the court of Khorshemish, but no one ever came out and accused Strabonus or his sisters of assassination. It was never proven that the king died by unnatural means, but he had been a healthy man.

The moment Strabonus felt the crown upon his brow, Koth changed. Low taxes and appeasement were cast aside in favor of squeezing the people to pay for an increasingly large army, supplemented by mercenaries. Under Strabonus' guidance, Koth conducted campaigns against neighboring kingdoms, but the people quickly tired of his taxes, to say nothing of his wars.

Now, Strabonus finds himself having to put down rebellions rather than conduct conquests. Rather than expand, Koth must first secure itself into a proper, obedient kingdom. The naked ambition Strabonus brought to the throne has revisited him in the form of rebellious princes and lords.

What is worse, ten years ago, the long-running feud between two sorcerers came to an end when Tsotha-lanti defeated his nemesis, Pelias, and imprisoned him in the Scarlet Citadel — which sprang from the soil in a single day and night. With his rival dispatched, Tsotha-lanti at last turned his attention on the throne. The sorcerer's fell power struck fear in Strabonus. It was clear who held the reigns of Koth now.

Strabonus chafes under the yoke of this unnatural master. He will not suffer it indefinitely, but he has yet to find a way of dealing with a man who makes pacts with demons. Once he does, though, Strabonus will send the meddling wizard to the House of Shades and reclaim the power that is rightfully his.

ATTRIBUTES

Awareness	Intelligence	Personality	Willpower
9	9	10	12
Agility		Brawn	Coordination
7		8	8

FIELDS OF EXPERTISE

Combat	1	Movement	1
Fortitude	1	Senses	3
Knowledge	4	Social	5

STRESS AND SOAK

- **Stress:** Vigor 8, Resolve 12
- **Soak:** Armor 2 (Royal Robes), Courage 1

ATTACKS

- **The Royal Sword (M):** Reach 2, 4⚡, 1H, Parrying
- **Shield (M):** Range 2, 2⚡, 1H, Knockdown, Shield 2
- **The Royal Name (T):** Range C, 4⚡ mental, Stun

SPECIAL ABILITIES

- **Respected King:** As king, he can command the obedience of any subject and has treaties that offer him extensive reach. Any Social test that scores a success automatically grants the king 2 bonus Momentum. Characters that win any Social struggle against the king automatically trigger two Complications. Tsotha-lanti is immune to this ability.

DOOM SPENDS

- **Coffers Full of Taxes:** Strabonus has a fully equipped army ready to take any order. By paying 3 Doom, the king can instantly summon an army of guards. Six Mobs of 5 guards in mail with spears and heavy shields will arrive every round.

ATTRIBUTES

Awareness	Intelligence	Personality	Willpower
11	11	14	10
Agility		Brawn	Coordination
8		10	8

FIELDS OF EXPERTISE

Combat	2	Movement	1
Fortitude	2	Senses	2
Knowledge	3	Social	5

STRESS AND SOAK

- **Stress:** Vigor 10, Resolve 10
- **Soak:** Armor 3 (Mail), Courage 3

ATTACKS

- **Sword (M):** Reach 2, 6🔥, 1H, Parrying
- **Shield (M):** Reach 2, 4🔥, 1H, Knockdown, Shield 2
- **Passionate Rage (T):** Reach 1, 7⚫ mental, Stun

SPECIAL ABILITIES

- **Enemy of Strabonus:** Any test to thwart Strabonus gains +1d20.

DOOM SPENDS

- **The Love of Yaralet:** Prince Than is never without allies in Yaralet. By Spending 1 Doom, he can summon a Squad of five guards (see pages 306 and 317 of the **Conan** corebook) that will happily come to his rescue. While in Than's presence, these commoners are *Inured to Fear*.

PRINCE THAN OF YARALET (TOUGHENED)

A striking figure with handsome, square-cut features, Prince Than looks the very role of king. His father, who rarely now ventures forth from the palace, once looked as mighty as his son. Than is the face of the monarchy, and the people love him. He is strong and wise, and looks as if the velvet cap and filigreed pantaloons he wears are slight embarrassments to him. In fact, they are. He would rather dress plainly, for Than is that rarest of Kothic gems — a genuine man of the people.

However, the people of Yaralet are in the grip of something sinister. They bolt their doors at night and hide in their homes, hoping the creature known colloquially as "The Black Charioteer" does not find them. At Yaralet's heart is a deep, old rot which no man nor woman speaks of. Even Prince Than's father will not offer counsel as to what it is that stalks the city and why.

The day-to-day affairs of the city are overseen by Than himself, though his father still makes all decisions of consequence. Than, for his part, keeps the counsel of one Atalis as close as that of his royal viziers. Atalis (see page 74) is not the sort a prince should consort with.

No citizen is blind to the fact that Yaralet is in decline. The worst has not yet hit, but the city's economy and influence wane. Prince Than's most heartfelt goal is to bring his city back to the golden age it once enjoyed. The Kothic people are on the rise. Than will not sit idly by and let Yaralet be left behind.

Than dislikes King Strabonus with the fire of Anu's own forge. The King of Koth is tyrannical, merciless, and singularly ambitious. However, Than agrees with the king that Kothians are destined to rule the western world. Also, Than is not currently in a position to make any move against Strabonus.

But the prince is young. He will restore Yaralet to its place as one of the gems of empire and, after that, turn his eye to Strabonus himself.

TSOTHA-LANTI (NEMESIS)

When one speaks of the inhuman nature and cruel deviltry of sorcerers, Tsotha-lanti's name embodies all the whispered fears of mortal men. His library of forbidden knowledge houses books bound in the skin of men he's flayed alive. In the dark pit of the Scarlet Citadel — of which the poet Rinaldo composed maddened, terrifying verses — Tsotha-lanti experiments on humans, turning them into frightful caricatures of life. He is without conscience and without restraint.

For many years, perhaps even centuries, Tsotha-lanti and his rival Pelias vied for power. A decade ago, however, Tsotha-lanti managed to defeat and imprison Pelias. Since that time, Tsotha-lanti has secretly ruled Koth, manipulating the people and forcing King Strabonus to do his bidding. This earthly power, though, is not enough to slake Tsotha-lanti's thirst. It is the Outer Dark which truly calls him, and he intends to visit every horror found there upon the world of men.

In appearance, Tsotha-lanti is lean, predatory, and striking. His face might be compared to a bird of prey were there any mortal bird so completely evil in its mien. His eyes are black — an inky dark that truly does reflect what is left of his soul. The better portion of that soul has been bartered to demons in return for knowledge which corrupted him. Yet, one should not misunderstand — Tsotha-lanti was never someone trustworthy, noble, or good. Whatever corruption his dealings with the Outer Dark has brought him, they merely pushed a debased, evil man further away from anything recognizably human.

It has been said that no wizard is truly human, but Tsotha-lanti is an extreme example. While his body is that of a man, no one looking upon him would mistake him for anything other than a perversion. He is powerful in the extreme, but knows the bounds of the very magic he wields. He supplements his sorcerous knowledge with trickery and treachery. He is possessed of a ring which harbors a secret needle ready to deliver an extract of purple lotus to his victims. This poison causes temporary paralysis in even the strongest of men. Various powders, too, are kept about his person to dress up rituals for the benefit of simpletons and fools.

Do not mistake any of these parlor tricks for the extent of Tsotha-lanti's reach. The demons and Great Old Ones taught him things few men could know. He rules from his Scarlet Citadel over the powerful kingdom of Koth, but his plans extend to the entirety of the world.

ATTRIBUTES

Awareness	Intelligence	Personality	Willpower
11 (1)	13 (1)	9 (1)	13 (1)

Agility		Brawn		Coordination
10		9		10

FIELDS OF EXPERTISE

Combat	1	Movement	1
Fortitude	2	Senses	4
Knowledge	5	Social	2

STRESS AND SOAK

- **Stress:** Vigor 11, Resolve 16
- **Soak:** Armor 2 (Reinforced Robes), Courage 3

ATTACKS

- **Hidden Talons (M):** Reach 1, 6 ⚔, Vicious 1
- **Threat of Sorcery (T):** Reach 2, 4 ⚔ mental, Stun, Area

SPECIAL ABILITIES

- **Fear 2:** Only against supernatural creatures.
- **Inhuman Awareness 1**
- **Inhuman Intelligence 1**
- **Inhuman Personality 1**
- **Inhuman Willpower 1**
- **Patron**
- **Sorcerer:** Tsotha-lanti has many spells at his disposal, including *Summon a Horror* and *Enslave*. The gamemaster should assume that he has access to any spell he might need.

DOOM SPENDS

- **Power Behind the Throne:** Tsotha-lanti gains +2d20 when trying to convince the king to act in any way.
- **Supernatural Presence:** For 1 Doom, he can make Threaten Act ions against creatures *Inured to Fear*.

HITHER CAME CONAN...

> "A short life and a merry one, say I — and with Conan the Throat-slitter in command, life is likely to be both merry and short."
>
> — Amalric, "Black Colossus"

His formative years in the barbaric north and the vagaries of the thieving life are behind him, periods addressed in *Conan the Barbarian* and *Conan the Thief*. After his roguish exploits, he took to his nature, that of a man born on the battlefield. His savage ferocity had yet to be tempered with the discipline of organized warfare and, where he first sought only coin in exchange for his sword-arm, he found the tactic of civilized warfare to his liking.

His naturally keen mind, coupled with the barbaric fury in his heart, grasped this new kind of warfare — something beyond raids and fort assaults — as naturally as his hand did a blade. Starting as just one soldier among many, Conan soon distinguished himself among the ranks, sometimes rising to command by strength of will or fortune of circumstance.

It is during these days as a mercenary commander that Conan gains a taste for leading men. In his future, he'll try to weld desperate wastrels and raiders into terrifying armies, all on the way to the throne of the mightiest kingdom in the dreaming west.

YARALET

Conan's knack for survival finds him the last man of a slain mercenary company. Stalking the dead like the carrion picking at their flesh, Conan's thieving ways set him to looking for valuables. There are none to be had, for the other mercenaries and camp followers had already stripped the dead.

Bleeding from a gash in his thigh, he stumbles upon a wounded girl he thinks is dying. Yet there is still life in her and, true to his nature, Conan refuses to leave a helpless woman behind. Hefting her over one shoulder, he heads for the crimson-stained river upon whose shores the doomed battle ended. A city lies along the end of this river, and an adventure that the scholars of Nemedia, in all their thoroughness, record only hints of.

BLACK COLOSSUS

Serving in the army of Khoraja as a sell-sword, Conan's life takes a fortunate turn when the king's sister, Yasmela, who serves as queen while the king is held captive by the Ophireans, follows a divine vision and puts the outlander barbarian in charge of her entire army. Predictably, the nobles and commanders receive Conan's promotion poorly, but Yasmela believes it is this bronze-skinned Northman alone who can defeat the 3,000-year-old menace of a wizard, Thugra Khotan.

Despite the interference of Khoraja's professional commanders, Conan defeats Thugra Khotan's army and the seemingly ageless wizard himself. Without Conan, Khoraja would have fallen and, quite possibly, the rest of the West.

IRON SHADOWS IN THE MOON

Conan's first effort to join the dread kozaki raiders sees him forming a mighty force comprising the Free Companion mercenaries, who he now leads, and the new wastrels of the Turanian steppes and deserts.

Conan's success so angers Shah Amurath, that the man worries he must either have Conan's head or the king of Turan will have his. He ambushes Conan and his men on the reedy shoreline of the Vilayet where, through treachery and overwhelming numbers, Conan faces defeat. However, he again survives where those around him do not, and happens upon the Shah in the reeds. After the clash of steel, Amurath begs for quarter. Having seen no quarter offered to his slain men, Conan butchers the Shah into a heap of gore. Witnessing this is a slave girl, who Conan at first terrifies. Again, a lady in need is not someone the Cimmerian will easily turn his back upon, and the two flee to a nearby island in the Vilayet Sea.

There, Conan and the slave girl, Olivia, encounter the remains of a green stone city, which will become a recurring find in Conan's wanderings. This city has but one hall remaining largely intact and, inside are found iron statues of such realism, that no society could now produce.

In the moonlight, these iron men return to life, as was the intent of their ages-dead master. Pirates from the Red Brotherhood land on the isle. Conan, having some experience with them, slays their captain, and eventually becomes their new commander when the crew is ravaged by the living statues. Conan has lost his first army, but he gains a pirate crew and a taste for the sea. This then leads one day to the love of his life, and the tragedy that follows.

XUTHAL OF THE DUSK

Conan joins Almuric, a rebel prince of Koth, in his war against King Strabonus. Yet the rebel army in which Conan serves is defeated and forced to push south through Stygia, and even Kush, until the Kothic army catches up with them.

In the whirling, bloody massacre that follows, Conan takes off on a camel with Natala, a Brythunian slave girl. They push into the deserts south and, near death, come upon a city that could well be a mirage for all its strangeness.

There, Conan encounters the strangeness of super-science, upon which Xuthal is founded. Its people lay in delirium, in dream-haunted slumber, while their every need is provided by the city itself. How this works, Conan cannot understand, though a Stygian woman, Thalis, attempts to explain it to him.

From her, he learns something more important — a terror from the Outer Dark stalks Xuthal. Conan eventually faces the beast, but is battered to within a breath of his own demise. At the last moment, he finds what he believes is

the monstrosity's head and, wounding it, drives it into a seemingly fathomless pit. The golden elixir given to the horribly wounded Cimmerian later miraculously heals all his wounds. This adventure behind him, he leaves the strange city on one horizon as his wanderlust takes him toward the other.

CONAN THE MERCENARY

Now a professional soldier, and sometimes leader of armies, Conan matches savagery with skill, talent with tactics. He is no longer the rude outcast of his youth, but understands civilization — even while his nature clashes with it. All the honor of most civilized men could fit into a forepaw of a Cimmerian rabbit.

Having learned the treachery of soft, city-bred enemies, Conan gains wisdom and a facility for deviousness that rivals the master viziers in the great courts of the West. Still, Conan is young and comparatively still inexperienced next to the generals he fights for and against. Some while must pass before the Cimmerian learns all the intricacies of command, and purposes them toward true power.

For now, he remains content to drink, to laugh, to find comfort in the beauty of civilized women and, as always, to revel on the field of battle gone red with gore. His sojourn with the pirates of the Red Brotherhood and his later exploits is addressed in *Conan the Pirate*.

CONAN THE MERCENARY

AGILITY — 10

Skill	TN	Focus
Acrobatics	14	4
Melee	15	5
Stealth	13	3

AWARENESS — 9

Skill	TN	Focus
Insight	10	—
Observation	11	1
Survival	12	3
Thievery	11	2

BRAWN — 13

Skill	TN	Focus
Athletics	16	3
Resistance	15	2

COORDINATION — 10

Skill	TN	Focus
Parry	14	4
Ranged Weapons	12	1
Sailing	12	2

INTELLIGENCE — 9

Skill	TN	Focus
Alchemy	9	—
Craft	9	—
Healing	10	1
Linguistics	12	2
Lore	10	1
Warfare	11	1

PERSONALITY — 8

Skill	TN	Focus
Animal Handling	9	1
Command	10	2
Counsel	9	1
Persuade	10	2
Society	9	—

WILLPOWER — 9

Skill	TN	Focus
Discipline	13	3
Sorcery	9	—

BACKGROUND

- **Homeland:** Cimmeria
- **Caste:** Barbaric
- **Caste Talents:** Savage Dignity, Uncivilized
- **Story:** Born on a Battlefield
- **Trait:** Born to Battle
- **Archetype:** Barbarian
- **Nature:** Proud
- **Education:** Educated on the Battlefield
- **War Story:** Defeated a Savage Beast
- **Languages:** Cimmerian, Nordheimer, Aquilonian, Hyperborean, Nemedian, Zamorian, Kothic, Shemite, Stygian, Turanian

SOAK

Soak	3 (Chain Hauberk, Helmet)
Courage	3

FORTUNE POINTS

STRESS

Vigor	
Resolve	

HARMS

Wounds	
Trauma	

ATTACKS

- **Broadsword (M):** Reach 2, 8🔥, Unb, Parrying
- **Dagger (M):** Reach 1, 6🔥, 1H, Hidden 1, Parrying, Thrown, Unforgiving 1
- **Brawl (M):** Reach 1, 5🔥, 1H, Improvised, Stun
- **Steely Glare (T):** Range C, 2🔥 mental, Stun

SOCIAL

Social Standing	2
Renown	4
Gold	6

TALENTS

- **A Born Leader:** Conan can, once per battle, re-roll any failed Command test.
- **Ancient Bloodline (Atlantean)**
- **Animal Magnetism:** Most women (at the gamemaster's discretion) take a one step penalty when trying to resist Conan's Persuade.
- **Agile**
- **Courageous**
- **Deflection**
- **Dodge**
- **Hardy**
- **Healthy Superstition**
- **Human Spider**
- **Knack for Survival:** Conan may spend 1 Fortune point to survive even the most seemingly inescapable death.
- **Master Thief**
- **No Mercy**
- **Savage Dignity:** Conan may roll an additional d20 for any test to resist being intimidated, persuaded, or impressed by a "civilized" person.
- **Strong Back**
- **Thief**
- **Traveler's Tongue**
- **Uncivilized:** Conan suffers one step of Difficulty in social tests when dealing with people from more civilized countries. However, his Upkeep is reduced by 2 Gold.

OTHER BELONGINGS

- Broadsword
- Dagger
- Chain Hauberk and Horned Helmet
- 2 Gold

THE MERCENARY WAY

> *With a Stygian host on its heels, it had cut its way through the black kingdom of Kush, only to be annihilated on the edge of the southern desert. Conan likened it in his mind to a great torrent, dwindling gradually as it rushed southward, to run dry at last in the sands of the naked desert. The bones of its members — mercenaries, outcasts, broken men, outlaws — lay strewn from the Kothic uplands to the dunes of the wilderness.*
>
> **— "Xuthal of the Dusk"**

Have you seen the enemy, his masses of glinting halberds appearing through a valley's mist? Have you, your dog-brothers, and your sword-sisters, rushed headlong into the fray, caring not who wins the day so long as your thirst for blood is slaked? No? Then you are no mercenary. You have not yet heard the cry of war in your breast. You are a city-child, made to sup at the fat tables of merchants. Your sword-arm is withered; your hands uncalloused from tightening round spears set against the charge of the enemy's cavalry. What know you of war and death? What know you of glory or the blood-bond formed between men in the fields of war? Go, soft one, fetch me another ale and listen to tales you can only imagine!

Such is the life of a mercenary. Sell-swords, dog-brothers, sword-sisters... they go by many names. In lands such as Koth, they make up the greater host of armies fielded by barons, lords, and other petty tyrants. In the course of a life, one may don many mantles — from youth to a stripling thief. Those who choose adventure as their path wear many guises. But it is in war, in the fierce combat where a foeman's eyes go wide as your blade drinks deep, where true men are made.

Whilst your tales of obtaining gems and gold both rare and coveted will pass an evening's season, they shall not keep you alive when the night turns against you, and those who listen would kill you for those treasures of which you boasted. Then, you rely on your profession of arms alone. You rely on the steel in your fist and the mettle in your warrior's heart.

CAMP FOLLOWERS

Supplying troops is never easy, and the armies of the era require vast amounts of provisions, equipment, and services. Supply lines largely do not exist, for it is far too easy to ambush a caravan if the army it furnishes is far ahead. The solution, then, is for the suppliers to accompany the army itself. A baggage train trails behind the army and, often, outnumbers it. This is especially true for the armies of kings and queens, followed not only by the necessities of war — food, weapons, blankets, tents, etc. — but their families, as well. In Koth and Nemedia, Aquilonia and Shem, a soldier can often expect to march to war with family in tow.

Mercenary companies, though, are... different.

TROSS

Mercenaries tend to call their camp followers, *tross*, a semi-derogatory term for a much-needed addition to any army-for-hire. *"Tross"* as a name can refer to the whole group, or to individuals within the group. It can also mean

My destiny never promised I should be a prince or king, but I have worked for both throughout the varying seasons of my life. The profession of arms has always relied on a rough-hewn code; the bond of brothers and sisters of the sword. Both trusting to their sword arm to see them through the bloody day and earn them coin. I look now on my assembled host, the Free Companions. The lights of their fires outside Khoraja are the winking bellies of fireflies in the still night. My heart is heavy, my sword arm is not as strong as it once was. It all ends in blood, one way or another.

I see the springs of my youth in these boys' bright eyes. I see my age in the nested wrinkles and deep scars of the veterans. Some, I have known for years. Dog-brothers and sword-sisters with whom, back-to-back, I have sent scores of souls to the House of Shades. Gauze-like clouds cover the moon, and I feel it in my bones that the days ahead may bring defeat. The Queen is a fool, trusting to the gods that this northlander will triumph against the thrice-cursed name of Natohk the Veiled One. The Cimmerian is wild and savage, but in his baleful blue eyes lurks some keen intelligence he does not readily share. Still, for all his prowess, I cannot see him winning the day, for he is an outlander and no true commander of men.

And so I write you now, Servius, so many years from where we both started. I write in the flickering of a candle's light and the edge of the moon that escapes from those gossamer clouds. You have asked your uncle what this life is like, and I will tell you.

Any god so kind as to mix royal blood into men's veins did not bless the likes of our family. This world is harsh, and we must make our way however we can. Your father chose the life a merchant, but the same blood that spurs my life toward the field of battle runs also in you. Follow that urge! Your father would boil with ire to know that I advise you thus, but that is no matter. We have our brief times upon this earth, and it is up to every man to make of it what he wishes. If he does not, the world will make it for him, and the result is usually ignominious.

Your father and I never saw eye to eye. I expect it would be no different now. Last I saw him, you were but a whelp. There is no room for such in the ranks of freelancers. Each soldier is expected to carry his own kit and keep his own counsel. But, Servius, I am more a brother to the men around me than I ever was to your father. The bond forged in the fray, where blood flows like cheap wine from a broken cask, that bond is the very heartbeat of life. There, true brothers, sisters, friends, and companions are forged. If that is something you want, cast aside your father's scales, the ledgers, the accounting scrolls and grab yourself naked steel, a worthy steed, and ride out into your future. Be prepared for adventure and for death. It is only on the edge of life that life itself becomes worthwhile. To kill the enemy is to know the power of your body, and the influence a man may have in this world.

The gods have their plans, and most of us are but paper dolls in such schemes, but your sword and the mettle of your heart can seize the very spark of life the gods impart. Decide if you want this life and, once your choice is made, do not look back! It is not a life of great wealth or silken finery, but it is the life of the warrior, and one in which you may carve your own destiny from the rock of the world.

Your first taste of blood…. literally, it is a metallic taste. When a foe bashes your face with the hub of his shield, you will know it. But that is not the only taste of blood I speak of. You must draw the blood of the enemy and decide if you like it. To kill a person is no small thing; for, while lives are cheap, the price of taking one is not. There is glory in the doing, though. Once you pick up the sword, you shall know it. Kill your foe face-to-face. Feel their last, hot breath upon your face as the life drains from their eyes. You honor them in the killing as you honor your life in taking theirs. This is the natural order. Those who are weak serve or die, whilst those who have the will lead and reap the rewards of being sell-swords.

Amalric

the area they inhabit behind a mercenary camp. The *tross* carry the bags, the equipment, the provisions, the medicine, and sometimes the wounded, just as other camp followers. Yet those who follow mercenaries are rarely the families of those men who fight for fortune. Instead, they are a strange mix of former soldiers, entertainers, orphaned children, prostitutes, merchants, charlatans, genuine healers, and professional gamblers.

Indeed, the *tross* is more like a raucous tavern in the Maul then it is a professional organization. *Tross* shape up when needed, though. Else, the army may well leave them behind and raze a village or two to supplement. In many ways, the mercenary army and their *tross* are like a mobile city or, if one is on the receiving end of their grim purpose, a host of locusts leaving desolation in their wake.

Jobs Within the Tross

Usually, the *tross* breaks down camp in the morning, and sets it up at night. Almost everyone participates in this work. Between camps, though, *tross* tend to specialize in certain roles. They rarely follow out of loyalty. Like mercenaries themselves, they follow for profit or entertainment.

Tross also don't have the same assurances as their counterparts in proper armies. Mercenaries are far more willing to cut their baggage train loose if the need arises. Likewise, it is rarely certain that the army intervenes on behalf of an attack on their followers. They may fight to protect their food, lovers, and supplies. They may even fight to protect people they have come to call friend, but it is expected by neither side, except where a company's reputation for honor is known. Like honest Zamorians, honor is a rare find indeed in savage times such as these.

Blacksmiths

Armor gets dented, swords break, and wagon wheels lose integrity. All this and more calls for a blacksmith. While a traveling forge isn't ideal, it serves in the field. Much of the blacksmith's work, too, is melting down softer metals on the march. These become horseshoes and nails, replaced pommels and stakes.

A mercenary must ensure that armor always fits. A dent which saved his life can cause a helmet to no longer fit. Pounding it back into shape is the role of a blacksmith. Few smiths in the *tross* are highly skilled, but there are some true artisan masters who send their indentured apprentices out after mercenary armies. One must, they say, experience the conditions of war to truly understand the sacred task given to an armorer, weapon-smith, or even wainwright.

z

w

u

t

s

r

q

NOSTALGIA

Combat is traumatic no matter how hardened soldiers become. While some few will never know the dreams of war and iron that visit many veterans, others still succumb to worse terrors. Soldiers call this "nostalgia", and it represents the aftershock that darkens the mien, slumps the shoulders, and causes soldiers to go mad. There are many horrors not of this earth, that which humankind was not meant to know, which can rob a mortal of sanity. However, there are many more all-too-human horrors humankind visits upon itself. Among these is war.

Whether it is battle or the pillaging which follows, the stress and fear, the tension, and continual threat of death erodes the will. Soldiers require rest not merely because they have marched for leagues without pause or built siege engines until dusk — they require rest because combat is a dire, thrilling, and ultimately destructive experience for many.

Some are born to this life, perhaps even born on a battlefield. They are never disturbed by the clang of steel ringing in their ears on a quiet night years later. Many more find themselves drowning in wine and lotus between engagements, and become but shells of men after many campaigns.

Carousing isn't merely the rewards one accrues and spends, it is also a much-needed venting of anger, hate, fear, and a skein of emotions and humors not otherwise extricable. Nigh every town bar, a corner in every city, or the lone shack in the woods children are afraid of, finds the old war veterans recounting events to themselves, muttering, recalling things in twitches and spasms of facial muscles. They relive war, day and night — their minds ravaged not by sightless, incomprehensible sorcery, but by the depravity and brutality of their fellow man.

Camp Boys

While some few girls chase after the mercenary bands that march from one end of this earth to the other, most children found in the *tross* are boys. Almost all of them are orphans. These children have nowhere to go. The villages, towns, or cities may have cast them out. Mitra's light or Ishtar's embrace has not found them. They are unwanted and of little use.

They scamper behind the other *tross* like stray dogs feeding on the detritus left behind by men. A sad lot, at least from the outside, their future is not promising. Yet these boys have a spirit about them few civilized adults can match. Life has been hard on these curs, true, but they have not been cowed by a lord to work his land or to live in the slums of Shadizar's Maul begging for food.

They pitch the tents with the others, fetch things for soldiers, scrounge supplies for themselves, and even sometimes act as undercover scouts. A group of dirty children at a city gate is no uncommon sight. The best among the camp boys know how to talk their way inside by playing on the guilt of guards, tax-men, and priests outside the gates. Once inside, they are unseen, the sort of dirty rabble one overlooks every day. Therein lies advantage, for they can see things, eavesdrop, and conduct reconnaissance for the soldiers just leagues away.

Some camp boys — by some accounts most — hope to join the profession of arms. Those strong enough, clever enough, or ruthless enough often get their chance. Most do not survive their first battle. However, in nearly every company are mercenaries who feel kinship with these motley boys. They take them under their wings, teach them how to wield a blade, and give them some slim chance at seeing adulthood.

Cooks

An army marches on its stomach, as all men of the blade know. But that same army grumbles, becomes irritable, and is more prone to desertion if the food provided is slop not suitable for a pig. Cooks are almost as prized as a large city ready for the sack. At least, they are to a hungry man.

The best cooks among the *tross* charge the most for their services, often partnering with sutlers (see page 91 of this book). None of them are liable to make more than a pittance, but it's enough to live on. A good cook is also a favorite of the soldiers. An account by Astreas mentions a cook in the White Company who, after accruing a large gambling debt in Belvarus, had his hands broken for him. The criminal gang who did so was found slaughtered in the street the next day.

Gamblers

Where there is money, there is gambling. Soldiers of fortune, who gamble regularly with their lives, are prone to gambling in camp. Sometimes, they do so only among themselves, but they also allow *tross* to join them. Such gamblers are either on their way up, scamming their way to a stake that gets them to a great city, or, having been tossed out of such a civilized jewel, are on their way down.

Only the most desperate men seek to earn their stake in the *tross* of a mercenary army. True, money flows plentifully, but a soldier taken for his hard-earned wages by a rogue is not someone you'd want to meet in a dark, Zamorian alley. The grifter here must skim only a bit. Greed will find them on the end of a pike before they have a chance to spend their ill-gotten gains.

MERCENARIES AT THE GAMING TABLE

Running a campaign centered on mercenaries is, in many ways, an ideal Howardian style of play. Like Conan himself, mercenaries travel all over the nations of the Hyborian Age. A sell-sword cannot stay — or slay — too long in one place. When their tenure in one army or another is over, they move on in search of the next war.

Mercenaries might be a scouting group, out ahead of the main army looking for intelligence on the enemy. This sort of activity is well suited to a small band. Having a large force only attracts attention. Similarly, mercenaries may be sent undercover to towns and cities to gather information. This could lead to adventures in which intrigue, rather than combat, is key.

Anything a small, specialized group is suited for works well for mercenaries. Taking a town by stealth might be the goal of a mission. Penetrating enemy lines, and even sneaking into the enemy's camp to rescue a captured noble, might also form an adventure. Imagine the mercenaries as a group of special troops — they take on the most dangerous missions where speed and quickness of action are paramount.

Think also about the weird and unusual things a mercenary group might encounter on a seemingly normal mission. The tower they must penetrate might be a ruin from the long-fallen Acheronian empire. The noble being held for ransom might have a pact with a demon, thus complicating his rescue. The supernatural and weird almost always make a menacing appearance, and Conan often finds a rather straightforward task turns into something much more sinister when those elements appear.

In other words, the regular work of being a mercenary can often be what the player characters do between adventures. Routine patrols, drills, and the like are not the stuff of high adventure. A standard scouting mission might instead lead to the discovery of a creature out of space and time. An adventure might begin *in media res*, during the final moments of the massacre of the player characters' army. Their opponents, hunting down survivors, drive the player characters toward a lost city none have set foot in since the days of Atlantis. A normal morning patrol might reveal soldiers are missing from the camp, leading the player characters to track them, only to find a mysterious castle shrouded in mist, marked on no map.

Though less common, gambling wagons do occasionally join the *tross*. They offer more than dice and games of cards, and often have direct connections to criminal networks in towns and cities. These gamblers tend to have a higher survival rate, as slaying one out of hand often gets back to the gang in charge. A soldier looking for fun in the next town doesn't want to alienate the larcenous thugs who are likely to provide it.

Healers

Most experienced mercenaries have some rude knowledge of medicine, but a battlefield wound is as likely to kill a man from infection as it is blood loss. There are few true healers, chirurgeons, and the like to go around. Most make their living in permanent residences or are ordered into the service of king and country.

Those who find themselves in the *tross* probably didn't get there by chance. It is fair to say that nearly every *tross'* life comprises a sad tapestry of bad choices and their attendant consequences. Even the educated are no different. That is not to imply every leech in a camp knows what they are doing. A great many are charlatans. Yet a smart commander sees to it that talented healers are paid. They may be lecherous drunks but, if they can dress a wound without killing the wounded, they are kept around.

Priests

Priests do accompany the motley bands of *tross* trailing behind mercenary armies like slime behind a slug. A few even do so out of genuine piety and the sincere wish to convert others to the faith of their chosen god. More do so because they have been cast out of the clergy, the monastery, or the town in which they brought the word of Anu, Asura, or whomever to those who would listen.

In the mercenary nomenclature, a priest is a term that refers to a special sort of holy person — one who knows how to brew strong drink or carries wine. There isn't one mercenary in five hundred who calls themselves a teetotaler. Mercenary camps are known for drunkenness. Sometimes, such spirits are taken as spoils of war. When that option is not readily present, priests step in and keep the camp drowned in the nectar of whatever fruit, grain, or mineral they can squeeze something halfway drinkable from.

By and large, while mercenaries are not a devout lot, few think it unwise to keep around representatives of several gods. One never knows which one might answer in the heat of battle. A mercenary bleeding to death in Nemedian mud cares not if Ymir, Erlik, or Tarim saves their hide.

Prostitutes

If a mercenary is to march through rain and snow, spill their blood for kings to which they would never bend knee, they desire companionship at the end of the day. After all, each night's pleasure could be their last. The oldest profession and the second oldest have a long history together. Where there are soldiers, there is sex for sale.

A woman or man who trades sex for gold in a town or city often finds themselves under the thumb of thugs. No so in the *tross*, where they make their own way, their own coin, and can come or leave as they choose. It is by no means an easy life, but some have no choice. Others, especially those of supple skin and star-like eyes, can trade on their looks in better places, but have a wanderlust inside them. Some, as with all mercenaries and *tross*, are simply crazy. Others quickly tire of life as a paid-for sleeping companion of drunk soldiers and take up the blade themselves. It is said that there is a company of mercenaries in the Black Kingdoms controlled and directed by a man who was formerly the consort of a mercenary warlord. There are at least two bands of desperate killers for hire who are led by women who, it is rumored, were once to be found at the back of the company they now ride at the head of. Such rumors may simply be meant to discredit those whose power has caused jealousy, but few who join the oldest profession in the world lack wit of one sort or another.

Sages

Oracles, diviners, prognosticators — call them what you will — are a common follower of mercenary armies. Few believe the gods do not take some hand in the affairs of mortals, and people who can read the signs indicating a god's favor (or lack thereof) are at least tolerated. Some are even consulted by company commanders on the eve of battle.

More commonly, the average soldier pays such a seer to tell them whether they will survive the day, come upon valuable loot, or find citizens to defile and pillage. Chance, fate, and death are bound up for all men, but it is rarely so clear how inextricable they are than amid bloody warfare. One that can extract meaning from that strange skein has value.

The haruspex, who divines the future from the intestines of sacrifices, is very common in mercenary camps. The enemy's entrails are spilled and must be read. So, too, must gods be appeased with animal sacrifices before and after battle. In these bloody viscera are the paths every man in the company will take, but only the haruspex can read these lines.

Seamstresses or Tanners

A mercenary can be expected to mend minor tears in his tunic, or to stuff a hole in a boot, but a torn pantaloon can trip you in battle and get you killed. A professional seamstress or tanner is called for. It's rare that any soldier would buy new clothes from such folk, and rarer still that they'd have them on hand. Marching for weeks, if not months, at a time is hard on all equipment, and clothes are the first to tatter and rip.

Ask any mercenary about a hole in their tent during rain, and they'll tell you the value of someone good with thread and needle. In a pinch, too, they serve to suture wounds. Some say the only difference between many healers and a seamstress is that the latter might help you.

Slaves

One of the spoils of war is human bondage. Your enemy may be ransomed, put to the sword, or allowed to surrender. They might also become your slave. It is uncommon for fellow soldiers to be enslaved, but citizenry, other slaves, and camp-followers are often pressed into service — at least in the armies of kings.

In mercenary armies, slaves are much less common. For one, they require guards, and mercenaries are a lean operating force with no soldiers to spare. Secondly, mercenaries tend toward indomitable humors, and pressing a man into bondage is not thought of highly. Of course, many mercenaries have no problem with this, and some companies even rely on slaves as a large portion of their *tross*.

Slaves sometimes want to be sold to mercenaries, too. This seems odd on the face of it, but part of the mercenary code — under certain interpretations — says that any who raises a blade to defend the company becomes a part of that company. In short, such slaves are freed.

Sutlers

Someone must provide provisions. Those merchants who have connections in smaller towns and villages can keep a mercenary well fed. Salted meats, preserved vegetables, and dried fruit are staples of the mercenary's diet. A good sutler, though, knows how to bake or has a baker along with them.

Often working in conjunction with one of the company cooks, sutlers can make a slim profit selling such necessities to the mercenaries they follow. Some companies even take these provisions directly out of the mercenary wages. A mercenary might be roused to fury over such an arrangement, but if they cannot hunt for their food, they may well be glad they have food owed them when their silver has all gone to whoring and games of chance.

RENOWNED MERCENARY COMPANIES

There are countless mercenary companies from the dawn of the sons of Aryas to the ultimate fall of the Hyborian Age under the brutal Picts. Most are forgotten, their names are lost to time and the vagaries of history. Cities rise and fall, and those who defended or sacked them are rarely noted in texts.

Some storied few, though, persist and earn a name which people from Messantia to Agraphur know as well as they know the names of their own children. These companies below are those whose name resonates in the Hyborian Age. These are the dog-brothers whose war cries inspire fear and loathing in equal measure.

THE ASSHURI

Long ago, the *asshuri* were just another nomad clan. They were not content to roam the desert like their brethren and took to hiring on with the rising Shemites to the west. Those folk were building towns and cities, mining gold and iron, and earning themselves territory through conquest. The *asshuri* were at first unwilling to settle in their cities. Instead, they would camp outside the towns and villages, still having the spirit of the desert nomad within. But the centuries wore on, and the *asshuri* became accustomed to the civilized comforts offered by the Pelishtim.

They did not freely mix blood with their western cousins, though, preferring instead to maintain their own bloodlines and traditions. While it is not unheard of for a Pelishtim Shemite and an *asshuri* to couple, the *asshuri* often disown any of their number who does so. While no longer nomads, they retain the privacy of that lineage.

Unlike other mercenary companies, the *asshuri* are not "dog-brothers" but related by actual blood. If you are not born into their ranks, you will never become one of them. They have allies who are outsiders, but the clans that run the *asshuri* are a large, extensive family. They disagree at times, and a majority of the three most powerful clans must agree to any contract. Though feuds occur, there are rules and rituals for vengeance. The *asshuri* share these secrets with no one.

Asshuri drill regularly. Any member must prove his worth in battle by the age of ascension — sixteen for boys and seventeen for girls — or be condemned to the life of a clerk, quartermaster, or money counter. Only those who can hold their own on a field of battle, where the dead are heaped like hillocks against the bloody eye of the sun, are accepted as mercenaries.

The mercenary code applies to the *asshuri*, but they also have more extensive rules. They do not turn their blades on fellow Shemites unless a blood debt must be satisfied. Should a city-state rebel against Askalon, the *asshuri* always sides with the crown. In the same fashion, they do not take contracts which would cause them to war with the nomad clans. Any *asshuri* unit which does so is castigated and exiled from the family.

Asshuri do not kill women or children. They readily sell them into bondage, as this is the way of things, but the *asshuri* do not slaughter those who cannot defend themselves. Warrior women, of whom there are a great many among the *asshuri*, are exceptions. They are treated like men.

Looting amongst the *asshuri* is more orderly than in other companies. Finders are not always keepers here, and spoils are divided by age and position in the family. The *asshuri* are also expected to give a percentage of all such loot back to the family. In return for this, all *asshuri* are provided with equipment, lodging, and protection anywhere and anytime their clan can provide such things.

Expert charioteers and archers, the *asshuri* nearly rival Hyrkanians in mobility. Shemites in general are expert archers if they serve in the military.

The *tross* (see page 85) of the *asshuri* is unlike the camp followers who trail other mercenary armies. Some are members of the family, and all are at least trusted as allies. The families of *asshuri* accompany them on extended campaigns in much the same way as the baggage trains of royal armies.

Contracts with the *asshuri* are precise and kept to the very letter. They always perform according to their word. However, if their employer in any way breaks that contract, the *asshuri* are known to take vicious revenge upon them. Outside of Shem, and even sometimes within her borders, the *asshuri* are rumored to be nothing more than a gang of criminals who use their connections and outland posts to smuggle various drugs, weapons, and slaves under the noses of local lords and their taxmen. This has yet to be proven.

Asshuri are described as a player character archetype on page 10.

> *Conan rode a great black stallion, the gift of Trocero. He no longer wore the armor of Aquilonia. His harness proclaimed him a veteran of the Free Companies, who were of all races. His head-piece was a plain morion, dented and battered. The leather and mail-mesh of his hauberk were worn and shiny as if by many campaigns, and the scarlet cloak flowing carelessly from his mailed shoulders was tattered and stained. He looked the part of the hired fightingman, who had known all vicissitudes of fortune, plunder and wealth one day, an empty purse and a close-drawn belt the next.*
>
> — The Hour of the Dragon

THE FREE COMPANIONS

In many ways, the Free Companions are the archetypal mercenary company. Comprising men and women of every race and background, a person can join the company and start a new life. The Free Companions do not care where you have been, or what terrible deeds you left in your wake. All that matters is that you can wield a blade and will stand back-to-back with your dog-brothers. A motley collection of rogues, thieves, slavers, kidnappers, murderers, disgraced knights, fallen scholars, and anything else under the sun are found in the Free Companions.

Simply because they ask no questions does not imply they make no demands. The Free Companions carry their own weight. A man brings his own kit, his own weapons, and his own strength. While strong leaders of the company rally troops on the field, the day-to-day slog through rain, mud, snow, and steaming jungle must by necessity be driven by the individual. Whether running from one's past or toward a future, Free Companions are motivated by a lack of other options.

They serve whoever pays, having no compunctions or moral quandaries. When they find themselves unemployed, they harry the borders of various kingdoms, killing and plundering as they may. Wages are decent, but most Free Companions expect to make their real coin in loot. The fields of the dead are not so cleanly picked by vultures as by the avaricious hands of Free Companions.

Yet they cleave to the mercenary code more often than not. Once a dog-bother is inducted, his fellows will kill for him. This may not go so far as dying for that cur who fights beside you, but it is enough that a Free Companion can largely count on the fact that the dagger which kills him won't come from behind.

The Free Companions work in the west, and most often in the kingdoms built by the Sons of Bori. They have been found in Turan and even fought in tribal wars as far south as Kush and Punt. The only real restriction on their range is how many men desert while on the march. A Free Companion is unlikely to trudge past the jeweled thrones of the Earth indefinitely without coin or loot.

As a company, they are good to their contracts and known as capable, ruthless fighters. Rebel princes in Koth, Nemedia, Corinthia, and elsewhere hire them to supplement their rebellious forces. The rightful kings of these same states, however, will also hire the Free Companions, and it is not uncommon for a soldier to have served for and against the same crown, on occasion simultaneously.

When not gainfully employed, and having turned to banditry, they are a terror no king wants visited upon their lands. Some kings even pay the Free Companions a ransom to go and loot their enemies instead. Bands of brigands, such as the dread kozaki of the Turanian desert, sometimes come into conflict with the Free Companions. There is no code between dog-brothers and outsiders.

THE NEMEDIAN ADVENTURERS

A class unto themselves, the Nemedian Adventurers are not knights, for they lack the money and the standing, nor are they mercenaries who hire out to the highest bidder. Instead, they answer only to the King of Nemedia, and it is from his ample purse which they are paid.

In Nemedia, the Adventurers are renowned for their skill in battle, their ferocity, and their loyalty to the king. They have dedicated their lives to the profession or arms. However, when the sun sets on any given day, they are still sells-swords. Their loyalty is perhaps the strongest of any known mercenary company, but it is still bought.

Living, and often dying, by the sword, the Adventurers hold no official rank, but neither must they bother with the trappings of title, nor the politics of rule. Their blood is not royal, but royal Nemedians respect that blood nonetheless. A Nemedian Adventurer is widely considered the superior in combat to all but the finest of the king's knights. Even then, the common man, if not the pampered noble, is like as not to put his coin on the side of the Adventurers.

And so, the Adventurers occupy a curious space in society, perhaps one which exists nowhere else in the dreaming west. Neither noble nor, precisely, commoner, they inspire tales, are given respect and well-treated in ways other mercenaries are not. Yet the king remains the king, the princes maintain rule and the individual Adventurer, however admired, shall never find their names listed among the greatest of their era. That is both their pride and their tragedy, serving anonymously to the history of empire.

Nemedian Adventurers wear gray mail and lack the affectations of knights and lords. Often, they command troops on the field of battle, but they answer not to generals — only to the king. Somewhere, it is rumored, they keep their own chronicle. If so, none but one of their own has ever laid eyes on it.

THE WHITE COMPANY

Legendary for their exploits in recent Argossean wars, the White Company is among the most professional mercenary armies in the west — a reputation gained because they have lost very few battles. The odds which they have stared down and won against are incredible. There is no other company of mercenaries that accrues victories for their employers like the White Company.

It is no surprise that they command high fees when contracted. Their victories are desired by nearly every king west of the Vilayet, and it is not unheard of for rulers in Vendhya to request their services.

Rigorous training is a hallmark of service in the White Company, but they never take raw recruits. All soldiers who serve under the white banner are already proven in the art of war. The White Company is the very height of the profession of arms.

Tross that follow the White Company are lucky for their ilk. The White Company protects those who serve them, and would not think of abandoning camp followers to enemy attack. Few other companies can say the same. Further, soldiers' families follow the White Company, though not in as great numbers as those of standing armies. Hangers on, who do not serve as *tross*, trail the actual camp followers of the White Company in hopes of gaining crumbs and security. Few armies would attack the White Company without cause, and nearly no brigands are fool enough to do so. The kozaki, however, are known to have tussled with these dog-brothers in the past, and there exists considerable enmity between them.

The White Company earned its name from the pure white standard they bear in battle. The snapping banner can be seen some distance away, and gives pause to even hardened troops. However, the banner itself is no longer white, at least not the main standard. Instead, it is blood-spattered and well mended, a veritable quilt of the company's campaigns.

New standards serve in lesser roles, and these are also white — at least when the battle begins. When it ends, these standards are used as funereal cloths to wrap the honored dead who fought, and died, best. At any given time, the

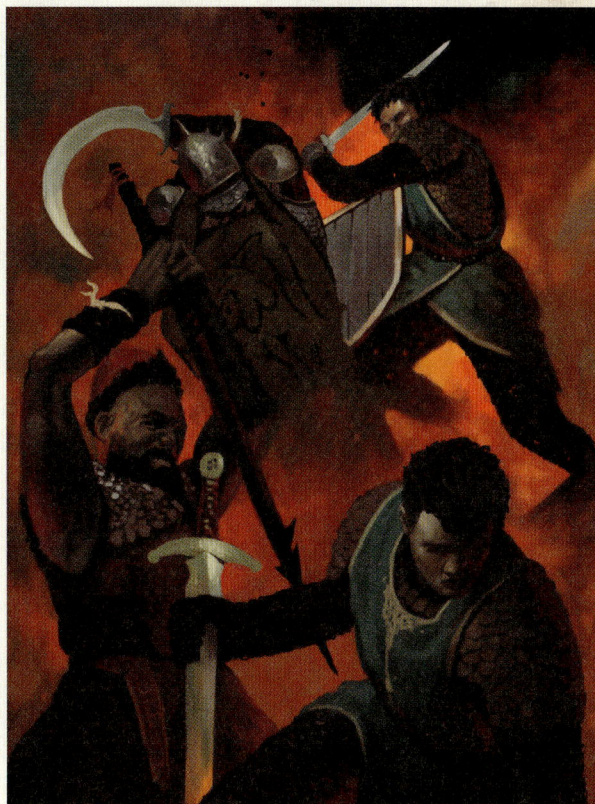

ON THE MARCH?

The player characters could be members of a well-known mercenary company such as the Nemedian Adventurers, the White Company, or the Free Companions. They might also venture on their own, hiring on where they can. In either case, the life of a mercenary gives ample reason to travel. Conan may have stayed somewhere for a time, but that's not what we read about. We read about his peripatetic adventures across the continent. Keeping the player characters moving is a key pillar to playing in a Howardian style. For mercenaries, this is easy.

They go where the next war is, where the next caravan needing guards is headed, where the next city-state rebels against the king of Turan. While you can certainly play out their travels between locations, Howard rarely spent more than a paragraph describing such events. The player characters go from one adventure to the next.

The rules section provides tables for what happens between adventures. Always bear in mind, in the fast-paced style of pulp, anything that isn't intriguing or exciting gets cut. If Howard wouldn't have put it on the page, you probably don't want to roleplay it out in your game. Cut to the big battle between opposing armies; don't play out the march getting there.

motley, blood-stained standard the company has borne since its inception is carried by the most respected rank-and-file soldier. Holding that banner gives a player character +3 permanent Renown, if the privilege was well-earned.

MERCENARY COMPANIES

A DAY IN THE LIFE

The life of a soldier, whether professional or conscript, is one of dull routine punctuated by blood-chilling combat, sheer terror, and savagery. Mercenaries march hard, fight harder, and carouse like no others. They live on a razor's edge, waiting always to fall on one side or another — death or decrepitude.

During a typical day, the men wake some while after the *tross* begin breakfast. They smell meat and eggs — should these be available — else they smell bread and oats of varying kinds. After eating, the camp usually breaks, unless it has come to a place to winter. Once camp is broken, scouts are assigned for the day — normally in three-hour shifts. The army marches nine to twelve hours a day when on campaign. When in search of work and throats to slit, the pace slackens to six hours a day average.

Prior to setting camp for the night, the last scouting detail reconnoiters the area thoroughly. These hardened soldiers know where a company might be trapped, where natural topography protects entire flanks, and where other armies usually march. Once the commander of the company approves the position, a very quick and orderly reversal of breaking camp occurs. That night, soldiers drink, gamble, and consort with the *tross* if they are not on duty. In any given week, a man can expect three to four nights of duty and the remainder to squander as he pleases. No matter what a dog-brother or sword-sister did the night before, it is no excuse for waking late, being unable to march, or not keeping their weapon well-oiled.

THE MERCENARY CODE

Though called "dog-brothers," "sword-sisters", and "throat-slitters", mercenaries are not thieves — at least not amongst themselves. They gladly loot the dead, but would find their hands cut off by their fellows were they to filch a purse off a living ally.

Unlike some armies serving under kings, mercenaries tend to have far less concern for the local population and, as noted, oft times turn to banditry. On the field, however, there is a code that all dog-brothers know, but none need speak — you have your brother's back, and he has yours.

More specifically, though almost never written as a formal charter, companies of hired soldiers practice and believe in the following:

- A dog-brother's possessions are their own — until death. Afterwards, they are fair game.

- The one who finds, keeps. When the battle is done, men and women scramble to find the best loot. Fights may break out over prying the gold tooth from some dead man's mouth, but the fight rarely turns deadly.

- Everyone works. While commanders and officers of significant rank do not pound the stakes into the ground for defense, nor pitch their own tents, they pitch in on patrols, cook if the company has no *tross*, and tend the wounded. No mercenary commander watches the field of battle from afar, for who would follow him?

- Blood for blood and life for life. A dog-brother is likely, even expected, to avenge a fallen brother when in this battle or the next. Likewise, any brother who fights beside you deserves your very best. You fight side-by-side, back-to-back and breathe your lasts breaths together — most of the time.

- When in a rout, it's everyone for themselves. When a company lies shattered under a grim, gray day, the ranks collapse and all flee. Some retain enough discipline to do so in an orderly fashion but, when this too fails, each dog-brother looks only out for himself and his immediate friends. You're fighting for money, after all, not a god or an idea.

- A man or woman's lover is their own. Do not interfere in the intimate affairs of your fellows. This is a blood debt most companies settle by combat to the death.

- That which happened within the walls of the city remains there. Drunken fights between mercenaries are common. Disputes get out of hand and, perhaps two women liked the same seraglio boy and fought over him in the night. That ends when the company returns to order. There is no room for real enmity save for the enemy before you.

- A contract is contract. You are paid to do a thing and you do it. If you cannot, you leave without pay.

- A contract broken by the employer is void. Woe be to the king that fails to pay or the rebel prince who betrays his hired men to the enemy.

- Do not fall asleep on watch. If you do, you are unlikely to live long enough to regret it.

THE STRUCTURE OF A COMPANY

Mercenaries companies are as varied as conscript armies in organization but, as mercenaries are all professional soldiers, they tend toward orderly formations. The company commander — sometimes referred to as a condotierri, captain, or other vernacular — sits at the top of the military chain of command. Below him are several lieutenants, battle-proven warriors who command sub-companies. The sub-company, too, is often simply referred to as "my company", by a soldier, and outsiders are likely to become confused.

Typically, a "sub-company" numbers between 50–200 soldiers. There may be only three such companies under the greater banners. These companies form families all their own within the larger unit. They see their lieutenants and sergeants as parental figures, with the company commander as the wise grandparent. They obey without question, for if the military machine breaks down, the men face a bloody death; whether it is a death delivered from within their own ranks or without depends on circumstance.

Under the lieutenants are sergeants. They command units of a dozen or more men each. A sergeant beds with the mercenaries, eats with them, and pitches in more than the lieutenant. However, unlike the army of a king, no lieutenant reaches his rank by anything other than skill and bloodlust. Sergeants under a mercenary banner respect those above them in a way rank-and-file types do not.

The rest of the company lacks official rank, though veterans have privilege over whelps yet wet behind the ear and, as may only be right, the better fighters make their position known as a lion might in their pride.

SUB-COMPANY NAMES

Within a company of mercenaries, sub-companies usually have names to keep them separate. These names are rarely known outside the mercenaries' own circles, though over a night at a raucous tavern, a commoner may overhear names like the following:

- Eagle Company
- Black or Red Company
- The Unclean
- Rolo's Reavers
- The Cruel Ones

A few free companies organize their names more rigidly by number or letter of a chosen alphabet. More commonly, though, the names derive from its leaders, its previous deeds, or its infamous stories. Outside the company, another mercenary has little clue as to the company's role in the greater unit. The Unclean, for example, could be fifty lancers or ten-score elite killers.

SIEGES

Should they live long enough, sooner or later, every sell-sword finds themselves pitted against the walls of a city. A city is the ultimate prize and the ultimate danger. Inside are the fat, soft folk of civilization with more gold and silver than easily counted. But, before getting to the underbelly filled with riches, many men pile against the walls and heaps of the fallen, the failed, and the broken.

Sieges are long, typically, and casualties mount rapidly — especially for the besiegers. Any city worth the name is built for defense, just as any castle. Soldiers must take battering rams to gates, launch missiles from siege engines, and climb ladders to gain purchase atop the battlements. In their way are archers behind slits, archers along the walls, pots of boiling oil, and other horrors. Siege combat is a long war of attrition. The most effective tactic in the besiegers' armory is often simply to starve out the besieged.

Once the walls break and the tide of avaricious dog-brothers pours through — well, there are few commanders who can, or try, to control them. Because of this, because of the indignities visited on the city's population and the destruction of much inside, cities attempt to buy off mercenaries. Or, failing that, buy the company to police the rest of the king's conscript army. Mercs promised all the secret gold in the city first are likely bought by the civilians. It is not common, but it has happened before, when a wealthy populace tires of an overly domineering monarch, and their overly onerous taxes, for example.

FORTIFICATIONS

While sieges involving cities form the greater number of stories heard, castles, keeps, and even forts or abbeys may likewise be besieged. It matters little to the mercenary what the folk behind the walls call their fortification. All such redoubts have weak points and, given time, a throat-slitter of any worth will find them.

THE SPOILS OF WAR

Mercenaries are guaranteed coin for service and, very often, this comprises the bulk of their recompense. Yet every mercenary expects supplemental income in the form of looting. In fact, a good day's work as a battlefield vulture can easily match a month's pay. Of course, the mercenaries must first win the fight, then race their greedy fellows to the spoils.

Pitted against an army, who now lie defeated in a bloody field, a mercenary company is like a swarm of flesh-eating insects descending on the dead and stripping them as quickly as the wind changes direction. Cutting the purses off fallen foes, pulling off rings and necklaces, prying out golden teeth, and even taking trophies of flesh are all a part of spoils.

Sacking and Looting Cities

Cities present a different opportunity for looting. A soldier will carry enough coin to get by, some personal mementos, and the like, but an army is rarely loaded with wealth. A city, however, is a giant treasury waiting to be plundered.

The folk inside, as well as their possessions, are all for the taking. Grim things happen when a city is sacked, and only a victim or a soldier can speak of them with any authority. Suffice it to say that chaos reigns and, unless specifically paid by their employers — or ordered by their commanders — mercenaries will assuredly strip a city clean of gold, silver, jewels, potential slaves, and anything else they want in a bloody, lusty moment.

Events While Looting

Upon the field of battle, where the dead are thick and the sky dark with ravens, little occurs. Sure, a dead man may prove yet to cling to life, and many a sell-sword tells a whelp over a campfire about the screams of those still living when one must cut their mouth open to get a gem-encrusted tooth.

In a city, though, where the tumult and fear and sweat and panic mount like a wave, many things can happen.

Pay

While loot is variable and open to the first comers, pay is steady and based on experience and rank. Novice whelps get the least, while commanders haul the most. The average dog-brother makes 2 Gold a month for service. This increases twofold (4 Gold) for any month in which they fight more than three days for their employer. Sergeants make another 1 Gold on top of this, while lieutenants usually make another 2 Gold.

The business of mustering for pay is usually followed by gross spending sprees in the nearest city or, failing that, tossing away some extra coin to the *tross* for food, entertainment, and lotus. Few mercenaries save their coin but, for those who do, they can gain a tidy sum, for they pay almost nothing for meals and sleep under the stars.

Of course, earning a living holds little excitement for mercenaries or player alike. It is the battle, and the looting that follows, on which real legends are built.

LOOTING TABLES

More things than even the philosophies of Khitai can reckon are found after a fray — bones and teeth, rings, necklaces, strange icons, and even fell fetishes might make their way into the purse of a sell-sword. On the following tables, some small sample of the spoils of war feature for one's looting pleasure.

RANSACKING EVENTS

Roll	Result
1–2	A child witnesses the player characters looting their parent's shop or home.
3–4	A priest, clutching a precious relic, is caught by your comrades, babbling about ancient prophecies.
5–6	An old, lame beggar lays feebly in the street. Perhaps he is blind; he draws mysterious symbols in the earth or sand on which he sits.
7–8	A lockbox too heavy for the occupants of a shop to make off with is discovered. It is heavy with silver and gold, or, perhaps, something more troubling…
9–10	A merchant seeks to make his way out of the city as a pregnant woman. A Stealth versus Observation Struggle reveals the merchant's deception.
11–12	A half-dozen of the enemy fight in a circle against your fellows. They are not long for the world, but seem determined to protect something.
13–14	A particularly sadistic member of your band sees fit to bleed a city dweller to death, cutting fingers and toes while laughing.
15–16	You come upon a pyramidal pile of severed heads, eyes open, staring. This must have happened before you entered the city… who committed such a barbaric deed?
17–18	A pack of stray dogs tears apart a hapless citizen too weak to fight them off — before turning on the invaders. Has something more than starvation driven them mad?
19	A near dead person wheezes pitifully in an alley, hands held out for aid or perhaps asking for a quick end.
20	A king or noble, disguised as a mere peasant, begs you to get them out. In return, they offer treasure outside the city gates or something else of great value.

LOOTING A BATTLEFIELD

Roll	Result
1–2	A simple purse filled with 2 🦅 worth of Gold.
3–4	A letter. Perhaps personal or perhaps bearing a royal seal?
5–6	A fine blade of Akbitanan steel.
7–8	A ring worth 2 Gold.
9–10	A diamond-encrusted tooth worth 3 Gold, but it must be pried or cut out.
11–12	A company's pet dog, scavenging the field like you.
13–14	A fine bottle of wine.
15–16	A helmet gilded in gold, worth 2 Gold.
17–18	A jade pendant from Khitai. What do the symbols on it mean?
19	A small idol made of unknown metal. A learned fellow in your ranks says it looks like a long-dead pre-cataclysmic god. He does tend to lie a lot, though.
20	A human skull, not of one killed in the battle. The skull is plated in gold and contains unknown gems for eyes. Who can say the value of the item? Or of the danger it might bring upon its owner?

> *He and the girl were, so far as he knew, the sole survivors of Prince Almuric's army, that mad motley horde which, following the defeated rebel prince of Koth, swept through the Lands of Shem like a devastating sandstorm and drenched the outlands of Stygia with blood.*
>
> — "Xuthal of the Dusk"

Roll	Result
	LOOTING A CITY
1–2	A secret compartment beneath the floorboard of a merchant's shop holds valuables totaling 5 Gold.
3–4	This statue before you is hideous, but even you can see the rarity of the stone and the glint of diamond eyes. 5 Gold.
5–6	In the attic, you hope to find hidden treasure. Instead, you find a long-dead corpse clearly hidden here from prying eyes. On its back, a strange map was tattooed. You recognize only one symbol — the pirate sigil for treasure.
7–8	A baby cries. Perhaps you try to ignore it, but the wail persists. If you investigate, you find a lone child swaddled in fine silk. Its forehead bears a tattoo which might denote royalty, but of what people you are not sure.
9–10	A stone box in the tunnels beneath the city. It is immensely heavy. The two men transporting it lie dead beside it, though there is no evidence of what killed them. Their eyes, however, have turned bright yellow. The stone box is oddly warm.
11–12	A silver tooth the size of your fist. It looks very realistic. Didn't another dog-brother once tell you of a holy relic venerated by a lost race whose god was made entirely of silver?
13–14	What appears to be a glass case contains a severed hand. The hand has three fingers and a thumb. Scales seem to coat the upper part near the wrist. A metal ring circles each finger. The case cannot be broken as easily as glass.
15–16	In a sack of potatoes or other foodstuff lies a stack of letters bound with twine. They describe a love affair between two opposing royal houses. Someone would pay dearly to get their hands on these.
17–18	A scroll citing the manifest of ship leaving the nearest port in mere days. It looks like some clever merchant wants to smuggle something of great value on a ship which routinely carries mere wheat or another common item.
19	A man gags in an alley then falls dead, turning blue. If you investigate, he has a large gem lodged in his throat. Two men burst out of the alley ready to cut him open to get it.
20	An unconscious maiden or young man of unrivaled beauty. Unbeknownst to you, this is the last surviving member of the royal family of the city you just sacked.

CAROUSING AS A MERCENARY

Between adventures, player characters take part in a variety of activities, among them Carousing. The Trouble and Carousing tables from the **Conan** corebook represent many intriguing and flavorful events, but mercenaries encounter still other diversions, whether sublime or debauched.

The following *Mercenary Trouble* and *Mercenary Carousing Event* tables are suitable not only for mercenaries, but other careers, as well. Certainly, these tables lean toward the dog-brothers and sword-sisters who spill blood (theirs or others) for coin. After all, they make a peculiar, dangerous lot.

MERCENARY TROUBLE

Effects	Example Trouble Caused
1–2	The player character is indebted to a gang this phase. The player character loses 2 Gold and has a debt that must be paid off or fled from.
3–4	The player character killed someone in a bar fight. Whether it was self-defense or not, the person had connections and the player character was to be hung. They managed a daring escape from their gaolers, but now have a bounty on their head.
5+	The player character assaulted a superior officer. Said officer goes hard on the character. Social tests will be increased by three steps of Difficulty until this is settled, possibly by a duel to the death. Regardless, if honor is not satisfied, the player character's Renown is reduced by –1. For each additional effect above 5, modify Renown by another –1, at the gamemaster's discretion.

MERCENARY CAROUSING EVENTS

Roll	Event	Description
1	Stealing and Seduction	The player character beds the wrong prostitute. The gamemaster should roll a 🦅. A positive result (1 or 2) indicates the player character loses 1 Gold as a result. A result of 3 and above indicates 2 Gold are lost. If the player character has thieving skills of their own, or an Awareness 9+, they may reverse the tables and steal from the prostitute. Of course, this may earn the ire of that employee's handlers. At the gamemaster's discretion, other skills or talents may substitute for a high Awareness.
2	Military Stockade	The player character violated even the magnanimous rules of the company in which they serve. As a result, they spend this Carousing phase in a military stockade as punishment. Fellow dog-brothers take pity on such fools and feed the player character, but they cannot pay Upkeep this phase. However, if the player character spends twice their normal Upkeep, they bribe their way out of the stockade. Bribery, too, is part of many a company's "unwritten rules".
3	Defended a Noble	Whether by choice or accident, the player character winds up defending the life of a noble or other important person. Were it not for the player character, the important person would now be dead. The gamemaster may award 2 Gold, 2 Renown, or decide the noble owes the player character a debt. Alternatively, the player can choose which option they like best. Of course, in having defended this person, the player character may also have earned a new enemy.
4	Killed a Powerful Individual	The player character killed someone of note. Perhaps it was on the field of battle, and they only now learn who they killed, or it happened during a raucous night. The specifics are left up to the gamemaster and player, but the end result is enmity of some sort. Important people have important friends, and they want revenge. Alternatively, by spending an extra 2 Gold for Upkeep this Carousing phase, the slain individual also had an enemy who now looks favorably on the player character for ridding them of such a nuisance.
5	Saved by a Fool	Either during battle or while Carousing, the player character becomes indebted to the company fool. Now, the company fool is not the butt of jokes and ribaldry. No, in a mercenary company, such deprecations are saved for camp followers. But, the fool of a company is a madman. He charges into battle with nary a care. He takes insane risks that, now, the player character is expected to join. However, should the player character pay the debt, by whatever means they and the gamemaster determine, they gain +2 Renown for their "fearlessness", however under duress it may have been.
6	The Drunken Rival	While drinking with other mercenaries or soldiers, one of them who was, or will soon be, on the opposite side of the field of battle spills tactical secrets. These valuable bits of information can be sold to the player character's unit for 1 Gold or 1 Renown. If either happens, the gamemaster may decide the drunk remembers who they spilled to, and thus a rival is gained.

MERCENARY CAROUSING EVENTS (CONTD.)

Roll	Event	Description
7	A Boast Gone Well	The player character brags about their deeds in battle, or in bed, and impresses those around them. They gain 1 Gold during this phase and 1 Renown. Of course, some folks might be jealous…
8	A Horse with No Name	The player character wakes in the middle of nowhere, lashed to a horse and saddle. How did they get there? Did someone slip the character a sedative or was this the result of a very bad bet during a very bad bender in Zamora the Accursed? More to the point, how is the character going to get back? And, is getting back the best idea?
9	Gang Favor	The player character somehow assisted a gang member, or friend/relative thereof, during a visit to a city. The gang pays its debts, and gives the character a signet ring which other members of the gang, in other cities, will recognize. They will assist the player character as a result.
10	Nostalgia	Not all wounds are physical. The ravages of constant war have taken their toll on the player character's psyche. Nightmares plague the character and, until he or she can rid themselves of them, they have one permanent Trauma. However, the experience also makes them more prepared for action, and they receive a one-step bonus on their first action in a combat.
11	Lone Survivor	The player character is the only survivor of a unit of mercenaries wiped out by an opposing force. The character ends this Carousing phase with only one Gold (the rest was lost in the battle), one Wound, and an extra +2 Renown.
12	Lotus Dream	During an episode of lotus ingestion, the character has a vision. Lotus dreams aren't rare, but this one appears to lead to a rare treasure, a lost friend, or something otherwise desirable. Is the vision real, or just another hallucination?
13	Addiction	Carousing usually takes place between adventures, but many mercenaries are hard drinkers and aficionados of exotic drugs. The character becomes dependent on one of these. At the gamemaster's discretion, the character must make a Willpower test once a session to resist ingesting the drug or brew of choice. Alternatively, this could simply be an opportunity for roleplaying. The player and gamemaster should agree on this result. If they do not, roll again.
14	The Black Market	The player character comes upon a trove of goods stolen from the company; unfortunately, he or she becomes the prime suspect. A black market operates inside the company, siphoning off supplies. Until the player character can prove otherwise, their Renown in the company is −2.
15	The Pretender	The painted boys and girls have found clients for the night, while you chatted away with a friendly drinker. As the dawn rises, the light illuminates more than the near empty tavern — the new drinking companion is a noble, one in disguise. Do you let on that you know, or follow them home to see what transpires? What brought a person of high station to such a lowly pub as this?
16	How to Treat the Locals	Some drunk members of the player character's company take good fun too far and begin to hassle the locals, even threatening them. The player character comes across this event as it unfolds. Fighting the dog-brothers will make enemies of them, but can the character allow such abuse of those clearly weaker?
17	The Heir	The son or daughter of someone you killed on the field of battle comes looking to avenge their parent's death. This person is little more than a whelp, and the player character could dispatch them easily. How do they handle this matter? The kid wants them dead, but they are still just a mere youth.
18	Bodyguard	The player character was offered work as a bodyguard while in some settled area. They declined, wanting to enjoy their time away from constant battle. Unfortunately, the would-be client was killed the next day and the constabulary knows the victim spoke to the player character the night before. Can they talk their way out of it? Perhaps they wish to investigate?

		MERCENARY CAROUSING EVENTS (CONTD.)
Roll	Event	Description
19	Lucky Streak	The player character gains 3 Gold this Carousing phase after a lucky gambling streak. Someone, however, was watching and believes the character's "luck" is the result of a god's blessing... They claim that god sent them a vision, and they now know that the mercenary is the one who must help them with some trial ahead. The player character may decline the offer, but the zealot follows them out of town, if so.
20	More Than Luck	The player character could not lose last night at the gaming tables — literally. The tables were somehow rigged, the games cheated by a local gang. The character won so much, they took the deed to this gambling den. That seems like a fountain of free coin... until the gang shows up and demands they hand the deed over to them. The man or woman who was supposed to win looked like the character and, while that conspirator was drunk in an alley, other cheats mistook the player character for their ally, who they never met. The den is worth a considerable amount of Gold.

MERCENARY ADVENTURES

Herein you have read of the mercenary life, been introduced to the rough-and-tumble sorts who swell their ranks, and visited those fractious kingdoms where a strong sword-arm brings good wages. While the bulk of a dog-brother's days are on the march, in camp, and often boring, they are punctuated by the thrilling, terrifying chaos of melee and war.

Yet battles alone are not the only stuff of legend. Howard's stories often veer from the prescribed career a hero inhabits and quickly stray into the weird. Thus, raw, bloody combat against foemen comprises part of their story; mercenaries also experience those things which most mortals could not face without descending into gibbering madness. This, then, are some of the adventures your mercenary campaign may encompass.

LET SLIP THE DOGS OF WAR

We have promised a glimpse into the weird fantasy of which the Conan stories are paragon examples, and we shall get to those. First, though, we explore the adventures which center on the mercenaries' ostensible purpose — warfare.

War provides the nourishment that feeds the body and the blood that slakes the soul of men of fortune and the blade. Lines of men in formation, armor glinting in the last rays of light they may ever see, comprise the bulk of those stories related about mercenaries. They are not, however, the full measure of the danger they face. Other tasks are ancillary to the wars ahead, but they are no less vital.

Incidentally, any of these more "basic" missions and adventures could merely be the set up for the weird horror ahead.

Scouting and Reconnaissance

Perfectly suited to small groups (such as player characters), scouting and reconnaissance is essential to any functional mercenary company. Even when they are not contracted to a kingdom or ruler, no company commander who has seen more than a few winters of war simply marches headlong into the unknown. Instead, scouts move ahead of the main body of the company to survey, and quite often assess, potential threats or opportunities.

A routine scouting mission isn't supposed to end in combat, but such is not the stuff of roleplaying adventures. Ambushes are an excellent way to turn the tables on a recon mission. After all, if one military commander is smart enough to send soldiers ahead, so is another. That other group may spy the characters first and set a trap for them.

Likewise, animals are natural predators and approach with stealth while striking with surprise. The forest ahead might hide cave bears, holdovers from the last Ice Age, or venomous snakes. Should a member of the scouts be terribly wounded (or poisoned), their best chance of survival lays with the main mercenary force. But if the scouts retreat, who is there to look out for dangers ahead? Perhaps some help the injured character back while others continue ahead.

The point is, even the mundane can create an adventure. Not everything need be infused with the weird and fantastical. Of course, there's no reason the scouts couldn't stumble upon a group of cannibals worshiping a perverse version of Jhebbal Sag.

Patrols

Patrols are like scouting but take place much closer to the main body of the company or army. Patrols are designed to spot enemy incursions, not forewarn of danger while on the march. Typically, everyone in the company must take a patrol at least every other day. There isn't a time, except in cities and towns, where mercenaries lie idle in defense.

The most common encounter for a patrol is either another patrol or the spearhead of an outright assault. The former seeks to test the enemy's defenses while the other already has. In either case, the player characters must fend off or kill the attackers while delivering a report to their superiors.

A potential reversal involves the character's patrol being overcome and captured by their enemy. Then you have the beginnings of great adventure. The player characters must resist interrogation, escape the enemy encampment, and, surely, warn their company of the dire plans they uncovered while in enemy territory.

Securing Prisoners

Scouting and patrols alone do not collect all the necessary intelligence needed by a wise commander. Direct reports from the enemy, extracted by whatever means, provide detailed information not otherwise obtainable.

Now, some enemy patrol of a lost squad may stumble right into the characters' hands, but that is nothing one bets their life on. Instead, sergeants and other commanders are likely to order groups out to find and capture prisoners specifically. Guess what? Tonight, the player characters are selected for that dangerous task.

Wandering about looking for an enemy patrol is not likely to reap quick or desirable results. The characters are ordered to penetrate the enemy camp, town, city, or other fortification and bring out live prisoners. The player characters may also be ordered to kill themselves in the event of their own capture. This sort of adventure requires a solid plan coupled with either swift, violent action, or stealth. Further, once prisoners are captured, they must be taken back to camp alive. That means either keeping them moving through threats, or knocking them senseless and hauling them home with brawn alone.

Rescues

Mercenaries are hardly the first soldiers to come up with the idea of nabbing the enemy and extracting information from them. Any mercenary whose spilled blood — their own or their foes' — knows that being captured is a genuine possibility. Whether prisoners are snatched in the night or taken after defeat in battle, those captured are often doomed to slavery. Particularly in conscripted armies, or those under tyrannical kings, a captured soldier's lot is bleak. Mercenaries take care of their own. Dog-brother is not a term used without genuine respect and loyalty.

A sizable percentage of mercenary commanders authorize, or overlook, rescue attempts. The adventure proceeds according to the information available to the characters — do they know where their dog-brothers were taken? Do they even know who captured them? Like securing prisoners, this likely leads to some sort of camp, keep, or fortification.

Perhaps it leads directly to a rival army, or even to a cult who intends to use the prisoners for sacrifice.

This sort of adventure has some raw nobility to it. Where the Hyborian Age is savage and unforgiving, so too are many of its heroes. Still, men who live by the mercenary code lay down their lives for one another. This situation is no different.

Banditry

Where war provides ample motive, so too does the lack of war. Mercenaries fight; it is their purpose on this earth — or at least for those days when other fortunes escape them. When fighting for coin runs dry, some companies take to marauding. If the king is not spending his money on war, surely it's in the hands of others in the kingdom. The desperate mercenary takes from those who have when wages are not available. Indeed, some companies even extort local rulers with the mere threat of turning to banditry. The king who has hired men in the profession of arms know all too well how effective they are against other soldiers. They do not have to stretch their imaginations to conclude what they could do to the roads and smaller towns of one's fiefdom.

It is a crude way to make a living for a professional soldier, this work as a highwayman. Yet the mercenary code applies only to those who have your back or pay you. It does not apply to the hapless merchants and peasants who might be easily separated from their money.

There are those companies who refuse to turn to such methods. Doing so can cause a long-fought-for reputation to crumble into the dust of ages. Some companies hang those among them who turn to this kind of "work". It should be noted this is not the same as looting. However, even in those companies who forbid banditry, groups break off on their own. Some of these become bandits in the hills, forests, and darker roads of the world.

EXCURSIONS INTO THE WEIRD

Robert E. Howard set his stories in a variety of genres. For Conan, he often mixed fantasy with horror, two-fisted pulp action, westerns, and war. The latter is the staple of the mercenary campaign. One of the features that set these tales apart from others, though, was the injection of the weird. Take any Conan tale, and there is a good chance he begins with a straightforward job — such as working as a mercenary — but winds up fighting an eldritch terror. Your game is liable to be the same, and this is highly encouraged.

Above, we briefly noted that any of the more "routine" missions a mercenary may be ordered to perform can serve as the set up for an excursion into the weird. Sure, a scouting mission could simply result in discovering an encamped army, but it might also end with time-lost ruins harboring a beast that ancient men worshiped as a god.

Weird fantasy and horror are the stuff of Howard's Hyborian Age. There is always a wizard, a demon, an unnatural beast, or strangeness that could drive men insane. Sometimes, such profoundly profane forces even influence great battles. The way of the sword does not prevent one from encountering that which cannot be solved or beaten by steel alone. What malevolent, sorcerous forces will your players come upon?

Cursed Ruins

Whether marching through trackless desert of darkest woods, mercenary companies venture far and wide from the dreaming west to the mysterious Far East. Along the way, they are likely to come upon ruins of ages past. Just as war is nothing new to Earth, neither is civilization. Cities have risen and fallen since man pulled himself up from rude primitivism. They have risen and fallen even before humanity's reign on this planet began.

Whether destroyed in the Cataclysm when Lemuria drowned beneath the sea, or burned and razed by one of a thousand wars, remnants of cities, monasteries, towers, and necropolises dot the landscape, poking forth from the past like skeletal fingers attempting to claw their way back into the light.

What lies within such ruins can be men of fortune encamped like the player characters' own company, but that alone is not weird. However, if the men so encamped were subject to a curse which haunts the ruin — turning them into grotesqueries mutated by the Outer Dark — then we have the beginnings of a weird tale.

Perhaps the city is still inhabited by the descendants of a people long supposed to have vanished. This enclave might be the last vestige of Valusia, Atlantis, or even a city of the serpent-men. Curious to be sure, but wary soldiers do not necessarily venture into danger merely to explore.

So, what if we take another part of the more combat-oriented missions? Perhaps the dog-brothers needing rescue were taken not by a foreign army but by the vestige of this lost race. Perhaps, they were not abducted by men but are being used as hosts for the Great Race of Yith, as that species projects itself through time.

Possibly, the characters' very goal lies inside these ruins. It could be a map, an arcane object, or even an enemy leader on the run. A scouting mission could result in the characters themselves being captured by the denizens of these ruins and are thus forced to visit them. The ruins might lie atop ancient sewers that lead into the city they are set to besiege... but what else lies inside those old sewers? There are many ways to get mercenaries involved in the exploration of weird locales where things dwell which are best left unseen by the human eye.

Ancient Battlefields

Over the course of millennia, man — and things other than men — battled on nigh every square yard of earth. Such violence can leave psychic echoes which shudder down through time like ripples formed in still water when a pebble is dropped. Certainly, not every battle leaves such scars upon the cosmos, but the great and most horrific ones do.

See here, where the Great Race of Yith met their final end, or there where the last knights of Acheron made their final stand. Witness this green, fertile field where once an entire town was put the sword by their cruel king. All of these places, and many, many more disturb the fabric of reality, touching the Outer Dark and the realms of nightmare and dream (see *The Book of Skelos*, pages 17–24). Hauntings are often nothing more than tears between this world and another made by trauma, fear, and violence.

A battlefield is a particularly appropriate weirdness for a mercenary troop to encounter. Men who live and die by the sword have some affinity for those who died likewise. Perhaps the dead do not lie still. Perhaps they merely haunt the dreams of those sleeping on their remains. Perhaps their final agonies ripped a hole between Earth and the Outer Dark which continues to offer passage for demons.

A necromancer might camp here with his retinue, seeking to speak with the dead who know secrets written in no book. Demons might use this as a hunting ground for mortals. Ghosts might appear from out of strange fogs to wreak aimless revenge on anyone who draws breath while they do not. War is part of the cycle of man and the eternal return of history. What can your characters find in the detritus of such all-too-human violence?

Abandoned Fortifications

These are not ruins, or at least not old ones. The fortification is either intact and abandoned or recently destroyed. Whatever caused the occupants to leave (or killed them, if you want corpses left behind) could still be in the area. The characters' commanders want to find out what happened, as the threat could easily endanger the company.

The characters are sent to investigate, for it makes little sense to send a larger group into the unknown. What do they find? Have Picts overrun a fort near the Black River, or has a mysterious plague killed everyone inside a keep and now infected the player characters? Finding a cure could be an adventure itself. Perhaps, the redoubt was a hill fort along a frontier. Inside, not a single person remains. There are no bodies, and it looks as if they simply got up and left in the middle of daily affairs. Fires still burn in hearths. Food on the tables has yet to rot. Nothing is disturbed, so where is everyone? Such a calm, even bucolic scene is suddenly tinged with tension and horror by the seemingly inexplicable.

Demons and Gods of the Outer Dark

While it is by no means common, battles have seen both demons and the spawn of abominable gods wreak havoc upon phalanxes of hardened troops. Sorcerers and their ilk call upon these unnatural entities to assist whatever side they favor.

There are tales recorded in fragments of Acheronian books that illuminate a time when Stygia and Acheron both employed these hellish forces upon one another. It may be that it was more common in that bygone day, for it is said that Acheron was an empire of sorcerers. Astreas, writing many of thousands of years later, finds it unlikely, for Acheron and Old Stygia both lasted thousands of years. If they regularly tore holes between reality and that Which Should Not Be Named, their empires would likely have crumbled to dust long before.

Battle is probably the rarest circumstance under which most characters might encounter something from the Outer Dark. All the previous weird locales are perfect for the presence of a perverted being of not-quite-flesh.

A fortification abandoned may have seen its defenders stolen into the air by winged horrors. A battlefield might be home to demons that feed on fear. Imagine, if you will, a character dying in the field. He is surrounded by flies and blood and the excrement of the dead. In his last moments, fear overcomes him as the great unknown void opens. He is about to shed his mortal coil when he espies a slender, shadowy form stalking amongst the dead and dying.

At first, he mistakes it for a survivor looting the unlucky fools who fell, but then he sees the form is not quite substantial and entirely inhuman. It is a demon, a servitor of the Great Old Ones come to reap the life-forces of men as they expire. This hypothetical soldier will not go into the real lair of Ymir, Crom, Mitra, or Erlik — he will be drawn into hell to toil for all time under the ministrations of creatures horrific but mercifully incomprehensible.

In weird fantasy, death itself does not always end one's terror.

MERCENARY CAMPAIGNS

A mercenary campaign offers a remarkable focus for a structured series of adventures. In a campaign, the gamemaster may tell the tale of an entire war or a single battle. The scale is as desired. The siege of a well-fortified city can last for months, during which the player characters battle, help sappers dig tunnels to weaken the wall, and even attempt to sneak inside.

The gamemaster may tell the story of a great Kothic rebellion (one such campaign is outlined, following), of the invasion of Shem by Stygia, or the rise of an army forged in the desert by a mysterious messiah. War is endemic to the life of a mercenary, but it need not circumscribe the imagination. On the way to the war, all manner of things may be encountered. The mysterious desert messiah may be a living god whose only weakness is the skull of an older god who died when menfolk still walked on four limbs.

As explored previously, being a mercenary may be the player characters' ostensible profession, but what happens between marches and camps and even battles, is often the headier stuff of Howardian sword and sorcery.

THE CONFLAGRATION OF KOTH

Koth exists ever on the precipice of open civil war. The penurious kings are far more common than those who might share the kingdom's fortunes. The barons, duke, earls, marquesses, and princes all have a thirst for more power. Almost as regular as the turning wheel of the starry night, Koth experiences revolt. This time, it's a powerful city-state in central Koth which is allied with other cities against the crown.

Further, the city-state is not alone in the rebellion, but garnered allies prior to revolt. Now, a genuine internecine war erupts in Koth. Strabonus marshals loyal troops, while both sides hire mercenaries. The fees begin to rise, and companies of dog-brothers flock to Koth. This could cause a dearth of work in other regions which, too, could have political ramifications.

For Koth, however, the very crown is on the line. Tsotha-lanti probably backs Strabonus, as the wizard is accustomed to lording over the king. However, it is possible Tsotha-lanti backs the rival contenders, should you wish to diverge from canon. Also, these events could take place in the power vacuum left after the events of "The Scarlet Citadel".

In that case, the destabilization of Koth has ripple effects all the way to mighty Aquilonia, whose barbarian king holds primary claim on the kingdom after his prior actions.

Whether Conan has anything to do with the war or not, Stygia, Nemedia, Ophir, and Aquilonia will all commit troops — for the kingdom that takes Koth whole gains a mighty advantage indeed. This could lead to an all-out war between nearly all the Hyborian kingdoms!

BATTLES

> *Conan, who had been watching the rolling mist with growing nervousness, bent suddenly and laid his ear to the earth. He sprang up with frantic haste, swearing.*
>
> *"Horses and chariots, thousands of them! The ground vibrates to their tread! Ho, there!" His voice thundered out across the valley to electrify the lounging men. "Burganets and pikes, you dogs! Stand to your ranks!"*
>
> — *"Black Colossus"*

Ho, dog-brothers! Does your blood not burn for the clang of steel against steel? Do you not relish the wide-eyed stare of your foemen as you cut his life's blood clean from his mortal coil? You do not face these savage hordes alone. Each man and woman is your kin in blood, and together you conquer your enemy, driving them before you!

The following are rules for company-scale, mass combat in **Conan**. They are designed to depict the furious combat in the thick of the fray. Player characters take the role as commanders of small Companies (or members within said **Companies**), and play out the combat as described below.

RUNNING A BATTLE

A player character can lead a Squad of warriors into battle. The rules for doing this can be found on page 306 of the **Conan** corebook. Given that a party of four player characters can lead another sixteen non-player characters into battle without additional rules, most skirmishes can be handled without new mechanics.

There are times, however, when a character might wish to lead greater numbers into the fray, time when a character takes control of greater numbers of troops; we call this a battle. In a battle, Companies made up of Squads and Mobs face off against each other.

Just as individual non-player characters are abstracted into Squads, Squads are abstracted into Companies, with the most powerful Squad forming the **Vanguard** of the Company and the weaker Mobs or Squads acting as subordinates. In a combat situation, where Company faces Company, the characteristics of the Vanguard — which are also the characteristics of the Vanguard's leader — determines the target numbers used by the Company in combat. In **Conan**, player characters play a very important role in overcoming the enemy. If a player character does not choose to lead a squad, they follow the teamwork rules as normal.

HOWARDIAN EPIC BATTLES

The battle rules serve to create more epic scenes as the backdrop to the player character's actions. If at any time the player characters unite to achieve a specific goal, this should take priority over the adjudication of the battle. Should an individual player character wish to engage in an action outside of the battle, manage this within the framework of the battle. See *Heroic Actions* on page 108.

TALENT UPDATES

When engaged in a battle, certain talents gain additional properties.

- **GENERAL:** Every rank of *General* increases the number of Squads allowed in your Company by 1. At the gamemaster's discretion, each level of General may increase the number of squads under a character's command by a factor of two.

- **CONQUEROR:** Gain +1d20 on attack rolls, up to the standard max +3d20, for each member of your retinue acting as the leader of a Squad within your Company.

- **BALLISTICS:** Gain +1d20 per rank to attacks using the Warfare skill while controlling a siege Company.

- **DEVASTATING BOMBARDMENT:** Gain 1 bonus Momentum on a successful attack with a siege Company.

- **INSPIRING LEADER:** Gain +1d20 on Defense tests.

For an item owned by a Mob or Squad — such as heavy armor or reach weapons — to be useful in battle, the item must be owned by half or more of the Company. *For example, to be considered mounted, half or more of the Squads or Mobs in a Company must be mounted.*

IMPORTANT SKILLS IN BATTLES

In battles, two skills are prominent: Command and Warfare. These two skills perform vital functions as forces clash and the dead pile in heaps of gore. Below are new uses for these skills.

COMMAND

Command determines the extent to which a player character can maintain control of a larger force. While any character can be a part of a Squad, and lead it with determination, Command Focus determines how many additional Squads can be controlled as a part of the character's Company. Every point of Command Focus allows the character to include 1 additional Squad or Mob in their Company. Thus, a nobleman with a Command Focus

of 2 can lead 3 Squads in their Company. Command also determines the ability to rally and maintain the Company in the face of casualties.

WARFARE

Warfare determines the effectiveness with which the Company fights. It measures the strategic and tactical deployment of all forces within the Company and, thus, the overall effectiveness of the Company in the field. If Command is what organizes and holds a Company together, Warfare is how a Company tears other Companies apart.

A ROUND OF BATTLE

Each round of battle represents at least several minutes of actual time and can last up to an hour. In a round, forces attack, fall back, rally, and return. We don't track individual charges in a battle. Just as in regular combat, Companies on the player characters' side act first, unless the gamemaster spends 1 Doom per enemy Company attacking first. Each round, every Company gains one battle action and one movement action.

ZONES, RANGE, AND MOVEMENT ACTIONS

In mass combat, zones are still used, but are much larger. They encompass a portion of a large palace, a city block, or even a small village. A Company can move up to one zone each turn, two if mounted. Melee attacks occur in the same zone as the target. Ranged weapons can attack from up to one zone away. Siege weapons can attack from up to two zones away. To make a Ranged attack, at least half of the Company's Squads must have ranged weapons.

BATTLE ACTIONS

The following actions may be attempted by a Company.

Withdraw

If a Company actively engaged in melee combat with another Company wishes to move, it must spend its battle action withdrawing instead. If it fails to do this, the enemy Company may immediately make an attack test with no opposing defense test. Mounted Companies may withdraw from melee combat without this penalty, unless engaged with enemy mounted Companies.

Fortify

A non-mounted Company can use its move action to fortify instead of moving. Fortify is a defensive action which makes defense easier, subtracting one step from the defense Difficulty. If the Company is already fortified, and spends a move action to fortify again, it becomes heavily fortified, subtracting two steps from the defense Difficulty.

A fortified Company loses the fortified state if it moves. There is one exception: a Company in which all members have shields may spend a move action forming a shield wall, becoming fortified, and then may move without losing the fortified state until making an attack.

> *"This day you become knights!" he laughed fiercely, pointing with his dripping sword towards the hillmen horses, herded nearby. "Mount and follow me to hell!"*
>
> — Conan, "Black Colossus"

Attack

To attack, the Company rolls the Warfare skill of the Vanguard's leader in a struggle against the Command skill of the defending Vanguard's leader. The attack receives teamwork dice that roll against the Warfare skill of the subordinate Squad leaders. For simplicity, it is recommended that the Company leader roll different colored dice for each different target number just as they would when leading a single Squad in regular combat.

The difficulty of attacks begins at Simple (D0), and the Difficulty Number is modified by the following:

ATTACK MODIFIERS

Attacker Conditions	Difficulty Modifier
Defender has shields	+1 step
Defender has mounts when the attacker does not	+1 step
Defender has Light armor	+1 step
Defender has Heavy armor	+2 steps
Defender has Very Heavy armor	+3 steps
Attacker has mounts when the Defender does not	−1 step

While the attackers roll their attack, the defenders test the Command skill of the Vanguard's leader, adding assistance from the Command skill of the other Squad leaders.

The test begins at Daunting (D3), and the Difficulty is modified by the following:

DEFENSE MODIFIERS

Defender Conditions	Difficulty Modifier
Defender has longer Reach weapons than the attackers	−1 step
Light cover (forest, light walls, etc.)	−1 step
Heavy cover (stone walls, etc.)	−2 steps
Light Fortifications	−1 step
Heavy Fortifications	−2 steps

Again, if half or more Squads within a Company have any of the above conditions (armor, long weapons, etc.), then the entire Company qualifies for the conditions.

If the attackers win the struggle, they deal 1 Casualty to the defenders, plus 1 extra Casualty per Momentum spent. If a Casualty has been inflicted, the weakest Mob or Squad in the Company is removed from battle. This does not necessarily represent them being slaughtered, but may also represent wounds or routs due to loss of morale.

If the defenders win the struggle, no casualties are inflicted from the attack, and the defender has the option of three Momentum spends:

- **Slog:** Momentum from the defense roll can be spent towards the Company's next attack, lowering the attacks Difficulty by 1 per Momentum spent this way.

- **Counterattack!:** Three Momentum can be spent to make an immediate Attack action against the Company that has just engaged them.

- **Stratagem:** Momentum can be saved to the group Momentum pool.

SIEGE WEAPONS

Each siege engine and its crew form a Squad. A Company of these Squads must be led by a character with the *Artillerist* Talent. These Companies function the same in battle as other Companies with the exception that the attack test of a Siege Company is never modified by the opponent's armor.

Successful attack tests have the following special Momentum spend:

- **BREACH:** One point of the attack's Momentum may be spent to remove the target's fortification status, or to permanently remove one level of cover from that zone (heavy cover to light cover, or light cover to no cover).

NARRATING BATTLES THE HOWARD WAY

Part of the thrill of a CONAN game is depicting the massive battles in which the player characters can take part. Now, while not every gamemaster expects to describe lurid combat during play to the degree that Howard did, attention to some details can help paint a broader canvas in the mind of the players.

Howard's Conan stories are rife with phrases that evoke bloody action such as "split his skull to the teeth". You can be as graphic as you like, but small details are key. A successful Siege attack results in snapping bones and iron helms crushed as flat as dry leaves. A vicious assault of Picts on Aquilonian footmen, as seen above, results in a "wild frenzy of blood as savagery tears apart civilized men".

You might describe a wedge formation piercing the heart of a Fortified Company, or the demise of a Company as "following the bloody butchering of their dog-brothers, the Kothian infantry flees for safety".

It doesn't matter how eloquent you phrase things, just that you give specific, concrete examples of what the dice rolls mean in the eyes of the player characters. A little goes a long way. While good detail heightens any melee, be it a group action or one-on-one, the more abstract nature of mass combat demands descriptive clues for the players to grab onto, so that the numbers turn into a true, gory fray inside the theater of the mind.

Example of Battle

A Company of Picts assaults an Aquilonian Company consisting of a Squad of knights and a Squad of footmen inside a forest. The gamemaster spends 1 Doom to have the Picts' Company attack first. The knights are in full plate (very heavy armor) on horses (mounted). The footmen have spears. The Picts have no armor and are on foot with axes.

The Pict attack is a Daunting (D4) test against the knights — who gain +1 from being mounted and +3 from the Very Heavy armor. The Picts are led by their shaman and she has 6 Squads in her Company. The shaman spends 3 Doom and rolls 5d20 against her Warfare skill. She scores 3 successes. The remaining five squads roll to assist, scoring 4 more successes. The Daunting (D4) Warfare test succeeds, with 3 Momentum.

Lord Cawdor, the leader of the knights, makes a defense test using his Command skill. His Difficulty begins at Daunting (D3), and subtracts −1 for the spears and −1 for the forest cover, bringing it to Average (D1). He spends 2 Fortune and rolls his Command skill, assisted by the footmen. They roll no successes! The Fortune gives Lord Cawdor a success with 3 Momentum, but the gamemaster spends 1 Doom to break the tie in favor of the Picts. Success with no Momentum on the attack roll means the Aquilonians suffer 1 Casualty. The footmen fall before the Pictish onslaught.

Lord Cawdor now rallies his knights. His attack against the Picts is Easy (D0). He spends his last Fortune and also rolls 2 successes, thus earning 4 Momentum. The Picts defend at Challenging (D2), having reduced the difficulty by

−1 step due to light forest cover. The Pict shaman tests her Command, assisted by the other five Squads. Together they get 5 successes, thus gaining 3 Momentum. Lord Cawdor's knights valiantly crush two of the Pictish Squads beneath mount and blade, one for the successful attack and one for the Momentum.

However, Lord Cawdor still has a desperate fight on his hands, as four Companies of Picts remain and are ready for their next attack.

HEROIC ACTIONS

Heroic Actions allow the player characters to retain the center stage, even among the swirling chaos of mass combat. Heroic Actions can sway a battle in favor of the player character's forces, but they are risky by nature and can bring tragedy as well.

Performing a Heroic Action

As a battle round is longer in game time than a regular round, the player characters can perform individual actions within these longer battle rounds. These individual actions are called Heroic Actions.

A Heroic Action is a cut-scene, using the standard action scene rules. In every battle where the player characters are split across different locations and goals, each player character can attempt at least one Heroic Action. Whenever a player character performs a Heroic Action, the objective should be clear. Some examples are: opening the gates to the fort, thus removing the cover provided the enemy; challenging an enemy leader to combat, thus taking him out of the battle if the player character wins; sabotaging siege engines, thus taking them out of the battle; or persuading an enemy Squad to switch sides or leave the fight. Basically, anything the players can think of attempting that could affect the battle.

Heroic Actions are in addition to any other battle actions. While the player character engages in a Heroic Action, the player character and their Squad still participate in the next battle round.

Challenges

Challenges are a special type of Heroic Action which cannot be run as a Quick Heroic Action (see sidebar below). A Challenge is used when a player character wants to attack an enemy leader directly. To perform a Challenge, a player character must be in a Company that is engaged in melee combat with the leader's Company. If the leader wishes to also engage the player character in combat, then the two Companies do battle using the regular action rules.

If the enemy leader does not wish to engage the player character in a Challenge, then the player character must succeed at a Melee, Athletics, or Stealth test with a Difficulty equal to the number of Squads in the enemy Company. If this test succeeds, then the player character's Squad uses the normal action rules to combat the non-player character's Squad. If this test fails, the swirling chaos of battle keeps the characters apart, but both characters and their Companies are otherwise unaffected.

TO THE VICTOR THE SPOILS

If the character fails at the Heroic Action, they escape with their life, but any Squad or Company they lead is doomed, and its members are either captured or killed in the attempt. Alternatively, the player can choose to have their player character take a Harm to avoid the loss of the Squad or Company.

Complications during Heroic Actions should revolve around resources lost during the battle, whether successful or not. Receiving a Harm, losing some of the Squad, losing a weapon, or breaking one's armor would all be appropriate Complications.

If the character succeeds in a Heroic Action, not only do they achieve the objective of their action, it may be a deciding factor in the battle

QUICK HEROIC ACTIONS

When the gamemaster doesn't want to slow down the game for the other players at the table, Quick Heroic Actions can be used. To perform a Quick Heroic Action, the player character makes two skill tests, the types and Difficulties are determined by the gamemaster based upon the Difficulty of the task attempted.

The members of their Squad or Company may assist the player characters if assistance for the task makes narrative sense. Heroic Actions are meant to fill the player characters with purposeful opportunities for glory, even during mass battles. If the players are instead abusing the system, the gamemaster may raise the Difficulty accordingly.

Non-Player Characters and Heroic Actions

Important non-player characters may also attempt Quick Heroic Actions, though these should be rare. For these cases, the gamemaster can allow players to pay Doom for Quick Heroic Actions committed by non-player characters which benefit the player characters.

To avoid situations where the players are relegated to watching the gamemaster make dice rolls alone for non-player character versus non-player character conflicts, the gamemaster instead pays Doom for non-player characters' Heroic Actions. The Doom cost is equal to the Difficulty of the action. *For example, a non-player character attempting the sabotage action described below would pay 6 Doom to succeed.*

Example Quick Heroic Actions

- Opening the gates requires Dire (D4) Athletics and Melee tests

- Scouting out a secret entrance requires Daunting (D3) Observation and Stealth tests

- Bribing a lieutenant is a Challenging (D2) Insight test and a Persuade vs. Discipline Struggle

- Sabotaging a siege engine requires a Daunting (D3) Stealth test and Craft test

CHAPTER 8

MERCENARIES OF THE AGE

And more than looking the part, he felt the part; the awakening of old memories, the resurge of the wild, mad, glorious days of old before his feet were set on the imperial path when he was a wandering mercenary, roistering, brawling, guzzling, adventuring, with no thought for the morrow, and no desire save sparkling ale, red lips, and a keen sword to swing on all the battlefields of the world.

— The Hour of the Dragon

FREYA THE RED

In Vanaheim, a woman can write her saga, and few Vanir men are foolish enough to underestimate a shield maiden in combat. Freya has red hair, but she is not named for those locks. She gained her moniker at the age of seventeen when she slew two Cimmerians in combat and did not wash their blood from her body for two days. Her clan said any who could withstand the blood and gore of a foe reeking on their person was a true warrior. It was something of a joke for the young people, as no real warrior wanted to smell rotting flesh. Nor did those who tried often make it through the trial without turning their stomachs inside out. Freya never wavered.

She fought under the midnight sun for three seasons before her fate found her, as it always does. There was a man in another clan she desired, and she sought him in a place secret to them both. Perhaps they might have been happy and had a family, but this was not to be. As each returned to their villages, they found their people slaughtered by Cimmerians. Rage bubbled again to the surface and the hill people of the south struck the final blow — or so they thought.

With nothing binding them to home, Freya and her man headed south and took horrible revenge upon the Cimmerians they encountered. They spared no woman or

BACKER CHARACTERS

Presented on the following page are characters created by backers for the *Robert E. Howard's Conan: Adventures in an Age Undreamed Of* Kickstarter campaign, provided here for use by the gamemaster or as player characters.

child, but cut a bloody swath through those stony crags. Ten years on, Cimmerians still speak of the red demoness and her lover who slaughtered their kin.

Such revenge proved hollow, and the couple drifted apart. Each, in time, came to regret at least the children — there was no honor or glory in such wholesale slaughter. Yet war was in Freya's blood, and it would not go away. She founded a mercenary company years later in Nemedia called the Sisters of the Blade (see page 60). Not all are women, but most of the commanders are. Freya chose them personally. She fulfills her contracts to the letter. She takes any job that offers enough coin. Her soul, and the gods she used to worship, are but dim candles inside her now. None say, at least not out loud, that perhaps she wishes fate to wreak its own revenge upon herself.

ATTRIBUTES

Awareness	Intelligence	Personality	Willpower
10	8	10	10

Agility	Brawn		Coordination
11	9		11

FIELDS OF EXPERTISE

Combat	3	Movement	1
Fortitude	3	Senses	1
Knowledge	1	Social	—

STRESS AND SOAK

- **Stress:** Vigor 12, Resolve 13
- **Soak:** Armor 3 (Mail), Courage 3

ATTACKS

- **Sword (M):** Reach 2, 5 🪶, 1H, Parrying, Vicious 1
- **Small Shield (M):** Reach 2, 3 🪶, 1H, Knockdown, Shield 2, Vicious 1
- **Throwing Axe (R):** Reach 2, 4 🪶, 1H, Thrown, Vicious 2
- **Rage of Folkvang! (T):** Range C, 6 🪶 mental, Stun

SPECIAL ABILITIES

- **Bathed in Blood:** All of Freya's physical attacks gain the Vicious 1 Quality.
- **Sister of the Blade:** Freya has all the special abilities and Doom spends of a Sister of the Blade (see page 60).

MAGNUS OF POITAIN

From poor beginnings and squalor under King Numedides, Magnus rose to make his own way by will and sword-arm alone. He never had a proper education, not even much schooling at home. He did not learn to read until he deemed it necessary later in life, though he possessed a keen intellect. Children of his station did not have any illusion that they would ever be other than they were, though of course they liked to pretend. For Magnus, the knights of Poitain were the shining example of what a man could and should do in this world.

The small farm on which his family eked subsistence from their lord was no place to achieve the distinctions of gallantry and bravery, though. Magnus set off after a fight with his father, who sneered that the boy aimed to be better than his birth. The two have not spoken since that day, though Magnus does on occasion think of returning home.

For the first years on his own, Magnus made do as an aide to mercenary companies of little note. He oiled weapons and armor, made himself known as the lad who could scrounge anything, and generally ingratiated himself with the men-at-arms. By the time he was fourteen, he hefted a blade in the fury of combat when a real soldier fell. After that day, no one called Magnus a boy again.

He has served in campaigns in Koth, Nemedia, Turan, Corinthia, and Shem. He has only seen thirty-some winters, and already his body is a map of scars. The older men in the companies he joins respect him, but in hearing their complaints, of old bones and wounds which won't heal, Magnus has begun to grasp his future... and he likes it not. There are few stories of old soldiers retiring wealthy.

FIELDS OF EXPERTISE

Combat	2	Movement	—
Fortitude	2	Senses	1
Knowledge	1	Social	—

STRESS AND SOAK

- **Stress:** Vigor 12, Resolve 10
- **Soak:** Armor 3 (Mail), Courage 3

ATTACKS

- **Broadsword (M):** Reach 3, 5 🌀, Unbalanced, Parrying
- **Longbow (R):** Range M, 5 🌀, 2H, Piercing 1, Volley
- **Steely Glare (T):** Reach 1, 3 🌀 mental, Stun

SPECIAL ABILITIES

- **Knight in All but Name:** Magnus can re-roll any d20 that fails to score a success when making a Melee attack, but must keep the new result.

DOOM SPENDS

- **A Poor Man's Luck:** For 2 Doom points, Magnus can get himself out of almost impossible situations. It is up to the gamemaster to narrate these, but Magnus has an uncanny ability to survive trouble.
- **Temper:** Magnus tends to fly off the handle. At any time, the gamemaster may decide something in the current scenario angers Magnus. Most often, it involves treating women poorly, cheating in games of chance, or showing cowardice. The gamemaster may then pay 1 Doom to grant Magnus +2d20 on any test to "resolve the matter". Player characters seeking to calm Magnus must pay 2 Doom and make a Challenging (D2) Counsel test.
- **I'll Not Leave Him!:** If a character is knocked down in front of Magnus, Magnus can pay 1 Doom to gain the *Inured to Fear* ability.

In recent months, Magnus' mind once again returned to the knights of Poitain. He grew a long mustache after their fashion and seeks a way to join them. He has no noble blood, no connections, nothing that would cause a fat king such as Numedides to grant him knighthood. As long as such a man sits on the throne of Aquilonia, Magnus must remain separated from his dream.

Even though Magnus cannot ever become a knight, he practices his own code of honor. He does not leave a friend behind, even should it mean his own death. Women are not chattel, and he suffers no one who treats them as such. He is not above looting or thieving, but he does not like a cheat. Nobles born into opulence are frequent targets of his harsh tongue.

ATTRIBUTES

Awareness	Intelligence	Personality	Willpower
8	8	9	10

Agility	Brawn	Coordination
10	12	11

INDEX

THE HYBORIAN AGE AWAITS YOU

BOOKS COMING SOON

Conan the Thief
Conan the Mercenary
Conan the Pirate
Conan the Brigand
The Book of Skelos
Conan the Wanderer
Conan the Adventurer
Conan the Scout
Conan the King
Nameless Cults
Ancient Ruins & Cursed Cities
Conan Monolith Boardgame Sourcebook
Conan and the Shadow of the Sorcerer
Legendary Beasts & Otherworldly Horrors

ACCESSORIES

Gamemaster Screen
Geomorphic Tile Sets
Doom & Fortune Tokens
Q-Workshop Dice
Card Decks
Stygian Doom Pit
Fabric & Poster Maps
Character Sheet Pad
Conqueror's Bag

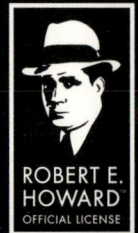

MODIPHIÜS™ ENTERTAINMENT

2D20™

CABINET

ROBERT E. HOWARD OFFICIAL LICENSE

HYBORIA

modiphius.com/conan